Just Once, When I was little

Just Once, When I was little

Brian Mynott

authorHOUSE®

AuthorHouse™
1663 Liberty Drive
Bloomington, IN 47403
www.authorhouse.com
Phone: 1-800-839-8640

© 2011 by Brian Mynott. All rights reserved.

No part of this book may be reproduced, stored in a retrieval system, or transmitted by any means without the written permission of the author.

First published by AuthorHouse   06/09/2011

ISBN: 978-1-4567-8251-1 (sc)
ISBN: 978-1-4567-8250-4 (ebk)

Printed in the United States of America

Any people depicted in stock imagery provided by Thinkstock are models, and such images are being used for illustrative purposes only.
Certain stock imagery © Thinkstock.

Because of the dynamic nature of the Internet, any web addresses or links contained in this book may have changed since publication and may no longer be valid. The views expressed in this work are solely those of the author and do not necessarily reflect the views of the publisher, and the publisher hereby disclaims any responsibility for them.

Acknowledgement

I would like to say a special thanks to my friends at PAB Studios, Wakefield (UK) for without their genuine understanding and verve, 'Just Once, When I was little' would still be on my laptop.

Just Once, When I Was Little

"Out of suffering have emerged the strongest souls; the most massive characters are seared with scars".

<u>Gibran, Kahlil</u>

A happy childhood is mostly an alien concept to me. I know they exist for most people but I only know this through listening to the experience of others. I often sit and listen to people reminiscing about their childhood. I hear them talk of wonderful Christmas mornings when Santa had been and the presents he had left. I hear them talk of happy holidays, of playing with their family on sandy beaches and a seemingly endless supply of other happy, holiday memories. I hear them talk of being cuddled when they had fallen and hurt themselves or simply a childish need for reassurance when they were scared. I hear siblings talk with love and fondness as they recall wonderful memories of 'growing up' together and the adventures they shared. And they did all this in a safe, loving environment.

I sit, listening, with a combination of feelings. Anger, regret, jealousy and sadness are all there. But the overriding feelings are of loss, isolation, of feeling different to those that spoke with such fondness of their journey to adulthood. And the simple, painful, truth is, I am different. Of all my childhood memories I have a single, solitary memory of feeling loved, secure and wanted. And, as precious as it is to me, I feel pain when my mind brings it, often unbidden, out of the shadows of my past. This one, wonderful, *memory, somehow seems to generate both sadness and happiness within me. Happy because I remember laughing on a warm summers day, and sadness because the memory includes a man that was to bring so much terror to my childhood that, to this day, some 50 years on, I still feel a sense of fear.*

The memory that has caused so much torment had remained buried, hidden for decades. Like many of my childhood memories; I had forced it from my conscious mind, burying it deep in a dark recess. Problem is that memories are not like computer files that you can simply delete. Good or bad, they are more akin to a virus, hiding in the background. And, a nasty memory, like a nasty virus, will eventually cause its host to crash.

But now, at last, after many years of anger and violence, tears, soul searching and therapy, I can look back to my formative years and remember that there *were* happy times. And, now, the elusive happy memories of my childhood years can be visited and separated from the bad.

The one and only happy memory of my life as infant is that of being carried high on my dad's shoulders through the dense woodlands that surround the village of Denby Dale. The memory is still so vivid that I can, even now, recall the musky smell of the woodland that we walked through that day. I remember it was a warm summer's day and I can even recall the low hanging branches brushing over my head. I can still feel my dad's powerful arms wrapped around my legs holding me firmly to his shoulders. I remember the feeling of security I felt in that lofty position.

There is, at least, one more memory from that same period of my life that should be there, as it should have been formed at, roughly, the same period. It would not a pleasant one, but nonetheless the memory ought to be burned into my memory because it would have been very traumatic to a little boy, yet I cannot recall a single second of the incident that left my right hand badly scarred and I think it highlights the value I somehow place on the ride on my dad's shoulders.

Just Once, When I was little

I only know how I acquired the long jagged scar on my right hand by the tale my mother told me. As you will discover, any information supplied by my mother should always be treat with caution and doubted. According to my mother I had injured my hand when I had fallen off a three-foot high wall that surrounded the small area where the village communal dustbins were kept. When I fell I caught my hand on an empty bean tin, the jagged edge of the open lid had sliced deep into the palm of my right hand leaving a gash requiring many stitches. Though it must have been both very traumatic and very painful I remember none of it, it's as if it never happened. But the scar remains as evidence that it did. Perhaps, even as a toddler, I was already used to feeling pain and feeling scared and, so, I simply don't recall a common memory.

Born in the corner of a small room on the ground floor of a block of flats on a sprawling council estate in Bradford 1955, was not, in it's self, a spectacular event. My parents, or so I have been told, were, at the time, nothing out of the normal. I was the latest addition to an ever-growing family that included one brother & sister. Based on appearance alone my family would not have stood out from the rest of the people of the estate, a young married couple with three children living in a council flat was quite normal and to everyone they would have appeared happy. But in the privacy of that flat things were already breaking down. Prior to my birth my mother had already served a short time in prison and had been arrested several times for thieving and much, much worse, and my father already had a reputation for violence and was 'known' to the police. I would come to know the force of his violence and sexual depravity.

According to her own mother, my wonderful Nana, my mother was then what I would always know her to be; a lazy uncaring woman that could not be trusted with anything of value that belonged to anyone else. She was a terrible mother in every sense of the word; even when she was pregnant, and that was to be very often, she found the whole process tiresome rather than tiring but having babies served the purpose of increasing child benefits. My own birth was a good example and I have scars that show that I was born with a double hernia and, as a consequence, I must have spent the first few weeks of my life in The Bradford Royal Infirmary recovering scared and in pain. Not a good start to my life I suppose, yet probably indicative of what awaited me over the coming years. The reason for my double hernia, according to my mother, and thus totally unreliable, was that the doctor was late arriving and, because I was eager *too 'get out and be born'* and that I was responsible for causing her a great deal of pain! The reality would probably be very different and it was more likely she was drunk and couldn't be bothered walking to the phone to call the midwife.

Whatever the reason, I came out of my mother's womb facing the wrong way and I would surely have spent my first days of my life in a state of panic and pain and I can only imagine the distress I must have felt as a newborn.

We didn't live in Bradford for long and we moved to Denby Dale only a few months after I was born and I couldn't possibly have known it at the time but constantly moving house was something that would get used to as it was to happen to the family at least once a year, often twice as my parents avoided the bailiffs.

I don't really know why my family moved to Denby Dale, but an educated guess would be that the bailiffs had turned up for the unpaid rent money that my father seemed to think was paid via the local pub landlord. Realistically all that I can recall from that busy period is the fleeting, yet wonderful memory, of summer's day I was carried high on my Dad's shoulders.

I remember that I had lost a shoe somewhere in the woods near to the house where we lived, it was the kind of thing that would have produced a severe beating from my father a few years later; however, at the time he had laughed and joked with me; he was being 'my dad' and he made me feel safe and I trusted him.

It must have been only six months or so before my family uprooted again, either by choice or enforced, and moved from Denby Dale to another little village just a few miles away called Scisset. It was, and remains, very much the same as Denby Dale in size and culture, although Scisset has more in the way of shops than Denby Dale, the people that live there are basically the same. I remember the house in Scisset. It was a modern council house with three bedrooms and an inside toilet and I can remember just about every part of the building. But what I remember most is the violence of my father and uncaring attitude of my mother. Scisset is really the start of my journey, it is where I first felt my father's fists and began to feel unloved by a mother that didn't care about her children. But it was only the start of my life and things would become far worse; as the family grew, so did the violence and privation. My childhood would be a long painful journey, by the time I reached puberty both my parents would be in prison. My mother for burglary and my father for incestuous rape against three of his children and I was one of those children.

The council house we moved to in Scisset was the standard semi-detached, redbrick building that seemed to be copied by every council in the north of England at the time. The small front garden consisted of a battered and broken picket fence that only partially surrounded an overgrown lawn and the remains of a flower border that was only just distinguishable from the rest of the garden. The overgrown garden measured about 10ft by 18ft, or whatever the metric equivalent is today. The green front door, all the doors houses on the estate were the same deep green. Our own green front door lead into a long dark hallway with the front room (or lounge if you were posh) leading off to the immediate left. It was a good house for the period, many people still lived in far worse houses, and this one had an indoor loo, a bathroom and would have been considered almost luxurious at the time.

I could only have been about five years old during my time in Scisset, and my time there must have lasted only a few months as I attending infants' school there but it wasn't long before I went to another infant's school when we moved back to Bradford. My over riding memories of Scisset are of feeling fearful of my father and lying in bed listening to shouting and doors slamming downstairs and hiding under piss soaked bedcovers with my hands tight against my ears.

The man that had carried me on his shoulders on a wonderful sunny day, the man that I called 'daddy' had gone; a man that looked like him had taken his place and this man was angry all the time and slapped me a lot and scared me simply by looking at me. I don't know why my father had changed so dramatically, it may have been some kind of pressure on the family finances because of the loss of his job, maybe my they didn't pay the rent again and the bailiffs were about to evict the family. Whatever the reason for my father's drinking and violence, it was now part of my daily life. at the ripe old age of 5 years old, I was getting used to being beaten and unloved.

The family had gone full circle when returned to the sprawling council estate of Buttershaw, to a house only half a mile or so from the flat where I was born only five years before. But this time I would remember Buttershaw, I would remember the house and the abuse, I would remember it all.

Our new home was council house in Bradford and was very much, like the one in Scisset, a typical 'green door' council house on a 'green door' council estate; this one was a bit older and smaller, with only two bedrooms. The house was not designed for a rapidly growing family, but that didn't matter, we wouldn't be staying long, we never did.

Being as I was about five years old I can remember a bit more detail about my life now and the people that were part of it, I can also remember far better details of my new home and the neighbourhood. The house itself was in the middle of a block of four or five terraced houses and had a heavy greasy smell that seemed to cling to the whole house. The open countryside and woodland of Scisset and Denby Dale had gone, replaced with dismal redbrick council houses. Outside the front door there was a large grassed playing area, however it did not possibly replace the openness and freedom I felt at my previous homes. No woodlands, no fields full of cattle, no sense of calm and quiet, just house with scruffy gardens and a playing area that was shared with all the children living on the sprawling council estate.

Being much smaller, our new home seemed almost chaotic at times and there was never enough room. The family was growing all the time now and my mother was pregnant again and there always seemed to be a baby crawling unchecked about the house. There was a 'nappy bucket' that was always full of shit stained nappies soaking in the corner of the kitchen; I can remember vividly the stink it used to give off, it filled every room in the house and even overpowered the strong smells that seemed to follow my family from house to house.

Father's temper was getting worse and the small house made it difficult to avoid his anger and I remember hiding under a bed once when he shouted my name in anger. I can't remember what I had done wrong; it wouldn't have been much, if anything at all. It was becoming quite normal to be slapped for making the slightest noise, or even just being stood too close to him when he was drunk. But I was to witness, and feel, a new level of brutality and psychological cruelty from my father that I didn't know existed. What had started as a wonderful day full of fun and laughter was transformed in to a bitter memory that was so distressing I buried it deep into my mind, and I left it there for over three decades.

I was at my new school and it had been snowing heavily for most of the day. I remember walking to Buttershaw Infants School and great white flakes of snow as big as I had ever seen were floating gently down to earth; slowly covering everything they touched, turning the whole of Buttershaw brilliant white and making everything seem clean. It was all so magical, and I remember watching from the classroom window with the other children of my class, I hoped it would never stop, and I remember the whole classroom of smiling children singing a well known children's chant *'snow snow come down faster ally—ally aster'*. All the children were looking through the windows happily singing along as the snow fell; watching wide eyed as it became deeper by the minute. As it deepened the snow was taking me away from a daily life of grime and poverty and my violent father. Forgetting it all as I became lost in a Disney like world of magic

I remember all the teachers had worried faces as they watched the snow deepen, but I was not in the least concerned about the snow. I, like the rest of the kids, wanted it to snow forever and ever. Ignoring the teachers' demands that we quieten down, we repeated the chant over and over again. In the blessed ignorance of childhood we pleaded with whatever god made it snow, to keep falling from the sky. The children could see only the fun it brought with no thought at all to the chaos that accompanied the snow; the cars slipping and sliding and getting stuck was simply part of that fun.

As the snow continued to fall and deepen throughout the morning, the teachers' finally decided to close the school and so, shortly after a very hurried dinner, all the children were on their way home. With very few people having phones in their houses, certainly no one I knew, and mobile phones being unheard of, it meant that most parents couldn't be contacted so most of the children were sent home in small groups accompanied by older kids or teachers. I remember that walk home as if it was yesterday, it was blissful. Snowballs were flying everywhere and even some of the teachers joined in the fun as we slipped, sometimes on purpose, into the ever deepening snow. I remember falling and lying on my back looking into the swirling mass of snowflakes and feeling them landing gently on my face. I felt free and alive again, slowly forgetting about my home life. I lay on the blanket of snow until I could no longer stand the cold on seeped through my threadbare clothes and slowly I got to my feet shaking but still laughing.

How I got home safely that day with no bones broken, I have no idea because by the time I opened our broken garden gate the snow was almost up to my knees and, as the wind picked up, huge drifts began to form adding another kind of beauty to the changing landscape. Those huge mounds of compacted pure white powdery flakes were wonderfully soft and ideal for diving in to headfirst: and I did dive in, several times. In my happy state I didn't care that I was soaked and frozen through to the bone, I was just a kid lost in a world of fun. Buttershaw and its bleak streets and houses seemed to be disappearing before my eyes allowing me to be what *I* really wanted to be; if only for a short time, I wanted just to be a child again.

When I opened the door to my home I was soaked through to the skin and my clothes hung off me with the weight of the quickly thawing snow, but I didn't care. Standing in the doorway I could only feel the sheer joy of the day; it was my first real experience, that I could remember, of a northern winter, and I was lost in the happiness of it, not caring that my mother was screaming at me to '*shut the fucking door*'.

I am entering into the part of my life when everything changed for me, and I would not remember the happiness of that day until 35 years had passed. The night that followed that day would be nightmarish. My father became a stranger to me, one to be feared. And I would battle with the desperate need of a young boy's need to be loved by his father and the emotional and physical pain I felt when I tried and failed. It was a night so bad, full of evil and cruelty that I would bury all memory of it, including the snow and the brief happiness it brought. Yet the terrible feelings of fear and sadness I felt that night remained, I could bury them. Even to this day I cannot think about that night with out feeling very emotional. My life, up to then, had been miserable and, in the few short years of it, I had come to learn fear and to withstand pain; but that night felt real terror, and pissed my self for the first time because of it.

Eventually the snow slowed and then stopped falling; leaving a deep layer of whiteness that covered everything that it had touched. As the early winter evening drew in, the gas lamps came to life, changing the whole world again with their soft orange light reflecting off the snow. I was full of the wonders of a child seeing the world change so utterly completely. I remember Christmas was only a few weeks away and I felt nothing inside but happiness. As I stared into the clear darkening night sky, I saw the moon stars as if for the first time and was sure I could see Santa and his reindeer, silhouetted by the moon, gliding across the night sky, flitting between the broken clouds. Of course it was only a wonderful, childish, fantasy; but it was a nice, warm, harmless fantasy and I loved every second of it.

Until the snow arrived I hadn't realised there were so many kids living on the Buttershaw estate, I'd only seen the few that lived near by. But the snow had changed everything and there seemed to be hundreds of them, and they were all playing on The Green outside my house. My mother had tried to ground me for getting my clothes soaked and I had been ordered to change my clothes and stay in the bedroom with my siblings but mother, not one to enjoy listening to her children at the best of times, certainly not when they were moaning, soon got fed up of listening to us and told us to get our arses down stairs and eat our tea.

We rushed hungrily through the usual teatime meal, a plate of chips, and then we begged our mother to let us play out again. She'd had enough so, with only the slightest hesitation, and little need for any begging, she said yes. I came to realise, eventually, as did my siblings, that she would just about always say yes to just about anything because she simply didn't care what we did, as long as it was not near her, and that most of the time she didn't actually want her children in the house at the same time as her. However, that evening, her children didn't realise nor did we really care, we simply wanted to play out again, and so before she could breathe another word, we were outside in the snow with the rest of the Buttershaw kids. We almost took the door of its hinges as we all charged at the door all trying to be first through it.

The snow, the gas lights and the laughing children had turned the sprawling estate of Buttershaw into a gigantic white playground. All the houses now looked the same and all the gardens were clean and white. House lights shone through windows adding to the wintry scene and parents would bring out cakes and hot drinks for their children, there was a party atmosphere and everyone was laughing. But I remember looking through the window and seeing my mother asleep on the sofa; I remember feeling both sad and angry that she wasn't joining in and bringing out treats for her children. I didn't look at my mother for long and I was soon screaming and shouting with the other kids.

Groups of children had joined forces to make small armies. All them must have felt as I did, feelings of sheer joy at the freedom of it all, and all of us eager to do 'battle' with each other. Soon countless snowballs flew through the air as 'war' broke out among the 'armies', the night suddenly getting much louder with our excited screaming. Huge snowmen were being built, under heavy snowball fire, and the crunching sound of snow being compressed added to all the noise. More than one giant snowman broke apart due to its sheer size and children were fleeing the intense bombardment of well-aimed snowballs. These now broken giant snowmen were now just piles of snow, the casualties of the 'war', but they were quickly turned into barricades where the children could shelter from the onslaught or suddenly fire off dozens of pre-made snowballs in one quick burst. There were generals, sergeants, corporals and privates, with me, being only a 'little kid', playing the part of a lowly private, with little hope of promotion.

We played in the snow for what seemed like hours and would have continued through the evening had it not been for the booming voice of my father bringing an abrupt halt to the war and striking fear into the heart of my siblings and me. Staring at my older sister who had suddenly ran to my side and grabbed my hand, I saw the same fear in her eyes that I felt in my stomach. We both knew that we were soon going to *feel* the anger that we heard in our father's voice, we could do nothing but hold hands a little tighter . . . and wait for the command from our father to go to him. The night began to darken and suddenly we could feel the bitter cold and I started to shiver.

Father had returned early from the pub because it had closed early due to the snow, but he still had had enough beer in him to make him loud and aggressive. It wasn't only my own brothers and sisters that heard my father's booming, drunken voice, just about every child on The Green had heard him and stopped playing and turned to stare at the man that had disturbed such a perfect night. But neither child nor adult dare utter a word in protest as my father glared at them, as if daring anyone of them to speak. All the fun and happiness of that wonderful day and night quickly began to disappear has it became obvious that father was going to turn violent.

Everyone stopped what they were doing. Children ran to their parents side and held their hands tightly, those children without parents simply ran away from the threat of violence. But my brothers, sisters and I could not run away, we dare not. Father screamed at us to get out *'fucking snow'* so with fear growing in our hearts with every hurried stride, we started to walk towards our house where our father waited for us, his finger pointing at the spot where we were to stand in front of him. And I began to shake, not shivering because of the cold that, since hearing my father's voice, had began to bite at my face, but shaking with fear as I looked at my father and saw his face contorted with anger.

The whole world was growing darker and I no longer cared about the moon and the stars or the snow. I felt my bowels tighten each time my father screamed at me and I tried to keep my feet from slipping from underneath as I almost ran towards my father. Gone had all the laughter, the magic; it meant nothing now; all I could see was my father's anger filled face and all that I could hear was my father's booming voice screaming at me to get into the '*fucking house*' and I remember the confusion I felt as we reached the garden gate. I desperately tried to obey father yet at the same time be anywhere near his violence. It was fear that made me want to flee from my father's command but it was pure terror that was screaming at me to obey. I was trying to move fast yet slowly at the same time, but then my father's voice became even louder and more threatening, increasing the terror I felt, and so ran towards him. As I reached the point where father had pointed for us to stand he looked at me, he looked fearsome at the best of times but with the bright room light glowing behind him, he looked even more terrifying. His face was contorted with rage and the smell of beer wafted over me and could tell that he was drunk. Father knew he was terrifying his children and we stood shaking with fear and cold as he stared at us, looking into our eyes: then suddenly he smiled. It was not a smile of happiness; it was a smile that held terror, a sick smile that I would see many times over the coming years.

It was then the cold started to really bite hard and, filled with fear, and I could no longer stop my body from shivering violently. With our reddened eyes and soaking clothes we must have looked a forlorn, pathetic bunch of children as we stood outside that door waiting for the inevitable; most people would have felt at least some pity for such a despondent looking bunch of children, but our father did not, he had achieved what he intended. The sickening smile disappeared suddenly father's face and was replaced by an empty stare; he stared at us in turn, daring any one of us to look back at him but none of us dare return that gaze. Then we waited. Always we had to wait. Before a beating started, father often took great pleasure in watching his victim shake with fear; he seemed to get as much enjoyment from his psychological games has he did inflicting physical pain. This time was no different and didn't have to wait long before father lashed out. I felt my bowels grip and my bladder ached for relief. Then I felt the piss start to run down my legs. It mattered little, I was soaked anyway and it wouldn't show. I remember hoping that my piss didn't turn to steam in the freezing night air. Father hated cowards and I knew that if he saw what I had done he would beat me even harder for showing the fear he had put in me. I remember looking past father and into the room hoping that mother would do something to stop father; but mother stayed quiet as she sat on the sofa, seemingly unconcerned, watching the television; making no attempt to stop what was about to happen to her children. Then suddenly father attacked

With amazing speed and aggression, father grabbed my older brother and dragged him headlong into the house. There was a tremendous crash when my brother slammed against the wall and fell to the floor. My brother screamed in pain has my father grabbed him by his hair, and screamed again, in pain, has he was picked up off the floor and once again thrown hard against the wall. My brother slid slowly down the wall back to the floor, he was shielding his face trying to fend off the blows that father drunkenly pounded him with, and I remember seeing blood smeared across his face and the terror in his eyes; my brother would have been eight years old and, and I knew within a few seconds it would be my turn.

The pain has my father grabbed my neck was intense, so intense I hardly felt the blow to the back of my head or the crash has I hit the wall and landed on my brother. My younger siblings faired a little better, my father grabbed them by the hair and frog-marched them, together, into the house. The youngest, my brother, would have been only three years old at the time, but that was of little consequence to my father. My baby brother was beaten just as hard as the rest of us; father didn't show the slightest concern as he lifted my brothers little body off the floor by his hair. He didn't seem to hear my brother's pitiful screams; he simply threw him into the chair next to the sofa where mother sat watching the television, but even mother must have realised that father was going too far. She didn't try to stop what was happening; but she did show a glimmer of concern.

It was not only the beating that I remember from that night, it was the depth of psychological wickedness my father would show for the first time. And it was as devastating as the physical violence.

When we had been beaten to father's satisfaction he sent us all to bed. No supper and no time to dry or warm ourselves by the fire that was blazing in the front room. We dare not complain or even look at the fire. As we passed father on the way to the bedroom steps, he kept pretending that he was about to hit us. If we ducked, and we all did, he would mockingly call us cowards and slap us anyway. We were ordered to sleep in our sodden clothes and warned that if we took them off then we would be thrown into the garden to sleep in the snow. He wasn't kidding, he would have done it. However, my older sister was ordered to take a bath and, with the very briefest of glimpses into her eyes, I saw sadness and emptiness in them, I knew she didn't want to take a bath, but I was only a toddler and couldn't begin to understand why only she had been told to take a bath. I remember getting into bed that night huddled together, a mass of misery and pain, and piss and snow soaked clothes. I remember lying silent in bed not daring to move as the sound of the bathroom door banged as my father went in to bath my older sister. Mother did nothing.

That night I cried, I think for the first time, silent tears. I was too afraid to make even the slightest noise; I knew that even a whimper would bring my father into the room, I lay in the bed with my brothers and sisters all of us too terrified to even whisper to each other, so we held each others hands until sleep finally overcame us. I don't remember my sister coming to bed; I only remember that she was in the bathroom for a long time with my father.

The following morning the bed was soaked and there were streaks of blood from my older brother's injury smeared across the grimy pillows. Dry blood clung to the side of my face and matted my hair; I don't know if it was mine or my brother's; I had a huge darkening bruise on the side of my face and my nose had been bleeding and when I sniffled I dry blood clogged the back of my throat.

I think we had all pissed the bed and soaked further the clothes that we had slept in. All the fun of the previous evening had now been forgotten, buried and replaced by memories of violence and a feeling of bewilderment. I think all the children awoke to a different world that morning. The snow had lost its magic and I remember looking through the bedroom window at the snowmen that had been built by happy children the evening before. But the snowmen now look back at me with sad eyes; they were just mounds of stupid snow with stupid faces, but, in my young mind, it was as if they were crying with me.

I didn't know it at the time and I don't know the details to this day, but my father raped my older sister in the bathroom that night. The muffled noises were the pathetic sounds of a seven year old girl being abused by the man that should have been protecting her and keeping her safe. And still mother did nothing.

The schools remained closed for what seemed an eternity; father hardly moved from the house, in fact nothing much moved, the world seemed to have come to a standstill. As a consequence, and to my, and my siblings utter despair, father could not go to work and, because the pubs also stayed shut, we had to suffer his mood swings and his fowl temper, fearfully watching our father as he drank the bottles of beer that seemed to appear from nowhere. We all knew that he would turn violent when he had drunk them; it only took a few to move his temper from bad to violent. I remember sitting on the sofa with my older brother only a few days after the beating, watching father eat a huge plate of chips and drinking beer while we sat hungry on the floor. We could not turn away our eyes away from the food. Not because of our deep hunger but because our father had told us we had to watch him eat every mouthful. We had been told we would not have any food because we had been '*little bastards*' by playing out in the snow and making him angry so didn't deserve any food. It was his attempt at making us blame ourselves for the beating and the hunger we now felt; it didn't work, we knew we had done no wrong; we had simply been children having fun, and if he had had the slightest love for us, he would have joined in. Instead he smiled at us has he ate and drank; but it was *that* cruel smile, and it carried no comfort or humour.

After a week or so both father's money and credit at the local shop ran out, and, because He still couldn't work because of the deep snow that stubbornly refused to thaw, he couldn't earn any 'beer money' so he could no longer afford to drink his daily fill of bottled beer. It was a living nightmare; his anger at not getting his daily fill of beer was directed at anyone that crossed his path. And no matter how quiet we tried to be around the house we were never quiet enough for our father; with the slightest noise or movement inflaming father's temper often bringing verbal or physical abuse; or both, to the unfortunate child. I remember the constant fear all the children lived under, banned from playing out and banned from making a sound

It took a few weeks but eventually the snow slowly turned to dark slush and then mud turning the estate into a filthy sloppy mess. I watched through the window with my siblings as the other children from the estate knocked down the slowly melting snowmen, and the kids seemed to be having just as much fun as when *we* built them during a wonderful evening what now seemed an age ago. Occasionally, as we looked longingly out through the window, one of the kids playing outside would throw a soggy snowball at the window and, when one of them hit the target, father would charge to the front door, throw it open and bellow obscenities at anyone and everyone that was even near the house. What a fearsome sight he must have presented to the children outside. Dressed in his string vest, work trousers and heavy boots he must have briefly appeared to them as he appeared to me daily: terrifying. With his powerful shoulders and thick muscular arms father was seldom, if ever, challenged by anyone. Even the other kids' parents would avoid any kind of conflict with my father and avoid attracting his attention. Even though every one of our neighbours must have been aware of father's temper and his enthusiasm for violence, they did nothing; and I ask myself today why no one intervened or even told the police of the violence they must have witnessed. They must have seen the bruises and the fear in our eyes. Yet they did nothing. But then, neither did our mother.

Neighbours didn't 'grass' or interfere back then, in most cases it was quite legal to beat your children; yet as a child I could understand none of it only the reality of it. I was only toddler still in infants' school and yet my world was already a fearful place, almost totally void of the love I had seen in other families. Yet strangely I missed my father. Not the brute that he had become, I missed and longed for the return of the man who had been my dad only a few short years before in Denby Dale. But he wasn't my dad anymore, he was no longer the man that made me feel happy and loved and it deeply confused the little boy that I was. And yet, in childish ignorance of the reality of what my father was, I tried desperately to make him love me.

I have a few more memories of Buttershaw but they are has mixed emotionally now as they were confusing when they were being formed. One such memory, a violent nonsensical one, is of being woken suddenly and dragged from my bed during the night and slapped very hard until my bowels opened and I shit bed. I was then thrown into a corner of the bedroom forced to sleep on the floor covered in my own excrement; the stench quickly filled the whole bedroom making all in keep their heads under the filthy bed covers. I dare not cry, I dare not move and I lay curled on the floor hugging my knees freezing until my younger sister found the courage to pull a blanket off the bed and curl up next to me. I fell asleep crying very quietly into her shoulder.

Suddenly I was dragged from my uneasy sleep by my sister. She was shaking me and whispering as loud as she dare that father was coming up the stairs. The noise of his heavy feet thumping on the stairs instantly made me lose control of my bladder. Father stormed into the room and I remember being dragged off the floor and being thrown back in to the bed and landing heavily on one of my siblings; neither of us made a sound. My father told me that I stank; called me a coward, and then slammed back out of the room. It was such a violent memory that it remains vivid in my mind to this day. I remember each thump landing, I remember the stench of my own shit, and I remember almost every second of the beating. But, to this day, I have no idea what I had done to deserve the beating.

    I have a memory of trying to ride a bicycle that was far too big for me and I remember falling off many times; but being a stubborn little sod, I just kept getting back on. My father had 'acquired' the bike from the scrap yard where he worked. He must have know it was far too big for me; and the laughter it gave him has he watched me struggle to master my newfound pride and joy wasn't the kind a dad would share fondly with his son, his laughter was the kind that was full of revenge and hate. But at the time I childishly thought I was making him happy and I remember not caring about the cuts and bruises I was acquiring every time I fell off that battered old bike. I didn't want to spoil my father's happiness.

    Another, profound memory is of being carried in the sidecar of my father's BSA motorbike and being bounced around inside as father rode too fast on the cobbled streets of Bradford. He was taking me and one of my siblings to Thorne near Doncaster to visit the only woman and man that seemed to care about me; my Nana and Granddad. I knew that my mother's wonderful parents loved me dearly and, at the time, they were the only bright light and source of happiness in my ever darkening childhood. It was worth being thrown about father's sidecar just to spend a few hours with them both. Even though I was scared stupid inside the small sidecar and the journey seemed to take forever; it was made easier just knowing that I would be seeing my lovely grandparents at the end of it. Nellie and Albert, my grandparents, lived in a lovely small semi-detached bungalow at the bottom a cul-de-sac. The cul-de-sac was the total opposite to Buttershaw in just about every way. All the gardens were well kept and full of fruit trees and flowers and it seemed like they lived in a different world. The garden of the bungalow backed on to a canal and a small boat yard was only a few hundred yards away and I remember watching boats being worked on. To the front of the bungalow, off to the left, ran a railway line and I remember sitting in the garden surrounded by sweet smelling flowers watching the great steam engines bellowing great clouds of steam as they thundered past, and I would wave to the driver and was thrilled when he waved back. I so desperately wanted to stay there with those wonderful people in that wonderful place. I wanted to live there and never feel scared again, never feel hungry, never feel alone and have loads of cuddles and laugh every day. But I always had to go back to Bradford and once, when I was getting back into the sidecar for the long miserable ride home I let my feelings show and I had cried and told my nana that I wanted to stay with her. I clung to her legs has tears ran down my face; I caught a glimpse of my father face and I could see the anger he was trying to hide and I knew I would be in for a beating. Almost as soon has we had pulled out of Doncaster my father skidded to a halt, I felt the terror build in me has he threw open the small door and reached in; he didn't drag me out, he didn't scream abuse at me, he beat me has I cowered in the sidecar. When he had finished I forced myself into the front of the sidecar and cried all the way home, I just wanted to be with my Nana and Granddad, I just wanted to be loved. The journey back was horrible, the bouncing about was even worse has father's anger made him push the motorbike to its limit.

When we finally arrived back in Buttershaw I was dragged out the sidecar and beaten again and sent to bed without food. I didn't ever cry again when I left my grandparents house.

Father's violence was becoming ever-present and everything had to be done the instant he commanded it. I remember the times he sometimes smiled as made his demands. It was that same cruel smile that I had seen many times; you didn't hesitate or return any kind of smile you just did as you were ordered, no matter what the command. This cruel and sadistic smile, that my father knew full well could terrorise his children, was, overtime, to become part of the abuse and I came to fear that smile more than the violence that followed it. However there was one occasion when the now instinctive response to father's commands may well have saved my life and, possibly that of my siblings. It was the night my father almost burned the house down and nearly killed the whole family.

The first thing I can remember of that night is being suddenly awakened by my father's terrifying voice booming up from the bottom of the bedroom stairs screaming for us to get out of bed. His voice was frantic and carried fear; and as I scrambled out of bed quickly became aware of a strong stench of choking smoke. I knew it was not the coal fire that was making the smell; it was much stronger than that, like a mixture of rubber & wood and it hurt my throat to breath. I assumed the smoke was coming from something father had chucked on the fire and that father was drunk again or he was mad at something or someone; and felt fear quickly build inside me hoping that it that I was not the target and searched my mind for what, if anything, I had done wrong that day. But before I had the chance to finish my mental searching, father burst in to the bedroom and bellowed at us all to get out of the house *now*. He screamed abuse at us for not moving quickly enough and began slapping those of us who delayed. I remember we were all coughing and I stared at one of my sisters and the panic I saw in her eyes increased my own, but we dare not scream or even ask what was on fire; the fear of attracting father's anger, and thus a beating, was far stronger than any fear of a fire. It was only when I reached the top of the stairs that I could see the smoke running along the stairs ceiling and into our bedroom that I realised that there was a real danger and as I ran past the kitchen door I could feel the heat coming from the kitchen and the hairs on my near naked skin began to singe. I was fascinated, even though the heat scary I couldn't help but pause and stare into the flaming room. I could see deep orange and red coloured flames clinging to the ceiling and black smoke was creeping along the walls coming out of the kitchen. It was only a brief glimpse however, father's panic driven fury would not let us stop or even slow down and he screamed at us move and get outside and, in a matter of seconds, we were all stood, huddled and shaking outside watching smoke escape through the front door.

Neighbours seemed to suddenly appear from everywhere and soon a great crowd of them had gathered to wait for the fire brigade. There was almost a party atmosphere as cups of tea and biscuits appeared and were handed to the family and remember someone putting a blanket around my shoulders. All this time my father was running about trying to put the blaze out by throwing buckets of water supplied by neighbours through the open door. It was quite strange for me to be watching the panic on my father's face; I had never seen him worried about anything or anyone before.

We could hear the bells of the fire engine well before we could see the big, bright red fire tenders. There were three of them and the crowd cheered as they turned nosily onto our street. Blue flashing lights reflected of windows and the sound of screeching bells echoed of the buildings, the night was suddenly full of light and noise. Men in uniforms leapt from the fire engines and began unrolling thick pipes along the ground shouting at people to get out of the way. It was both scary and fascinating has the firemen went about their business, and they took little notice when father screamed obscenities at them for taking so long to get there. But it had only taken the Fire Brigade a short time to arrive and they knew it and my father knew it; so they simply ignored him and went round him, it was the first time I had seen my father ignored and I thought he would thump one of them. But he didn't; he just stood there swearing at them; telling them to get a move on. I remember wishing he would shut up and help them or at least pay his shivering, scared children some attention; but he ignored us and carried on shouting at the men that were working hard to save our home. Even though I was just a little boy I knew my father was acting like an idiot.

It was not long before the fire was under control and the cause of the fire was identified and dragged, unceremoniously, out of the house. It was my father's motorbike, his once pride and joy was now a burnt out wreck. All the chrome that father had spent hours polishing was now twisted and blackened. The machine was a mess and a write off and now stood abandoned and useless on the front garden along side its detached sidecar.

Father walked the few feet from where he was and stood with his arms folded and stood at the side of his smouldering bike. He had a fierce look on his face and his fists were clenched ready to strike out, even the police approached him with caution. But he hit no one that night, however he made up for it over the following weeks as we struggled to live in a smoke blackened house that now stank of smoke. The sight of my father's burnt out bike outside the front door was a constant reminder to him of his own stupidity (he had left a cigarette burning in an ashtray underneath the bike and petrol had dripped onto it) ensured my father remained in a bitter, dangerous mood, whether drunk or sober.

Eventually, after weeks of living in a house with blackened walls the foul stench of smoke that I never got used to, several council officials turned up; however they were far from sympathetic, and whether because of the fire or for not paying the rent they evicted the whole family.

The men from the council only gave the family a week or so to move and during that time something happened that should have warned the powers that be that my father had something wrong with him. it doesn't in anyway excuse the things my father did and continued to do, nothing could do that, however it should have alerted the authorities.

I remember one evening father did not come home for his tea from work. Mother kept his tea warm in the oven for what seemed hours and it was only when it the food was dry and blackened that she shared it amongst the children. We didn't mind the dried up mess, it was food and food was never wasted no matter what it was or had been. We were sent to bed after that small meal and had fallen asleep but awoken later when the heavy knocking rattled the whole house. I could hear muffled voices and plucked up the courage to go to the window and see who it was. It was the police and two burly officers were holding up, with some difficulty, my very drunk and very wet father. They were talking loudly at my mother saying my father had tried to drown himself in the small, and very shallow, beck that ran along the bottom of the estate a few hundred yards from our house. My father was crying and saying sorry every few seconds and he kept babbling on about 'life' and how he hated it and himself. Roughly manhandling my father through the front door and onto the settee, the officers' told my mother to cover him up and let him sleep it off and saying that, if he could remember anything in the morning, he would no doubt feel stupid. As they turned to leave they said they would be coming back the following day to check on him and *'have a word'* I do not remember looking at my father and not feeling any pity or concern for my him, if I recall anything from that night then it is of feelings of shame and disgust at my father because he had cried and I remembered the countless times he had belted me for doing just that.

What I didn't know, what I couldn't have known at the time, was that my father was screaming out for help that night, he knew he was a monster, but he couldn't stop himself. Why oh why did no one listen? Why didn't those police officers ask him why he hated himself and why he tried to kill himself? If they had then maybe the misery that followed could have been avoided and a family could have been saved.

Leeds Road

Being evicted or doing a 'Moonlight Flit' was to become quite a normal routine, but in the early years it was very traumatic for me to be suddenly told we were moving. I seldom had enough time even to say goodbye to new found friends and neighbours and I would often wonder if I would see my school friends or teachers when I left school for the day. That's what happed when we left Buttershaw, I was shaken from my sleep one night ordered to get up and we simply disappeared into the dark, pushing prams and carts laden with our few possessions the four or five miles to our new home on the other side of Bradford. All I remember about the move is that I was heartbroken about leaving my school behind knowing that I would never see my friends or teachers again. So I helped my brother to push a pram loaded with furniture silently crying as we walked through the night.

The house we moved in to on Leeds Road was a definite come down from the house at Buttershaw. It had no bath, no inside loo and no electricity, and not nearly enough room to accommodate two adults and five children, plus another family member on the way. There was always another baby on its way.

Our new home was an ancient 'back-to-back' house that was virtually derelict even before we moved in. With just one room downstairs, and a tiny filthy kitchen, and two small bedrooms on the first floor and a huge dark attic at the top, it was not a place I wanted to live. It was a bleak, dismal place both to look at and live in, and every room held a strange musty smell of damp walls and age. The small enclosed yard at the rear of the building was overshadowed and the sun never penetrated and it always seemed dark and damp whatever the time of day. Almost all the houses were in the same state of disrepair with tattered grubby curtains hanging on wires or string that were too long and allowed the curtains, in some cases old blankets, to sag in the middle. This only added to the gloominess of the houses that stood in line on the same row. The whole area around Leeds Road housed the workers for the dozens of nearby mills and factories that pumped out thick smoke or dark greasy steam that smeared the windows of all the houses. With the exception of one house that stood out from all the rest. The house had a small well-kept garden instead of a paved yard and all its windows were clean and the curtains hung straight, and I remember the curtains had a bold flowery pattern; the house was like looking at a nice picture hanging on a filthy wall. It didn't take my mother long to find out that the house belonged to a woman called Vera. It would become the norm that whenever and wherever we moved to, mother would soon find someone soft enough for her to '*borrow*' things from. But this time mother would not get her way so easy. Vera was a formidable woman that always had rollers in her hair no matter what time of day it was and, from the very first time I met her, Vera stood no nonsense from her new neighbours with me in particular seemingly having the ability to annoy the crap out of her without the slightest difficulty. Many times during my time there she would drag me by the scruff of the neck and boot me on the backside for trivial things like using her nice clean loo instead of our own stinking crap house, or climbing on her midden and jumping off. Even so, I liked the woman very much; probably because she always had buns or cakes to hand out when she wasn't kicking my arse, but more importantly, she was fair with me and never once told my father when I had been naughty. She reminded me in many ways of my paternal grandma, very strict but very fair: and an excellent cook. And Vera, like my grandma, definitely didn't like my mother.

It was not long after we moved in that a new baby brother was born. My brand new little baby brother became the latest addition to our ever-increasing family. Mother was annually increasing her own little band of urchins and we could find mischief just about anytime and anywhere as long as our father was not looking or was drunk in bed; which was almost every day. And, due to mother's reluctance to give a crap about what we were up to, as long as we were out of the house, we were always up to some mischief or other. When the new addition to the family arrived I remember the midwife calling daily to day to check on both her and my new brother. I found that boring; but there was a fun bit that I wouldn't have missed for an ice-cream. Every day the midwife would administer an injection straight into my mother's oversized arse, apparently she was lacking in iron as well as motherly skills. Every day for weeks after the birth of my brother she had to hoist up her skirt and bend over and every time I heard my mother screech as the needle pierced her skin I smiled. As a bonus the large syringes the midwife threw away after each jab were quickly recovered from the dustbin and used as water pistols by my siblings and myself. We never did find any of the needles however hard we tried to find them, which, perhaps, was a good thing.

About half a mile away from my new home was a gasworks and the smell of gas was always present but after a few weeks you got used to the heavy smell and very seldom noticed it. The gasworks being so close, though smelly, was a positive bonus when the summer turned to autumn and the house began to cool, as it was a very good place to acquire free coal. The gasworks used coal and there was mountain of the black stuff piled high just a few yards away from the road and most evenings during the autumn and particularly winter, I would accompany my older brother and sister during the dark evenings and sneak through a small hole in the security fence that surrounded the coal mounds and help ourselves to a pram load of the black gold. How we were never caught god knows, we weren't the quietest of thieves and the old pram we filled used to rattle and clanged ever step of the way under a burden it was never designed to carry. But we were never caught and so, needless to say, we were never short of coal and thus able to, at least, keep warm during the freezing nights. One problem with the coal was that it was not designed for domestic use and, as it was both cheap and damp, used to send huge clouds of deep brown smoke pouring out of the chimney when it was lit. Perhaps we were spotted occasionally as we loaded the pram, and I am sure now that we must have been, but maybe the workers felt sorry for the young Dickensian like urchins and let us be, we were hardly stealing truckloads, and we must have looked a very sorrowful sight in our tattered clothes and our mucky faces struggling with a heavy pram.

When we returned to our house, covered in coal dust and sweat, with the plunder, we would deposit the coal in the small coalhouse that made up the other half of the communal toilet block. Once the pram had been emptied we would clean the pram as best we could ready for our new born brother to use the following day; but there was no way we could remove all the damp coal dust and the baby would end up looking like a tiny coalminer.

The house was old and very basic. There was no bath, no electricity, and no running hot water and the only lighting in the bedrooms came from the ornate gas lamps that stuck out of walls. The lamps were a throw back to the Victorian era and used to scare the crap out of me every night. The stuttering flame cast by the rusty old lights would cast flickering orange flames that would create dancing drunken shadows across the bedroom walls and ceilings. The slightest draft would send the shadows into a frenzy of wild dancing; even the bed seemed to move in some chaotic rhythmic dance, it was as if the whole bedroom was moving in different directions. Every night I would bury my head under the blanket, suffering the stench of piss soaked blankets in doing so, so I couldn't see the dancing shadows. I would wake up gasping for breath and wish I hadn't when I opened my eyes and the room was in total and utter darkness. But there was sometimes another reason I would wake suddenly; it was more of a feeling than seeing something, a feeling of someone or something standing near the bed, or maybe the blanket had been lifted and released causing a draft of cool air to flow in: but it was more than a feeling. But it would be a few years before I realised what it really was.

For a short time all the children slept in one double bed in the bedroom at the back of the house while my parents slept in the front bedroom. My however father didn't like the noise of the main road that ran passed the front bedroom so it wasn't long before he kicked us out of the back bedroom and swapped. Although the house was back-to-back the front bedroom was over a barbershop that faced onto Leeds Road and although it was a much bigger room father had decided the extra space was not worth the sleepless nights; the constant traffic noise was too much for him so, bless him, he put all his children in there, including the new born.

Father had been right, if not fair, it was bloody noisy. At first I found the life generated by the busy main road fascinating. Trolley Busses were really very quiet machines, powered by electricity carried by seemingly endless cables that were present on all the main roads of Bradford. And there lay the problem. The cables were suspended and hung in mid air and held in place by insulated steel cables and when the runners, two long metal poles on the top of the bus, ran across these, it was like a mini lighting storm that would waken even the deepest sleeper. They crackled and sparked every 15 minutes or so and it was made many times worse because the buses made little noise and there so few other vehicles on the road that the buses seemed to sneak up on us. Put together, the spooky gaslights and the late night explosions created by the Trolley Buses ensured I didn't sleep until the last bus had passed at about 10.30 pm. Then the bedroom would grow dark and the creepy feelings would start again and I remember trying to fall asleep before my siblings did, I hated being awake on my own.

Foe some reason my father decided that he wanted to move back into the front bedroom and I was glad when father said we were going to change bedrooms and he announced one day that he was going to '*do the attic out*' for us. I hadn't seen the attic because it had been blocked off, but I thought that it had to be better than the front bedroom. But the attic would turn out to be far worse, and what father had meant when he said he

Just Once, When I was little

was going to '*do the attic out*' was that he would open the door leading up to it and carry the bed up the few stairs dump the bed and rotting mattress in the room. And that was it, no new paint, no scrubbing, and no sweeping up. Nothing

In theory, the attic was not part of the house we were renting and father had been told quite clearly by the woman that had foolishly rented the place to my parents that it was '*out of bounds*' and we were not to go in. But that didn't bother father, he would have ripped the door off on the first day if had wanted to or if he had needed the room, but we hadn't needed the extra space until the new addition to the family arrived however when the baby was born we needed the extra space and so, without a second thought about the restriction, or even a slight consideration of his children living at the top of a tinderbox, he pulled at the locked attic door until it gave way, it didn't take much effort, and we were in.

Even during the daylight hours the attic was a child's worse nightmare, especially one that had become terrified of the dark as I now was. To me the attic held every ghost and demon ever created and the fact that there were no gaslights up there stimulated my imagination to new heights and I imagined that demons were even hiding in the walls.

Just behind the attic door there were several very old dust covered boxes and when we lifted the delicate lid we discovered they were full of very old style clothes. I don't know why, but a black ladies hat with a long black feather sticking out of one side was taking up most of the room in one of the crates and for some reason scared the shit out of me, so much so that when I was ordered by my father to move the crate out of the way, I hesitated. It was only the briefest of hesitations and for the briefest of moments but it was enough to bring father's hand crashing to the back of my head. As I fell to the floor he was screaming that I was a "*soft twat*", a "*useless weak-kneed fucking coward*". The pain from father's constant backhanders hardly bothered me any more; I had become used to the pain. In fact I was getting so used to the pain that, unless it was a severe beating, I hardly felt a thing anymore. But his words were beginning to hurt me deeply. To my father I was nothing more than a coward and a piece of shit; he told me every day at least once. I remember, at times, thinking that maybe he was right; after all I was scared of an old hat and a feather and a few flashing lights and the dark. I would sometimes get so angry with myself I would even called myself a few names and tried desperately to be brave and I remember feeling ashamed when every night I would feel terrified of the dark; and felt the same shame and anger has I looked at the terrifying black hat and I tried to conquer my fear of it and the black feather. But no matter how I tried the hat still petrified me and it was only the much deeper fear of my father that moved the crate, I was wincing when it scraped across the attic floor, keeping has far away from the crates contents has possible.

When I had moved the crate away from the door, father pushed me violently away from it and then threw me violently towards the side of the attic so he could rummage through the crates contents. I lay on the floor watching him. His powerful frame was illuminated by the light from the stairs and his features were darkened in a deep shadow. He looked like a monster and was laughing to himself and shaking his head as he pulled various bits ladies of clothing out of the crate. Suddenly out of the shadows the black hat landed only a few inches away from my face; the feathers touching the skin on my leg. I froze with fear; terrified as the feather seemed to scrape down my leg, terrified that my father would notice my cowardice. And I struggled to keep the scream in my head and not let it out.

Whilst I could hide the terror on my face in the darkness of the attic, I could not stop my body shaking and it wasn't long before father noticed. The response from him was instant. "*You soft little cunt*" he threw more clothes at me screaming at me that I should "*grow balls*" … "*you're shit little coward*". The angry words flowed from his mouth; when he finally calmed down, I was almost buried under a mound of clothes that reeked heavily of moth balls. I was six or seven years old at the time.

I avoided a beating that day only because one of father's drinking buddies turned up when my father had run out of clothes to throw at me and was about to knock the shit out of me; after a few more insult and a few more heavy slaps and a threat to knock some courage into me he went off to the pub. I remember that I attacked that stupid hat and that stupid fucking feather as if it were a living thing; beating it with both my fists, screaming at it has I ripped it to shreds.

The contrast from sleeping in the front bedroom to sleeping in the attic was huge. From a room full of flashing lights and endless noises to a room full of dark shadows and almost deathly quiet and, even though it had been removed, all I could see in my minds eye was that black hat and that stupid feather. I started to agree with my father; perhaps I really was a coward.

It was only when we went to bed that I realised just how big the attic was. It seemed vast compared to the other rooms in the house and dark and strange shadows were being created by the candle I held in a death like grip in my hand. The candle was the only light other than the dim light that came from the wall-light on the landing. Strange long shadows seemed to be floating in every direction, distorted by timbers that ran across the slanting roof. Nothing made sense and it all seemed surreal to my young eyes. The dancing shadows would suddenly flicker and grow every time the flame of the candle wavered and then they would bounce around crazily before they returned back to normal size again. That night I did something I seldom did, I fought my way to the centre of the bed so I would be surrounded by my siblings: let the monster get one of them; not me.

The comfort and feelings of safety I gained from sleeping in the middle of the bed allowed me to eventually fall to sleep. But after a while I woke gasping for breath and pushed my head out from under the blankets; I lay there feeling the cool air waft across my face, drying the sweat that covered my head and face. I lay there listening to the shallow breathing of my brothers and sisters. They were all asleep and I was glad that I was in the middle of the bed when I started to get a feeling that someone or something was in the attic. I could hear a it breathing, it was much deeper than my siblings and I knew it wasn't one of them. Slowly, I pulled the blanket lower so I could see over the edge and looked around the attic, in the dark shadows of the room I was sure I could make out the shape of someone bent over near the crates that held more old cloths. Images of the hat and the black feather crept into my mind and my imagination ran wild. Was it a witches hat and she was angry because I had wrecked it? In sudden panic I ducked my head back under the blanket; but after what seemed an age, the suffocating heat, the stink of piss, and my own curiosity forced me to pull the blanket back down. Ever so slowly I peeked over the edge of the blanket. Desperately trying to show as little as possible of my face I peeked over a look and my panic grew: I could definitely see someone, or something there. Was it the ghost of someone looking for their clothes? Was it a real ghost? That was it, the clothes must have belonged to someone that had died and they were now a ghost and now the dead had returned as a gruesome beast: and the ghost was now looking for the person that had dared to open their boxes of clothes and the ghost was now going to take me away from my family and torture me forever and ever. I remember I wanted to shout that it was my dad that had opened them, not me; but I dare not utter a sound, I was terrified. I started to silently cry, I was trying desperately to wake my older brother from his deep sleep. Surely the ghost could not drag me screaming away me if someone saw it do it! I was crying quite loud now; the panic and fear rising has I convinced myself that the thing I was watching was a ghost; and the ghost was going to do horrible things to me. Then the 'ghost' must heard my muffled cries and seen my frantic movements when the bedclothes moved has I continued tried frantically to wake my siblings: then it spoke to me and it was a human voice; and it brought a new type of terror and I suddenly wished the shadowy figure had been the worst demon from hell. The voice was that of my father.

 Father moved faster than I had ever seen him move and he covered short gap between the crate and the bed with startling speed. Calling me a little bastard has he grabbed me by the hair and he pushed his face into mine until his forehead was touching mine; breathing heavily he started to push my head back under the blankets, then he seemed to change his mind and dragged me back until I was almost sitting up straight. I pissed uncontrollably as he screamed quietly into my face, his voice hissing and full of threat. He almost breathed his words at me telling me over and over to keep my *fucking mouth shut*. His face was still only inches from mine and even in the darkness I could see his face was twisted in anger and he had pure hatred in his shadowy eyes. I could *feel* the threat of violence in his voice and I knew he meant every word when he said he would kill me if I didn't keep my mouth shut. In blind fear I kept whimpering, pleading with him, *yes dad, yes dad, yes dad, sorry dad, sorry dad*, over and over again. Promising, swearing on my life that I would never tell anyone. But not tell them what? What had I to keep my mouth shut for? What had I done wrong? Why was my father squeezing my face with his powerful hands, threatening to kill me? I had spent most of my short life thus far afraid and confused by my father's actions and seldom knew why I was being beaten. But that night I was totally and utterly confused and really thought I was going to die and not know why. Then, has sudden as the attack had begun it stopped. Pushing my head back into the pillow and making sure I realised, and fully understood, that I would die if I said anything to anyone he repeated his threats. And then with one final heavy thump to the top of my head; hard enough that it made my head spin and my teeth bite into my tongue, he was gone. I lay there for several minutes wondering what had just happened. I was shaking and my tongue was bleeding and my head hurt, but I was used to pain but the utter confusion scared me. My tears had finally stopped and even though I was still terrified I was finding difficult to stay awake: then I saw another shadow, much smaller, move towards the bed, I begged that it was just a ghost, a demon, anything or anyone except my father, and I ducked has far down under the blanket as I could. I didn't care if I died of suffocation and even attempted to crawl under my siblings sleeping body. Then I heard something I had heard many times before and would hear many times again; the gentle sobbing of my sister. It was a sound I recognised straight away. I pushed my self back to the surface gulping in the fresh air and feeling the coolness of it. I watched has she slowly crept into bed. I tried to talk to her, I wanted to know if she had seen father and if she had done to me and did she know why. I wanted to ask if she had done something wrong that had made father angry. But my sister was shaking and almost naked and I knew she didn't want to talk. I could see she was in pain and crying quietly so I just pulled back the blankets to let her snuggle up to me; but she just pushed me away and lay at the side of me crying quietly into the pillow. I was still too young to understand what had taken place; in my innocence I had been cross with my sister because I thought she may have made father angry. It was a childish assumption, I just wanted to be angry with someone and hide my own fear and I would have hugged her had I known. But I was only a child I wouldn't have, couldn't have known what had really taken place.

The following morning father decided that the crates had to be taken downstairs. It was one of the very few times that I agreed with my father and I remember dragging a box full of very old clothes down the stairs before he changed his mind. Mother didn't normally care what we did but has soon has the crates were downstairs she pushed the children away and started rummaging through crates. I don't remember much about the crates or their contents after that, no doubt mother sold the lot for a few quid; she wouldn't have cared that they were not hers to sell. After that night I don't think I slept a full night in that attic. I would lay awake wide eyed every night until my eyes burned and sleep at last forced itself on me. It was horrendous. The room had no windows at all, not even a skylight to break the darkness so I didn't even know that it was morning even when it did arrive and during the dark winter mornings we had to find our clothes and then dress in the freezing darkness whilst desperately avoiding the piss bucket that was just dumped somewhere near the door. With four kids pissing in it, the bucket was nearly always splashing piss over the sides and it didn't take long for the floorboards to be covered in piss, and sometimes shit, so that even when the bucket was empty the urine that had over flowed had soaked floorboards ensured the room held the acrid smell of piss.

One day father carried something that looked like a small shiny cabinet into the house and it was only when I saw the small screen that realised that it was a television. The small screen was encased in a brown shell and had two knobs on the front;

the thing seemed old even in the 60's but that didn't matter, it was a television and the children, including myself, took some quietening down and it was only when father belted my older brother that we calmed down. My father was a lot of things, a brute, a bully and a drunk to name a few, but he was also very resourceful when he needed to be. We had 'acquired' a TV but lived in a house with no electricity; however the shop at the front of our house did and, within a few hours of the television arriving a thick cable appeared that ran magically from the top of the cellar steps to the TV. Not only did it power the TV it also supplied power to a light bulb that now swung precariously from the ceiling by a piece of string that was fastened to the old gas light. The electricity came, unknown to occupier, from the barbers that was to the front of our back-to-back little house, apparently the two dwellings, our house and the barbers, had once been one building and the cellar ran under both so father simply plugged into the barbers' fuse box. I can still see those bare wires hanging from the ceiling and the cable running from the television and I often wonder how father didn't actually kill one of us.

The smog that seemed to be everywhere, even when the sun shone, held a kind of eerie magic during the winter evenings when the gas lamps were lit on the main road. It would move in giant swirling clouds that made strange orange halos around the street lights. I remember often sitting on the window sill of the barber's shop that, unknowingly, supplied the power for our light and TV. When the shop was closed I would sit on the narrow ledge and watch as the smog roll up and down Leeds Rd; I found it strangely comforting and would wait patiently for a car or trolleybus to pass by so it would cause the smog to spin in giant eddies around the gas lamps. I would watch the people on as they sat on the bus. Often with their faces peering back at me through the circles they had made in the steamed up windows and I would wonder where they were going. Were they happy? Why were they on the bus? When I saw children I would often wonder if their lives were like mine; or were they happy. I would sit on that ledge for hours sometimes, only leaving when the cold began to bite or there was a danger of

Brian Mynott

my father catching me; then I would return home to the stench of filth and the sight of mother watching the television. I can still see her in my minds eye; sitting on the grubby sofa with a cigarette in her hand surrounded by filth.

It must have been a school holiday and we were all bored; after going to the nearest school to receive our free school dinner, there was always a school open to feed the poor kids, our little gang was on our usual tour of the neighbourhood looking for something to get up to and, as usual we ended up at the abandoned cars. I'd call it a scrap yard but really it was just an open area of derelict land on which people dumped their old bangers and, once they had stripped them of useful parts the shells were left to rot. We didn't care why or how the old cars and vans got there we just wanted to play, to escape the life we lived if only for a few hours. And on this certain day has we approached the cars day we noticed that there was a new addition; a car that had not been picked over, so it became the usual race to see which of us would occupy the drivers' seat and, as usual, it was me that won the mini race. I was faster and more agile than any of my siblings and I always won. So with a big grin on my face I wrenched the door open and claimed my prize as I gripped the steering tightly. My brothers' and sisters' were busy searching the old car for anything of value, but there was nothing, there seldom was, although we would find the odd coin now and then and that was enough to ensure a thorough search of each vehicle just in case there was more. Whilst my siblings conducted the search I had been checking the car, pressing pedals, pressing buttons and messing with switches that I had not the slightest idea what their function had once been and, when I released the handbrake, the car moved, only very slightly, but it moved. Within seconds my brothers' and sisters' were sat in the vehicle with me, eager screams of excitement filled the inside of the car now, all eager to get the thing moving and we were rocking backwards and forwards as hard has we could trying to get the thing moving, but after a few minutes we began to realise that we were not going anywhere: the car needed a push. Volunteers or rather victims were bullied into volunteering to get out and push, and soon two of my younger siblings were grunting at the back of the car. Though the car had not been stripped, the engine and gearbox had been removed making car much lighter and it began to roll slowly down the slight incline, just slow enough for the pushers to jump back in to the car. At first it was great, I was *actually* driving a car, or so I thought, but in reality the car was just rolling forward and picking up speed at an alarming rate and I had no idea what I was doing. We stopped laughing when we noticed that, no matter which way I turned the steering wheel. Somebody must have removed a vital part of the steering and the thing did not respond and going wherever it wanted. Looking at my siblings I saw their smiles change looks of fear has they realised I couldn't stop the car. It can only have been a few hundred yards but we seemed to travel for miles and we were so busy holding each other and screaming that we didn't notice where the car was heading. It was not as if I could have stopped the car even if the brakes had been working as not only did my feet not reach the peddles but I didn't know which one was the brake anyway: so I screamed along with my brothers and sister and the we all watched in horror as the car rolled inexorably towards a high brick wall of a derelict house. The house had been empty for some time and had been partially demolished, it seemed that we were about to finish the job. We had picked up speed and were going too fast for anyone to jump out; so we watched the wall get closer and closer, clinging to each other while we screamed. Then, with a loud bang and the sound of things breaking and metal bending the car hit the wall, crashed through with some ease and came to rest in the enclosed in the back yard of the house. The whole episode only lasted a few seconds but it took several minutes before the small gang of children emerged from the, now, totally wrecked old banger but, other a few bumps and a bit of blood here and there, we were all ok. A look of total shock was on our all our faces, and although shaking, we had survived and I remember laughing but not finding it at all funny.

We quickly left the scene of the crime. It had been just another scary adventure for us and we all soon recovered and it wasn't long before we were back up to mischief.

Brian Mynott

Much of Leeds Road, and streets that ran off it, was being demolished and many of the old houses that still stood, and still had doors, were left unlocked and partially stripped, others had been levelled and all that remained was rubble, however among this rubble lay hidden wonders. Every now and then we would find the entrance to a cellar and the cellar would become another hideaway, a den. We would take candles, bottles of water and, when we could, we would take sweets and stay hidden in our den for hours. It was our place of safety, a way of escaping the real world, a place where we could be children, and a place where we could laugh out loud without fear of being beaten. Once we even found a gas meter that had not been emptied of money. The shillings stunk of gas so we washed them in a toilet bowl then we bought bread, milk and sweets with the money. I felt safe down there with just my brothers' and sisters' for company. I would often try and imagine the people who had lived the house, how they lived, and their names and were they happy. We were always reluctant to leave our den and return to our home; in our den we were happy and could make noise and play; at home we stopped being children.

One day when we were looking round an old mill that was due to be demolished, we found some old metal bins. The bins were empty and huge rusty, old things with pictures of red skull in the middle of each one. We didn't really think that much of them at first and we just rolled them at each other, then we realised that the smallest of my siblings would fit nicely into one of them so my youngest sister *volunteered* to be the passenger and, struggling, she was placed in the bin which we had dragged to the top of the same hill that had carried the car so swiftly into, and through, the garden only a few weeks before and with a gentle push my young sister was on her way. It went well, or so we thought. When my sister emerged seemingly unscathed from being bounced around the bin we all just laughed has our sister screamed at us, however after about half an hour her hair turned bright green. We couldn't stop laughing, even my sister eventually joined in and even the battering my father dished out to us all later that day for turning one of his children a deep green, couldn't stop us bursting into spontaneous fits of giggles for weeks after. But happy memories like this are few and very far between.

One day father brought a dog home, a small Jack Russell crossbreed that bit anything and anyone that moved, but it was a game little thing and in no time at all it was part of our little gang and didn't bite us too often, father however wasn't so lucky and we had to hide the dog upstairs when he was around, it used to go berserk when it heard father shouting. More than once my father had tried to catch the little thing and, although we dare not show it, we found it very funny watching father being made a fool of. It made him seem almost human. One day however he did catch the dog and although the dog fought bravely, biting and scratching, it stood no chance and father threw it into the back yard and beat it to death with a spade. I think that was the first time I had seen death let alone anything killed, and it broke my heart and, though the pain has gone, I can still see the spade being swung and hear the slight whimper has the heavy blade connected with the little dog's body. But father didn't just hit the dog once, he kept striking the limp body with the spade until there was just a mass of broken skin and brains and blood. It is an image that is immovable from my memory.

It was while we lived at Leeds Road that I started to be aware of how others perceived my family and the reason why we were isolated and ignored by our neighbours. We were the poorest family living a very poor neighbourhood. We had nothing of any value and my father's violent temper ensured that we had very few visitors. Parents would not allow their children to play with us in case we infected them with something nasty, either with nits or, somehow, our general poverty. Nothing highlighted this more than our treatment at school, not so much from the teachers as from the other pupils. Every day we would have to queue for our pink free dinner token. The queue was for the poor kids only, whole families of children would be forced to run the gauntlet of derision from the children who paid for their food. The teachers must have been aware of this and the acute embarrassment it caused and either they could do nothing, or simply choose not to, either way it encouraged bad feeling and cleared the way for many playground fights at break times. At least these fights offered some release of the anger that seemed to be growing inside me.

Most of the fights in the playground were short lived and soon over but I remember my first *real* fight and I remember how much I enjoyed it, the feelings of shame would be replaced with of power and the respect, or so I thought, that came with it. I was beginning to enjoy feeling that power and I was beginning to enjoy fighting; and school was the perfect place to meet bullies, and I hated bullies.

Mrs Skinner was the first teacher that I can remember with any real clarity. Mrs Skinner was my form teacher at Bradford Moor Junior School. She was a small, pleasant, woman that took the time, and had the patience, to teach me basic stuff like my birth date and how to tie my shoelaces. Simple, basic, stuff that most of my class took for granted yet I was just learning. I was seven or eight years old and being given 'special' attention made me a target for the school bullies. But I was not an easy target, I was the opposite and many of the bullies I would meet during my school years would find that out to their cost.

One Monday morning, as I stood in the meal ticket queue with the rest of the local poor kids, one of the older boys in the 'rich kids queue, had come up with the idea that those in my queue were 'scroungers'. His father, apparently, had told him how he was paying for us via his taxes and we should all be put in workhouses. The lad's dad had put words in his son's mouth, words that stung me and as he stood mouthing off in his own sniggering queue, I could feel a strange new feeling building inside me. I wanted to hurt him, even though he was bigger and older than me, I wanted to *really* hurt him and shut him up. The boy's constant insults had had the impact the lad had wanted, but I don't think he was anywhere near ready for the response he got from me, it even surprised me: not just what happened but the ease at which it came.

I picked up my pink meal ticket as usual from the desk at the front of the assembly hall, I had stood in that queue absorbing the snide remarks and direct insults for too long and I knew I was building up to thumping someone. Every Monday morning it had been the same, the pushing and name calling, lads sniffing the air and holding their noses then pointing and chanting that we all stank. The bullies had pushed and pushed until I had to push back, and that day the bullies had gone too far this time so I pushed back the only way I knew how, with extreme violence. The boys that did most of the bullying had turned their attention from me and picked on my younger sister, laughing when she had begun to cry. The main protagonist was beaming with pleasure at making her weep, it was a victory to him and he revelled in his achievement hurling more abuse at her even when she ran from the room sobbing. The boy I was about to batter was about two years older than me in his final year at the school, and he was a good three inches taller; however he was tiny when compared to my father and I had been at the receiving end of his beatings often enough, so much so that I had lost all fear of kids, even those bigger than me and, as I walked towards him he would have had no idea as to what was going to happen next because even I didn't know, I just knew that I was very angry and that something would happen.

Walking towards the bully the rage began to build up inside me, I could still hear the name-calling; still see the fingers pointing at my sister's shabby clothes and her tears has she stood sobbing outside the room door. There was no fear in the bully's eyes, why would there be? I was only small in height and my shoulders had only just begun to take shape. But I was fit, deceptively strong and full of adrenalin and hate and before he realised what was about to happen it was too late for him. Not altering my step I walked straight at him pushed him hard in his chest, forcing him to fall back and before he could respond I punched him full in his face several times. He fell crying and swearing, his friends lifted him from the floor held him back, echoing the bully's words that he could and would kill me at playtime. But I didn't want to wait that long and went for him again; ignoring his mates and screaming with my own rage, I thumped him several more times. His 'friends' just backed away from the fight leaving him to suffer a beating on his own and, even though he begged me to stop, I hit him several times before I stopped. It was then that I noticed I was crying.

Teachers appeared from all around the assembly hall and I was carted off to Mrs Skinner's room whilst the bully received treatment for his bleeding nose, his fat lip and his hurt pride. Fully expecting the cane I stood, still shaking with rage, in front of my teacher. I wasn't scared of the cane, I had been caned many times before and it didn't hurt nearly has much has I thought it would and I would have happily taken the punishment that I thought was inevitable, Mrs Skinner, however, was great about it, she had witnessed what had been taking place for some time and, though she had tried to stop the bullying, she had failed. It seemed that by humiliating the main bully I had put a stop to it. Mrs Skinner only gave me a few hundred lines stating that '*I must not fight in school*' and advised me to be careful walking home as she felt that the bullies would try and get their revenge when I was alone; I smiled at that, Mrs Skinner had never meet my siblings and, as we always walked home together, I knew that I was safe. However I didn't have to wait long for the bully and his gangs' response, and it wasn't when I was walking home.

Dinnertime came and to reach the dinning hall the children had to walk in twos across the busy main road outside the school and has I walked with the '*free lunch brigade*' clutching my free meal pink ticket, I was very aware of eyes glaring at me and I could hear the threats being spoken quietly, but with venom, about what was going to happen to me after dinner. The bullies, it seems, had not finished with me yet. One or two of the gang nearest to me asked if I was scared of them now, was I scared of having my legs broke etc, strangely I was not. I was looking forward to continuing the fight. I still had vivid images of my sister sobbing, the images bringing the feelings of rage flooding back. The lad I had beaten stood to the back of his mates this time and well away from my eager fists, they certainly knew I was not scared of them because I just stared at them with no signs of emotion at all, and that seemed to unnerve them.

I think the fact that I ate all my dinner and even asked for seconds unnerved the bullies even further, they could do nothing but stare at me, trying to strike terror into me with his eyes, but all I returned was a smile, a wicked little smile that told them I was not scared. Leaving the dinning hall the children were allowed to walk back to the school at their own speed and in small groups. We could call at the corner shop to top up our dinners with sweets and pop but I had only got within a few yards of the shop when I felt a powerful shove in the middle of my back, I knew immediately who was responsible and, letting the momentum of the push carry me forward I ran, only a few yards, but it was enough to make the gang think I was running away and a cheer went up; but I had run only to give me space so that I could turn round and face my attacker and sure enough it was the bully. He was shouting out to his friends just what he was going to do to me, by running away I had given him misplaced confidence and he took off his jacket throwing it to the ground and striding towards me, his face full of anger and revenge, and confidence. But he was hopelessly exposed and held his fists down by his sides, his already bruised face was a tempting target and I knew I could not miss, I think I smiled at him as the rage burned again from deep inside me and my young fist slammed into the side of his head.

I thumped him again and again, until his only defence was to put his hands up to protect his head, then the tears started, not mine, his, I was in full fighting mode and had lost all sense of control. Tears teemed from him, the bully; the 'hard man' had fallen from his lofty position as the 'tough guy' and school bully. A boy much smaller than him had beaten the crap out of him, not once but twice, and he hadn't even got a single decent punch in: and I smiled again as he cried. His mates, once again, had deserted him.

Mrs Skinner had no choice this time but to cane me. I took the punishment without complaint and Mrs Skinner had used as little force as possible when she caned me; it had been worth it and I felt good about myself. I think that Mrs Skinner felt good about the lad being thumped. He was a known bully and had picked on the wrong person to bully, it was has simple has that. Maybe he learned a lesson that day, but I doubt it.

That caning was to be, as far as I can remember, the last time I would see Miss Skinner. The family was to be evicted from Leeds Road and, as usual, we would sneak off during the hours of darkness to a new life in a new home without the chance to say farewell to anyone. But our new home wasn't really new. The house may have different rooms and we would have new neighbours, but life remained the same, same shit in a different place, a drunken father and a hapless mother. Constantly moving house also meant that I couldn't establish any kind of solid friendships outside the family. All I ever seemed to do was fight the local kids when they tried to establish a 'pecking order' and put me in my place. Fighting was becoming a way of life and almost every day would I would be involved in a scrap with someone. And, if I am honest, I enjoyed every fight and I felt it was the one thing I was any good at, and it was the only thing that my father seemed to like about me.

I remain, to this day, very sorry that I didn't get the chance to say goodbye to Miss Skinner and the few friends that I had made. She had taught me many lessons; and not just academic, she was a wonderful woman that taught me a little bit about *me*

Why we moved from Leeds Road I could only guess that it was for the same reason we never stayed in any house for more than a few months. My parents seldom, if ever paid any bills. There was also the strong possibility that the free electricity, supplied by the unsuspecting barber, had been discovered. Seeing as there was a thick length of wire running from the barber's meter to our house, it was a distinct possibility. But whatever reason, we moved from Leeds Road in the middle of night. A caravan of children pushing prams and carts laden with their meagre possessions would skulk away during the hours of darkness. We were used to it. To the children it was nothing special and, at least, this time I was not sorry to leave the house. It held some terrible memories. Of gas wall lights, the sticking dank attic, the flashing trolley buses, a black hat and a black feather and a little dog being beaten to death.

Ripley Ville

It was always the same when we moved house. In the dead of night the sleeping children would be roused from our bed and set to work, still half asleep, packing our meagre belongings into boxes or wrapping them in blankets. Then, after putting all the furniture on handcarts, prams and carrying bags and boxes, we left the house that had briefly been our home. I can remember feeling sadness when we trundled past the homes of our recent neighbours. The main Leeds road was deathly quiet and there was not a single vehicle to break the silence, the only noise was the thundering noises the wheels from the carts and prams of the family that were fleeing. Someone must have heard the racket. Pots and pans rattles and every so often a bucket, or some other metallic object would fall from a cart and crash to the ground; and bounce at least a thousand times before it was stopped. A great sadness came when I noticed a bedroom light on making the flowered curtains glow in the darkness. I tried to imagine the family that lived there, and I wondered if they had ever done what we were doing, or were they a 'proper' family, and I remember crying silently. There had been no chance to say goodbye to my few friends, no chance to see Mrs Skinner or the other teachers and no opportunity to thank them, and no chance to say goodbye to the few school friends I had made. We simply disappeared into the night.

Before dawn we had reached our new home. Tired, cold and very hungry, I looked along the deserted streets of Ripley Ville trying to guess which of the rundown houses was to be our home, they all looked the same, smog blackened and ancient, with more cardboard in the windows than glass. Making our way along the narrow uneven potholed streets and with the noise of the carts echoing back off the houses, I felt depressed and pissed off with life as curtains twitched and heads popped out of open windows asking what the hell we thought we were doing. We hadn't even moved in and I already felt ashamed. Looking at the back of my father's head as he tried to force the kids to be quiet by belting them as they pushed the heavy carts, I felt my first real sense of hatred towards him, I wished my father were not with us, with all my heart I wished it. I even wished him dead.

Ripley Ville was a small estate made up of houses that seemed even older than those on Leeds Road. Closely packed together these houses had, like most of the houses in Bradford, been built to accommodate the workers of the previous century that once operated the sprawling mills that made Bradford a magnet for the unemployed, attracting families from all over Britain and, in later years, from around the world.

By the mid 1960s however, the huge factories were closing down leaving many of the workers unemployed and Ripley Ville reflected this change with many of those living on the estate being jobless and '*drawing the dole*'.

Narrow potholed footpaths separated small front gardens. Broken windows had been 'fixed' with cardboard or wood and everywhere there were piles of rubbish. Small front gardens were mostly neglected and old broken or unwanted furniture had been left to rot where they it had been dumped. In the enclosed backyards of the houses were the outside toilets and coal sheds. The toilets being shared by at least two houses and was always going to be a problem for all concerned considering father's habit of spending hours in there. No one dare ask him to hurry, and it didn't matter if anyone was waiting; he would stay in there until he had read his paper; or whatever it was that he did in there. Has we arrived at the front door of our new home, I remember thinking that the new neighbours had no idea the trouble that was about to move into their street.

The house itself was small but at least it had three bedrooms, a front and back door, a separate kitchen *and* electricity. It was a slight improvement on Leeds Road, but not much; the only real bonus was the electricity because I knew that meant no more terrifying gaslights. The décor consisted of two tones of brown paint separated by a dado rail, I think the colours had, at one time, been distinctive different shades of brown, but over time the colours had faded so much that they had blended and now looked the same. There were no carpets anywhere in the house and the kitchen floor was flagged in well-worn paving stones. Throughout the house there lingered a rancid smell. I never did get used to that awful stench, nor did I find out what caused it. The house, like Leeds Road, had an attic but with, the added luxury of a skylight offering some light during the day so I knew it wouldn't be too bad during the day, but the electricity didn't extend to the attic so those that slept there would rely on candles during the night. And that meant more nights of dancing shadows.

My life changed in several ways during our time there, some good and some bad, but mostly bad. My older sister seemed to distance herself further from the family each day; she withdrew further away from the rest of us and would go days without speaking to anyone, and she had stopped laughing. Something was wrong with my sister, very wrong, but I was too young to work it out. We had grown together; we had laughed and cried together: now she neither laughed nor cried and I hardly knew her anymore.

It was while we lived on the Villa that I first felt the deep sadness the death of someone I loved could bring. My granddad lost a battle with cancer and died. I didn't even know he was poorly, I hadn't seen him for a long time and then, suddenly, he was dead. I remember the shock and then the tears when my mother came home one evening and calmly told us our granddad was dead. Even my father seemed to be affected by the loss, whilst I cannot remember any tears from him or even mother, he was very quiet for a few days and I remember he even tolerated the children crying.

My granddad Albert was my mother's father and he was the total opposite to my own father. Granddad Albert was patient, funny and loving. He could make me feel safe and loved with nothing more than the ruffling of my hair. He was much smaller than my own father and almost as round as he was tall and when he laughed his belly would bounce up and down. I know he loved me, he told me he did, and I remember it thinking that I would never see him again or his little bungalow in Doncaster again, and I remember the horrible feeling of loss I felt.

I had left Bradford Moor School with feelings sadness and regret at not having the chance to say goodbye and I was not looking forward to going to yet another 'new school' and having to make new friends, and enemies, all over again; but I needn't have been worried, my new school would be my favourite of the many schools I attended. My new school was St James' Junior, a small school about a mile away from The Villa, and even though I had initially resented the enforced move, the little school was to play a pivotal role in my life. It was at this wonderful school I started to gain a sense of me and who I was and also discover that I loved reading.

I remember every room of St James School. Every sound and smell of that old school building and the classrooms are fixed in my memory and I loved every day I spent there. From the very first day I started at St James' I felt welcome. Even the little scruff that I was, the teachers treated me as an equal. There was no separate queue when collecting our free school meal tickets and the teachers soon remembered my face and name and would just hand me the tickets. No fuss, no snide remarks—just a pink ticket.

It was around this time that my siblings and I first started to receive free school clothes from the local government and even though it was great to get brand new uniforms, it would again be a cause of embarrassment, not just to me but also all the children that received the government handouts. All the clothes were marked in some way, even the shoes had a hole on the side near the lace-holes and it didn't take the other kids long to pick up on this, however unlike Bradford Moor school, at St James' there was very little harassment and, the little that there was, was quickly stopped by the teachers. Maybe it was because, at St James', more pupils received these handouts, including free meals, than didn't, but I also think it was down to the teachers and how they discouraged any kind of *'them and us'* feeling to develop.

There was the same kind of 'we are all in this together' feeling within Ripley Ville where most, if not all, the families that lived on that old estate were poor with most of the men unemployed. Few had any money to spare and all the houses were in the same state of disrepair. Much of the estates social life revolved around the pub in the centre of the estate and the church at the top of bumpy the main road that ran between the houses splitting the estate in two. The church ran a Sunday school, and I remember well playing in the small graveyard and reading the headstones, amazed at how very old some of the people were when the died. Far older than my granddad was when he died: he was 56 and some of the graves were for people that were as old as 68! I remember more than once pretending that my granddad was buried there and would sit on the low wall and talk to him asking him why he died and could he hear me. And more than once I was sure I heard his voice, heard his laugh and felt his hand ruffle my hair. It's difficult to understand death when you're so young, it just didn't make sense that I would never, ever see my granddad again, that he could just not be there anymore. I cried a lot, only realising that I loved him when I couldn't tell him anymore.

There was a real feeling of community on The Villa, and my family were very much a part of it. Even father seemed more settled and I remember that every week he would check that mother had paid the rent by checking the rent book; he must have wanted to stay there, as did his children. We had started to make real friends and, although we were the poorest family with the scruffiest house, we were equals. Even father had seemed to have lost some of his anger and hardly hit any of his children and, with the exception of my older sister; he would sometimes even talk to his children in a normal voice. Even though I felt no love for my father, and hated him only slightly less when he wasn't belting the crap out of me, it was the closest I had felt true happiness since I lived in Denby Dale. That is until my mother did her best, and then succeeded, in isolating us from the rest of people on The Villa. Within a few months of being welcomed on to the Villa, we were to become the most hated family on the estate and forced to move again.

My mother was not, physically, a cruel woman; she was cruel in a way that was much harder to deal with. Mother simply didn't care about her children, or anyone else for that matter, and she didn't care what took place in the house or what her children got up to when they were playing out, and she always made excuses to the doctors and police for the bruises our father gave us. It was mother's total apathy for all her children, not just me that was hurtful and cruel. In many ways it was easier to deal with the physical pain of father's beatings than deep sadness that I felt being unloved and unprotected by my mother, and it was not as if my mother didn't feel the force of father's violence, on more than one occasion my father would beat my mother in full view of me and my brothers and sisters. Yet still my mother did nothing to protect her own children; and in later life I would realise exactly why.

The full horror and terror of witnessing such violence is etched, in pictures and feelings, into my memory. The screams of my mother, the smashing of furniture and of children cowering has they huddled together for imagined protection; crying quietly as they watched their parents destroy all our lives. These are a group of memories that I could not remove no matter how hard I tried and, even though I have never loved my mother though always wanted to, the sight of her semi conscious on the floor of the kitchen with blood pouring from her face can still stir emotion. No person should suffer like that. Not a man or woman, and certainly not a child. But my mother never seemed to worry about the beatings she knew father would give her when she '*forgot*' to pay the rent or *forgetting* to have his tea ready, and she seemed to recover from the beatings within days. But I don't think mother realised just how angry father would get when she caused us to be evicted. However before we would be evicted my life would change in a way that I would leave me both grateful and angry. I would be grateful that

I had seen things, nice wonderful things, and anger because I realised that my life was *not* normal.

A Bradford charity helped impoverished families send their children on a two-week respite holiday and I had been offered a place at Cinderella Home in Morecambe. At first I was nervous at the thought of being away from my family for two whole weeks but I remember a few days before I was due to start my holiday my father had encouraged me to go by beating me senseless. I don't know why he battered me, I don't think he did, but knew I needed to get away from him and so I started to look forward to going. And I remember feeling excited about going on my first holiday; I was going to see the sea.

Although being told that I was to have a holiday in Morecambe had scared me at first the beating from my father had removed all doubt and I read the letter from the Cinderella Club full of childish excitement. I was to live with about forty other kids for two weeks and I was to sleep in a dormitory with a bunch of other kids, however that in it's self did not worry me, what really worried me was the fact that I pissed the bed every single night without fail. How was I to get out of the embarrassment of waking every morning soaked in piss? It was a thought that I could not get out of my mind, and for several nights before my holiday, I practised getting out of bed and using the piss bucket to get every drop of urine I could out of my bladder. But it didn't help; I still pissed the bed.

One thing that the club insisted on, that nearly cost me my place, was that all the children could take no more and no less than £1 each. A £1 in the early 1960s was a lot of money the fixed amount was to make sure we all had the same money to spend and thus equal, however it represented a good couple of nights boozing for my father and there was no way he was going to give me any money and I received a good slapping from him when I plucked up the mountain of courage I needed to ask him for it. he screamed at me, telling me I wasn't worth a penny, that he worked hard for his cash, that he wasn't going to waste it on a piece of shit like me and he told me I wouldn't be going. I felt heartbroken.

Father forgot that he had banned me, maybe he thought that I wouldn't go because I didn't have a £1, maybe he didn't care whether I went or not, maybe he just didn't want to waste a £1.

I really believed I wasn't going to see the sea and had resigned myself to staying on the Villa. Then my wonderful Nana came to my rescue when she raised the cash and sneaked it to me the day before I was due to travel, it was the first time I had ever seen or held so much money and I remember feeling quite scared of it, and scared of my parents finding out and taking it from me and I'm sure that father would have if had known I had the money. But the excitement would be put on hold when my mother committed a crime that was terrible even by her standards and would cost us the friendship and support of the people on Ripley Ville.

Almost every evening, when it was dark enough and wasn't raining, my mother would go 'for a walk'. As soon as she was sure father had gone to the pub and was safely getting pissed she would set off; looking for a house to rob. Often she would take my two younger sisters with her and wander the streets of Ripley Ville until she found a suitable house to rob. Mother had developed her own system for breaking into houses, and she had it off to a fine art. First, one of my sisters would knock on a door and, if anybody answered the door, she would ask if so-and-so was playing out, inventing a name and they would, of course, be told they had the wrong house, if no one answered then the house was burgled. A simple yet very effective strategy or, as the police preferred to call it, her MO. This meant of course that when the police did catch up with her she could, and did, blame the children knowing full well that my sisters, due to their age, could not be prosecuted. However on one occasion the police found the evidence they needed to arrest our mother for one particular burglary. Although I was getting used to watching mother being arrested, this time she had gone too far and the whole estate turned against the family; and I felt deep shame as two officers walked my mother the few hundred yards to their car and heard our friends and neighbours shout obscenities at her. Mother had burgled the house of one of the nicest people on the Villa. Her actions had left an old man broken hearted and lead to her family being hounded off the Villa, and I didn't blame them one bit.

Opposite our house on Saville Street lived an elderly friend of my aunty Pat, he was a smashing bloke who always had a kind word for anyone who took the time to stop and talk to him, however he was from a different generation, a generation when you would leave your door unlocked without the slightest fear of being robbed by your neighbours. That was, of course, until my mother became one of them.

I cannot remember the old chap's name but I remember that he nice and lived a pleasant, quiet life harming no one. He had spent most of his life on the Villa and I would often watch him pottering about the little garden at the front of his house. The old man was one of the few people who bothered to plant, and care for, flowers. His small front garden bringing just a much needed touch of brightness to the otherwise dull and blackened streets and he always had his old dog with him. The dog, a small very old mongrel, was quite harmless but it would yap at anybody and anything that moved. But everyone knew that the old dog was totally harmless. When approached it would suddenly stop barking, and then roll over on its back so you could scratch its belly.

I remember the night my mother robbed that lovely old man and also remember the anger it caused. The ethos of Ripley Ville was one of *'we may be poor, but we are all poor'*. This simple but wonderful community spirit didn't concern my mother in the least; she didn't care who she robbed and had already burgled a few houses on The Villa and many of our neighbours had already begun to suspect our family. Mother knew of the suspicions but simply didn't care and, when the time came, she didn't hesitate to mobilise my sisters to rob the old man. One evening watched through the window has the old man left his home; waiting until he was out of sight before mother sending my two sisters the few yards across the street to rob him. The man's old dog was no problem and I remember watching it toddle down the street wagging its tail, my sisters' had left the door open slightly and the mongrel just trotted out making a beeline for the pub to visit its master. I may have been still only a young boy but I knew that, has soon has the dog went into the pub, the old man would know something was wrong; but mother didn't seem to care one bit

The pub was only a few hundred yards from the old man's house and, within minutes of the dog reaching the pub; the old chap was walking back towards his house. My heart nearly burst and my bladder empty, and I felt a great urge to run away when I saw my father walking the old man and his dog home.

My father caught my little sisters carrying an old radio and some other stuff out of the house; he went crazy and beat them all the way our house. They were both screaming that their mum had made them do it, pleading with him to stop, but he wouldn't, father never listened to his children pleading for mercy. As they got closer to our house, father literally threw the youngest of my sisters at the front door of our house. The force of my sister crashing against the door swung it violently open; slamming the door against a chair sending it spinning across the floor. In a state of panic I tried to hide behind the sofa but found I could hardly move. My legs were shaking so bad that I couldn't get them to carry me without falling. The screaming, the crying, was terrible and the sheer terror I saw in my sisters face as she landed on the floor nearly me made me piss my self again. I was in a state of blind panic, but adrenalin must have kicked in because my legs suddenly stopped shaking and started to work so I raced through the small cluttered room towards the kitchen avoiding my sisters' has they lay trembling on the floor. Climbing over my sisters that day, has they lay helpless on the floor is a memory that I cannot shake. And for years after I thought myself a coward for not helping them; but I now know and understand that I dare not stop, I was just a small boy trying to survive. I ran through the small kitchen and ran up the bedroom stairs. I was shaking with fear and the screams and shouts of what was taking place downstairs followed me. I dived onto the bed and buried my head into a pillow and pulled the stinking blankets over my body in a pathetic attempt to find safety by hiding. My heart was racing and my blood was pounding so loud in my ears that it sounded like the steam train thundering passed. But it loud enough to drown out the noise out that was coming from downstairs. I could still hear the screams of my sisters. Terrified that I was going to get a beating I pissed myself again, soaking my school trousers and the bed. But the beating never came and, after what seemed like hours, the slamming of the door announced that my father had gone back to the pub and the only sound that remained was the sad noise of my sisters sobbing. Deep inside I felt my own fear growing. I knew, has my sisters' did, that when father returned from the pub things would be even worse; he would be even more violent. But I was lucky that night. Exhaustion must have overtaken me and I eventually fell asleep. When I eventually awoke I was alone in the bed and I wasn't sure if it was the same day that I had fallen asleep; it took some time to realise that the whole night had passed and then I started to remember the violence of the night before; and I started to shake again has the memories returned. Even though the house was silent and it was daylight I was terrified and I lay on the top of the bed knowing that I had to try and remove the strong smell of piss that clung to me before I went to school. My clothes were damp with piss and they had creased terribly while I had slept. But I dare not move; I dare not make any sound that may bring my father screaming into the bedroom, so I lay on the bed listening for any sound from down stairs that would indicate that all was well. There was nothing but silence. After lying on the bed for what seemed like forever, I knew I had to get out of bed and go downstairs I did so with a feeling of dread, fearful of what I would find down there. Slowly I made my way down the stairs, cringing every time the old wooden stairs creaked and as I got near to the bottom step I could make out voices. I recognised my older sister's voice. She was whispering but I could not make out what she was saying or where exactly they were coming from. Leaving the stairs I stood in the small kitchen straining my ears to make sure that father was not on the other side of the door that I was about to open. After few minutes, and when I was sure it was safe and that father had gone to work, I slowly I turned the door handle and pushed gently. And when I opened the room door fully and looked into the room where my mother and sisters were; I was shocked at what I saw and couldn't help but let out a small scream.

The room had been totally trashed, furniture had been upturned and there were stains all over the walls as if someone had thrown water around the room. My mother was leaning against the small grease covered table; her face was smeared with dry blood and there were bruises and swelling covering most of her face; her clothes were torn and she was shaking almost as much as I was. Father had obviously beaten mother very badly but I felt little pity for her. There were none of the feelings that a son should have for his mother when seeing her in so much pain and distress; the sight of her scared me, but I felt little else. It was my two sisters that I was concerned with and looked around the room and noticed that my older sister wasn't there and I thought that maybe she had escaped and had gone to school. Then I heard sobbing coming from the kitchen and I knew immediately that it was my sister, I had heard my older sister sob too often and knew the sound too well.

My sister was lying curled in a ball on the floor of the kitchen, her hair was matted and she was trying to cover her small body with a towel. She had squeezed herself between the grease smothered cooker and an equally filthy cabinet that stood only a foot or so to one side of it. It was a poor hiding place, but it was the best that she could do to hide from the violence of my father, but it obviously hadn't helped. Father had got to her. Has I write about this I am feeling very real anger, the image of my sister lying helpless and abused on that filthy kitchen floor is another memory that is branded into my brain.

It turned out that the previous night my father had not returned later that evening, he didn't return home until the early morning. Before he had gone out he had ordered my sisters, and my mother, to stay in the kitchen and not move until he came home warning them that he would deal with them when got back. They had obeyed and stayed in the kitchen the whole night, not daring to move a single step from where father had left them. Then he had gone out and stayed at the pub all night getting pissed. When he did arrive early morning he was still very drunk and had set about beating my mother until, according to my sister, she was unconscious. He then took my older sister into the kitchen so she could '*make his breakfast*' leaving my younger sister to look after my unconscious mother. Of course my father did not want my sister to make his breakfast; he was to vent his anger on her in a very different way. But I didn't know it back then what was really happening. To me it was just another form of violence.

I would have been about 8 years old then, and my character was being formed and my perception of right and wrong was being established. I had started to fight again, mostly defending my sisters and I from the other kids on the Villa that had turned against us since my mother robbed the old man. I had even started to steal things. Only bottles of milk at first and really that was only because it was the only sustenance I could get, but I would also steal sweets from the shop. Though I felt guilt at this I was beginning the feel that if the world hated me, then I hated the world and it could fuck off and I would steal whatever I could. It was how I felt. I was getting angrier by the day and before I knew it, I had started to take things and sometimes smash them, simply has a way of fighting back. I hated my life and the people in it and it was starting to change me inside.

My trip to Morecambe could not have come at a better time. I was becoming the kind of son my mother would have been proud of; a thief. And it burned my conscience, and I was beginning to hate myself even more. But at the same time I was feeling empowered by the simple act of taking things from people and being able to find or buy food whenever I wanted. If it had not been for my holiday to Morecambe, I am sure that I would have carried on stealing and breaking things and my life would have taken a very different path.

Although I was desperately looking forward to my holiday, and the fun I was sure to have; I didn't know it at the time but I would not just have days and nights of fun, my two weeks at The Cinderella Home would bring. Those two weeks would not only take me away from the violence, filth and stealing that had become my normality, it would make me challenge everything I thought of as normal, and challenge the person I was becoming.

Anyway, the big day came for my two-week holiday and I was surprised and more than a bit scared to find out that my father would be taking me to Foster Square train station to begin my journey to Morecambe. I was to meet up with the other needy children of Bradford at the station and also some of the people that would be looking after me during my holiday. My father taking me to the station had convinced that he had found out about the £1 I had tucked away in the little suitcase. I had decided I would just hand over the money to him at the first mention of it, it was not worth the beating I would receive and, in all honesty, during the short drive to the station I was beginning to have doubts about going to Morecambe and was seriously considering pretending that I felt sick. What would happen every morning when they found my pissed wet through bed? But as the car pulled up at the station and before I could change my mind, father told me to get a *'fucking move on . . . get out of the friggin car'* and that was enough to convince me to go. I had to get away from him and the daily feelings of terror I felt in the pit of my stomach every time he came near me or even spoke.

I have no idea why father had borrowed my aunt pat's car to take me to the station, it wasn't as if he was going to tearfully bid me farewell, he had made it quite clear that he was glad to get shut of me for two weeks. As for my mother, well I don't think she even noticed I was going anywhere let alone that I had gone.

We had arrived at the station well before the prearranged time meaning I had to spend a miserable hour or so alone in my father's company. All the time I expected him to demand the cash out of my suitcase, but he didn't. Then; without saying a word he just slumped down and fell asleep on a bench and was soon snoring loudly. Even the huge steam engines bellowing steam and shunting backwards and forwards failed to disturb father's deep slumber. I sat at his feet looking at him, and I remember feeling anger and disgust has I watched saliva dribble down his chin. I had seen him asleep many times, it was father's favourite pastime on a Saturday afternoon when he returned from the pub, pissed. He would put the TV on (when we had one) and watch the wrestling. Most times he would want to wrestle with his children. It was not a fun thing. Father would pin me to the floor and bend my arm or leg back so far that I would scream in pain. Then he would get angry and call me a soft bastard, a coward, a piece of shit. Then he would pull me back to the floor and pin me down. I now know that when father pinned me down and rubbed himself against me, it had nothing to do with punishment or the wrestling.

The smell and all the sounds of the station were a new experience to me; people were everywhere busily boarding or getting off trains, guards in uniforms were helping people find the right platform or carrying heavy bags for those that seemed to need help. Then I saw a group of scruffy kids, sad faced and dressed in tatty clothes just like me, each carrying a bag or suitcase and holding their parents' hands. All the children seemed just as scared as me and a few had even started to cry. I knew that it was getting close to the time to start my holiday and I needed to move from the bench. This left me with a decision to make: how do I wake my father without getting a thumping? I started to gently prod him as if he was a delicate piece of glass. But he just carried on snoring so, forcing myself to prod him a little harder each time, I continued, scared to death that I achieved what I was trying to do and wake him. But it was no use he just grunted and carried on sleeping his snoring seemed to grow even louder. Eventually a big bloke that was standing in the waiting group noticed my suitcase and me and gave me a cheery wave. I smiled sheepishly back and returned to prodding my father, screaming inside my head for the fat bastard to wake up. I knew that unless I shook him hard I had no chance, and I simply dare not do it, there was a serious risk of being thumped there and then. Father had never shown the slightest reluctance to beat the crap out of me in the company of others. In the 50's and 60's very few people would have gotten involved with '*domestic issues*' and I often felt the back of my father's hand in the middle of Bradford on a busy road. No one ever even tried to stop him.

The man that had waved walked over to where I was trying to waken my father. I didn't notice him approach and he made me

Brian Mynott

jump when he said hello and put his big hand on my shoulder. I looked up and our eyes and I felt immediately liked; he was one of the biggest blokes I had ever seen in my life, his voiced boomed but gently. He could see what I was trying to do and he shook his head knowingly; and he must have seen the fear and confusion in my eyes. Even the vigorous shaking my father was now receiving from me failed to wake him; he just grunted and farted. The huge man smiled and put a finger to his lips indicating for me to be quiet and clam down. As I looked at the man's face knew that that I could trust him, though he was massive with huge arms and hands, and I liked him instantly. As I looked at him, I saw only kindness in his face and eyes. "*Hello, little chap, are you going to Morecambe with the Cinderella lot?*" his voice was calm but very deep and I nodded vigorously in response "*having trouble waking your dad then?*" He looked down at the man that was snoring, grunting and farting like a pig with salvia running down the side of his face. I shrugged and nodded ashamed of my father. The bastard was asleep in the noisiest and busiest place I had every seen, and he was oblivious to the world. "*Now, little chap, you just give me your case and go and tell that lady over there your name and leave your dad to me*" he pointed towards the group of waiting people and waved to get the attention of a round middle aged woman. She looked happy and kind and waving at me beckoned me to go to her. I waved back and reluctantly handed the big man my suitcase, the suitcase contained my quid, yet I felt not the slightest hint of mistrust when he took the suitcase that now seemed very small in his huge hand. As I walked away from the bench and my sleeping father I turned my head and watched astonished has, after a few punitive attempts at waking my sleeping father the giant simply raised the bag above my sleeping father and let it fall on to my father's chest. I held my breath. Father grunted and suddenly, and violently, knocked the offending suitcase off his body. I quickened my pace to put distance between my father, knowing, or rather thinking I knew, what was about to happen. Father would batter him. But I was in for a surprise. Father sat up looking fierce and felt my bowels turning to liquid as he then sprang to his feet his hands curled into fists. I had seen that face many times and I nearly pissed my self with the fear it always created. The big man didn't flinched though and stood straight in front of my father, his massive bulk towering above my father. Father baulked at the sheer size of him. My father was many things, a brute, a bully and a drunkard but certainly no coward, I had seen him on several occasions go up against more than one bloke without any sign of fear, however even he realised that it would be a mistake to suddenly lash out at the giant of a man that stood in front of him. The man seemed to grow even taller when father faced him, he towered above my father and glared down at him and I thought, for a brief moment, that my father was going to belt him. But he didn't he, father just stood there glaring back; craning his neck to look up. But the big man didn't flinch and I knew by the look on his face that if father did start a fight, the big man was more than ready, in fact I think he was hoping my father would throw a punch. After what seemed an eternity the giant told my father in his deep gravely voice that he could leave his son, me, with him and go back to bed if he was so knackered and without another word he suddenly turned and walked towards me. I was in a kind of shock and had stopped walking and stood watching events unfold. When he caught up with me the huge bloke ruffled my hair and, swapping my suitcase from one hand to the other, he held out his massive hand and, taking hold of my comparatively tiny hand with his other and totally ignoring my father, he walked me over to join my new friends.

When I looked back my father had gone, no goodbye, no cheery wave and no words of concern about staying safe or having a nice time, there was just an empty bench where he had been sleeping. I remember suddenly feeling lonely and afraid and even before I got on to the train I had trouble holding back the tears. I was feeling 'home sick' just like most of the other children waiting to board the train, but they were free to cry and some even got a friendly hug from the people that were now charged with our care. I didn't cry, my father had taught me that it was pointless and that crying could also bring about a beating. So I fought back the tears with little difficulty: and I was angry with myself when I realised I was missing my father.

Brian Mynott

When I eventually boarded the train with the other children and our carers, I was feeling quite nervous, yet at the same time the train fascinated me. The sights, sounds and smells were all new to me and I felt excitement building inside me. As the train began to pull away the noise increased tremendously has the huge engine pulled at the carriages making loud metallic thumping noise. Great clouds of steam seemed to fall like a dense fog all over the station. It was both scary and beautiful at the same time and I peered through the window of the train fascinated and watched as the other children's parents' waved their children goodbye. Mothers cried and children cried as the distant slowly widened between them. My own mother was probably still in bed and my father would have almost certainly gone to the pub as soon as he had left the station; I had no one to wave me goodbye. I waved anyway pretending that my parents were there but it hurt too much pretend so I watched the other children wave tearfully to their real parents and so I waved at theirs instead. Suddenly I felt a surge of emotion, a sense of loneliness that I couldn't understand, I stopped waving at pretend parents and went to the toilet and sat cried alone. I felt utterly unloved.

I stayed in the toilet until I stopped crying; but when I stopped crying I felt trapped. The toilet was a tiny box like room and I felt like it was crushing me; my recently acquired claustrophobia kicked in so, quickly drying my eyes, I returned to the carriage window and watched as the train began to pull slowly away from Bradford, taking me away from my normality.

The train had pulled free of the dark mills and streets of Bradford and seemed to suddenly be bathed in sunlight. The train was now travelling through open countryside and the tremendous noise inside the carriage was reduced to a gentle rumble as the noise of the engine became lost in the open air. I sat with my face pressed against the cool glass of the window watching the changing scenery. I listened to the rhythm of the train increase in tempo, feeling the side-to-side motion steady as the steam train picked up speed. I was leaving Bradford and going on holiday for the first time in my life, the feeling of homesickness had gone as quickly as it had come; replaced

Just Once, When I was little

with childish excitement and I started to smile. I was free of my home and all the shit that went with it.

Soon after we had left the station all the children were asked to pay attention but I was enthralled by the open fields and villages we were passing through and it took a bit of gentle persuasion and coaxing before I turned my gaze from the window. I wanted to see it all, drink in the openness and freshness of the countryside. I was having the same magical feelings that I had when snow covered Buttershaw. But an image of my drunken father's angry face standing at the front door came unbidden into the memory and the feeling left me

All the children were given crisps and a bottle of orange pop and then asked to wait until those charged with our care had spoken to us before we opened them. We were told about the Cinderella Home, where it was and a few instructions on what we would be doing. We were told we would still have to do schoolwork; this caused a few groans until, after a brief pause, we were told that whenever possible the classes would be held on the beach and would be mostly about marine life and only have to do a few sums! This brought a loud cheer from all the children that continued when we were asked to quieten down and told we could eat our crisp and drink the pop.

The giant that had escorted me away from my father was called John, Uncle John to the children, and he was making gestures to quieten the children. It didn't take him long to bring calm the excited children. But he did not do this through fear; he did it with a big beaming smile that seemed to cover his whole face. "Now then" he said in a booming voice that seemed to rattle the windows in the train. He stood looking around at the smiling faces of the children, none had a bigger smile than my own "you lot are a happy lot aren't you" he then paused and made a slight grimace "I want to ask you a question, but first I want to tell you something that may help you answer honestly" his smile returned and he held our full attention "until I was fourteen I wet the bed, it wasn't my fault . . . because I was always asleep when it happened" his eyes were watching, judging the reaction of the children but only a few smiled at his attempted joke. He knew it was a deep and personal question but he would also have known that many of the children on that carriage would wet the bed that night. When he asked who wet the bed a blanket of silence fell over the carriage as all the children fell silent. Uncle John held up his hand "I don't wet the bed any more" he spoke softly, his voice calming "but *I used to do*" he continued. His deep voice had a calming effect that demanded honesty and I felt a strange urge to stick my hand in the air; so I did, then others started slowly to do the same. Within a few minutes almost half of the children had their hands in the air; but I don't think any of the children felt embarrassment, if anything I felt relieved when I realised that I was not alone. I think that that is exactly what uncle John had intended, he may well have wet the bed until his early teens but whether he did or did not, it didn't matter, Uncle John had already helped the children feel less isolated, less dirty.

As the train pulled further away from my home and my family I felt a kind of freedom I had not know before. For two whole weeks I would be free. I would not have to avoid my father's drunken rages, I would not be ostracised by my friends and neighbours for the actions of my mother. I would be free of it all. Free. With every mile that passed by the window, the new experience of feeling free increased until I felt almost giddy at the thought of not seeing the miserable face of my mother and facing the unpredictable rages of my father every day and night.

Throughout the journey uncle John wondered about the carriage talking to each of the children in turn as he introduced the children to each other; helping us form friendships by encouraging the children to talk to each other. He succeeded with even the shyest of children and I found that I was eagerly waiting for Uncle John to get round to me and I wasn't disappointed when he did. Placing his huge hand on my head he ruffled my hair and I couldn't help but smile in response; his face never seemed to stop smiling, and his laugh was infectious. He reminded me of my real uncle, my uncle Joss, my father's brother a man who I have many fond memories of throughout my childhood and a man who I will write about at length later.

Just Once, When I was little

Uncle John asked me about all sorts of trivia, could I run fast, did I like swings, did I like the moors and what school did I go to? He insisted that I *would* have a nice time on my holiday or he would fasten me to a donkey and let it drag me up and down the beach. He ruffled my hair once more then introduced me to the lad sat next to me, telling us both that if we didn't talk to each other then he would sit us both on the roof of the train until we did. The threats were pure fun of course, and it worked, and so I made the first of many friends on the first day of my holiday.

When the train reach Morecambe station and came to a noisy halt, there was a flurry of activity as we all picked up our little cases and made for the exit door. There was an explosion of general mayhem as kids jumped over seats to be first to get off the train. That was until Uncle John blocked the whole doorway and put a finger to his lips. It was Uncle John's sign to calm down and we had learned it quickly so we all responded in an instant; well, almost. When calm was restored uncle John asked us all to wait a few moments until the other passengers had got off the train so no one would be lost or left behind telling us that the next stop for the train was Holland, I had no idea where Holland was but it sounded a long way off, and he assured us we wouldn't get off the train for at least two days! We all waited quietly, doing as we were asked not through fear of Uncle John, but because we all liked him; and we all wanted uncle john to like us.

Standing on the platform I could see the full length of the train as it curved along the track. It seemed to go on forever. Shiny dark green coaches with golden writing on the side stood ready, as if alive, for more passengers get on board. It had been, as far as I can remember, my first train journey and I would remember almost every minute of it, but I had two long weeks ahead of me. Two full weeks, I felt sure, of fun and freedom. And I would remember them, not just for all the fun and laughter, but for many other reasons. My life was about to change and over the following two weeks as I would be shown a very different way of life. A different kind of *normality* that would clash in almost every way from my own perception of it; and when I returned to Bradford things would never, could never be the same.

When we first arrived at the Cinderella Home I was in total awe of it. It was a flat a large flat roofed building at the very edge of Morecambe Bay. But it wasn't the building that grabbed me; it was the vast expanse of the sea that was directly behind it. I stood looking at the scene in front of me so the first thing I did when we got clear of the old double-decker bus that had carried us from the train station was to run to the wall that ran behind the building, separating the Cinderella from Morecambe Bay. When I reached the wall I stood on my tiptoes and looked over the wall and I stared in wonderment across the vast open water watching seagulls' swirl about the sky listening to their loud squawking. I could smell the sea; I could feel the cool breeze hitting my face: I took a long deep breath, filling my lungs until they hurt. Freedom, I now knew what it felt like.

I must have stood there for a long time taking it all in and it wasn't until Uncle John came over and gently placed his huge hand on my shoulder that I awoke from the trance like state I was in "if you want some tea lad, you had best come with me before it's all gone" but before we returned to rejoin the rest of the children Uncle John suddenly lifted me in the air, I felt like I was suddenly flying. Placing me on the wall had lifted me about three feet of the ground, heightening my sense of amazement of Morecambe Bay. I felt sure I could see the whole of the world from up there. Uncle John left me there for a few minutes but he remained only a few feet away in case I fell, he had no way of knowing that I had been in far more dangerous situations with my siblings but I felt happy just to feel the security his company gave me. I knew that no one, not even my father could hurt me when Uncle John was with me.

Lifting me off the wall Uncle John gently placed me back on terra firma "right little un" he half whispered "let's go get some grub eh lad . . . I am starving" and I suddenly realised that I had only had the crisps on the train that day and the rumble in my tummy confirmed that I was hungry so, holding my hand in his huge paw we walked the few yards back and joined in the chaos that was taking place.

I had seen only a few houses clean and organised before, my nana, my grandma (my father's mother) and some of my aunts and uncles' homes were always spotless and would smell of fruit or polish or even both, so I knew that not all houses had filthy kitchens and overflowing piss buckets. But the Cinderella beat them all.

I remember the strong smell of apples filling my senses as I first walked through the front door. Everything was spotlessly clean and the smell of polish mixed with the smell of fruit as I went further into the building. There was a sudden rush for the toilets when uncle John 'suggested' that we needed to wash our hands before tea and I was amazed when I opened the door the bathroom was massive. The room had a clean, not unpleasant, smell about it and on each of the sinks there was soap, a towel, a toothbrush and a comb and each sink even had its own little mirror placed at just the right height for a child. The noise from the children, including me, echoed of the tiled walls, but there was no attempt to quieten us down even though Uncle John stood in the doorway with his hands covering his ears. But I still had a nagging fear that my father would suddenly appear; that was not free of him. It would take few days for me to finally accept that he wasn't hiding somewhere.

Before we left the bathroom we were all asked if we wanted to use the toilet, which most of the children did, including me, and in each loo I found another luxury. There was toilet paper. I had only ever used the shiny stuff at school or old squares of newspaper that hung on a piece of string in the stinking toilet at home, the paper that in those toilets was soft.

There was a long queue for the toilets but there were about six toilets so the queue that had quickly formed disappeared just as quick. After washing our hands again, a strange experience for me to even wash tem once, we were shown the dormitory where we would be sleeping and, as we walked through the dormitory door, I was once again in awe of what I saw. There were two lines of beds, all with crisp clean covers neatly made up and tucked in. At the side of each bed there was a small wooden bedside cabinet where we could store our few belongings. The place was beautiful and clean, the daylight blazed through the huge

Brian Mynott

windows that seemed to frame a view of the sea within them. We were all told to choose a bed and then store our clothes in the lockers but to bring what money we had with us; we were given time to change and then left alone for about ten minutes. During that brief time all the children hurriedly unpacked our few belongings. Once that was done we pushed and shoved to get a good look at the sea through the dormitory windows. It was all done in good humour and started a bonding process among the children that was to continue to grow over the following two weeks. It was only when Uncle John reappeared that calm was once again restored to the dormitory; and in his deep voice uncle John asked if any of us were hungry to which we all responded by nodding our heads with great vigour.

Forming two lines in the dorm we were walked quietly to the dinning room; after such a long day I was starving and my mouth started to salivate at the very thought of food. As we approached the dinning room I could smell the meal, whatever it was, it smelt divine. When we reached the dinning hall and Uncle John opened the door; once again I was amazed. It was not so much a meal but a feast. Never before had I seen so much food. Not even at school dinners had I seen so much meat, chips, fruit, cakes, and never before had I been told to eat as much as I wanted. There was little noise once we had overfilled our plates and sat down. We had all refilled our plates and ate until we could eat no more and, with our bellies full, Uncle John stood facing us at the front of the food table and asked if we had all eaten our fill, and if we had would we like to go outside so we could have a little chat in the open air about the Cinderella Home and the few rules that we needed to follow to ensure we enjoyed our time there whilst staying safe at the same time.

Standing in the mid-afternoon sun gave me a chance to look around. I had been too busy in my excitement and eagerness when rushing to the sea wall to notice what else the Cinderella had to offer. The grounds of the home were mostly grass covered and there were swings a see-saw and a huge round-a-bout shaped like a witches hat that not only went round in circles but also from side to side. We all played on the 'hat' and, today, I think the PC brigade would have a giddy fit if they had been around in those fun filled days as the children turned green or flew off in all directions. In those far off days children were encouraged to have fun, in spite of the risks. The lush grass that grew quite long underneath the roundabout cushioned any child unfortunate enough to fall accidentally, however most us made a point of jumping off as the hat reached its highest point. Bliss

Outside the grounds and just along the main road, about 500 yards to the left, was a railway bridge running over the busy holiday road that ran alongside the Cinderella leading to the Lake District. It was a fantastic site when a train passed over the bridge on its way to or from the Lake District. Huge bellowing clouds of steam that poured from the train swirled as the giant machines thundered along making the whole area temporarily fogbound. Uncle John had to shout at the top of his voice so he could be heard because one of the biggest trains I had ever seen thundered past just when he started to speak. But his voice was so loud that we had no problem hearing him. And we all laughed when he continued shouting well after the train had passed and peace had returned; I've never made my mind up as to whether or not he was kidding, but the laughter Uncle John had created was very real.

Sitting on the grass, all the children were asked to calm down a bit and pay attention for a few minutes while we were told what we would be doing over the following two weeks and, of course, a few rules and regulations. We were told how we would always try and hold the schoolwork on the beach and that we would be going to church on Sunday's and that at no time, and for any reason, were we to go over the wall to explore the beach on the other side. We were told quite firmly, and with all seriousness, that it was dangerous and that we should stay away from the sand that, although looked safe, was very dangerous and people had been swallowed up, never to be seen again. It was a scare tactic that worked and there would be no incident of a child climbing over the wall: though it remained throughout the two weeks, very tempting for some of us.

It was to be the only time during our holiday that we were actually *told* that we couldn't do something, the rest of the time we were always *asked politely* if we would do something; we were never ordered. Uncle John introduced the rest of the staff to the children and I wish I could remember their names, or even their faces, but I cannot. But needless to say I they were all caring people and they all smiled a lot. There was a woman that I will call Aunty Janet, and she was to have an impact on me in a way that would make me think about my self. Janet would show me the kind of kindness, warmth and understanding that my mother should have shown. She would be my surrogate mother for only two weeks and but think she knew more about me in that short time than my mother had through my short lifetime.

Has the mini-meeting was drawing to a close Aunty Janet told us all that we could ask for anything they had, if we were hungry then we *must* ask for something to eat, if we were thirsty then ask for a drink and, whenever possible, we would receive what we asked for. And that was it really, no harsh 'behave or else' no threats of punishment any kind, however we had to hand over the money we had and it was explained that we could all have a certain amount each day to spend. Although I was, at first, reluctant to hand my money over, I realised that they were right, I would probably spend it all at once or probably lose it so I passed it over to Janet without any fuss. After telling us to go inside and get out of the clothes we had travelled in and change into clothes we could play out in, the outdoor meeting ended so we all, including the staff, raced back to the front door of the building, screaming wildly as we went. We were all laughing as we charged across the grassy playing area towards our temporary new home. Each child feeling a kind of freedom we had never known.

Some of the children, including me, had very few extra items of clothing to bring with them, but it was not a problem and aunty Janet produced boxes of clothing to fit everyone. Janet obviously knew what to expect, yet she made no fuss, simply passing out clothes to those of us who asked for them, or those she felt needed them. She asked us all to make sure we pinned little white cloth tags to our own clothes and write our names on the tags so they wouldn't get lost. Aunty Janet told us they would be washed and ironed ready for when we went home: and I remember thinking then that I never, ever, wanted to go home.

When we had all got changed there was a period when we could do as we pleased. We could sit and watch television or we could play out on swings. All the children chose the latter and it didn't take long for us to burn off all the food we had eaten only a few hours before and, like all children, we were soon starving again. As teatime approached we could hear uncle John's booming voice above all the noise the children were generating. Standing outside the double doors that lead into the building he bellowed at the top of his voice "*if your hungry come and get washed and changed and if your not then you can play out a bit longer*" he knew what the response would be and all the children immediately stopped what they were doing and charged as one across the grass leaving swings swinging and 'the hat' spinning wildly. Blocking the doorway uncle John stopped us all and asked us not to run into the house, he wasn't unpleasant when he asked, he never was, but we all knew he was serious and we knew he was right: thirty odd children running through the narrow corridor could have caused some damage, in fact we almost certainly would have.

Our tea that evening was a feast, like the previous meal, there seemed to be an endless supply of food only this time there would be mountains of chips, beans, stew and Yorkshire puddings rather than sandwiches. No sooner had we finished those off than pudding was being placed in front of us. I have never tasted custard like it, it tasted like pure cream, poured over a fat wedge of steaming apple pie, and I, along with the other kids, could hardly move when we had finished eating: some even groaned. I later found out that the custard was made with Carnation Milk; whatever was added, it tasted wonderful.

Uncle John stood at the door of the dinning room and said that as we had had such a long day we could have a bit of an early night. No one argued or complained, we were all burned out and exhausted, so instead of playing out the staff took, those of us that wanted, for a short walk down to the beach to watch the seagulls have their tea. As the huge birds screamed and swooped or strutted along the beach, I was amazed at the sight. My belly was full; I was away from the privations of my home in Bradford and I felt as if I my whole world had changed for the better. And it had, but at that time and in that place, I gave no thought to the fact that it was temporary. Perhaps I didn't want to have those thoughts.

During the short walk I couldn't ask enough questions or see enough sites, I wanted to know and see everything. The smell of the sea filled the air and my lungs, the blue evening sky was full of sea birds all, as uncle John had said, looking for their supper. I saw families out walking together. I saw fathers playing with their children on the beach. People were laughing and happiness seemed to be everywhere. I stared at them; feelings of deep regret and even jealousy filled me. I couldn't help but compare what I saw with my own life in Bradford. A little piece of me remembered my father and what he *was* like when we lived in Denby Dale; before he changed. A time when I was happy and we had laughed like the sons and fathers that I saw on the beach.

But I was too happy to feel sad for long and so I didn't linger on any thoughts of home: and what my father had become.

When we returned from our walk I was utterly knackered and, after sitting in the television room with the rest of the children for a short time, we were all given a mug of Horlicks or Hot Chocolate made with milk and a ginger biscuit for our supper. It didn't take much persuading when aunty Janet told us it was time to go to bed. All the children had quietened down and our drooping jaws and blood shot eyes were more than enough evidence that we were ready for a good nights sleep.

When we went into the bathroom to get washed and ready for bed it was then that I realised that I didn't have a toothbrush, I had never had one. It was the reason that I had lost several of my milk teeth years before most other children my age had. And also the reason I had to endure painful visits to the dentist, I can still smell that awful gas and feel the mask being pushed against my face. And I remember the taste of blood as it seeped from empty space left in my gums when the teeth were yanked out. Again the staff seemed to have pre-empted the children's' lack of supplies and new toothbrushes were handed out to each and every child whether they had one of their own or not. I had, of course, brushed my teeth before that evening, but only rarely using *toothpaste*. Toothpaste was expensive and I have vivid memories of using soot and salt on my family's communal toothbrush. It tasted vile and for several minutes afterwards my gums would be black from the soot. This was not unique to my family or me and many families used the same black paste, it was both cheap and readily available; there was certainly no shortage of soot in the area. The toothpaste that evening was the real stuff and it tasted divine and left my mouth tingling.

When I had finished in the bathroom and had put on the new pyjamas my grandma had given me I made my way to the dormitory where several of the children had already climbed into bed. The lights had been dimmed giving the dormitory a soft warm feel and as climbed between the clean white sheets I felt so tired my eyes hurt; yet I would not allow myself to succumb to sleep. The feel of the sheets and the sheer cleanliness of the dormitory were not at all what I was used to. It felt so nice just to lie there feeling clean and warm. And I so desperately didn't want to spoil it all by falling asleep and soaking my clean pyjamas and those clean white sheets with my piss. I decided that I would stay awake all night. But it was a foolish decision of course, and one I could not maintain, but I managed about 30 seconds after making the decision. When Uncle John made his final round, as he would do every evening, before turning off the dorm lights; replacing them with a single blue light that made the whole dorm seem surreal. I must have woke briefly as I remember feeling scared when I saw the dark shape walking between the rows of beds and then feeling silly when I realised it was only Uncle John just checking that all the children were safe. He must have noticed that I was awake and he walked quietly over to my bed. He asked me in a deep low voice that still seemed to boom, if I was ok and even though I knew I wanted to go to the toilet, I don't know why but I lied and told him I was fine. He seemed to know I was lying and asked me if I wanted to go to the toilet, I nodded, once again feeling silly for lying to him. Uncle John understood, he seemed to understand everything, and just ruffled my hair and then walked with me over to the bathroom door and left me when I went in. When I had finished and forced every drop of pee out of my bladder that I could he was waiting for me outside to door. "If you need to go to the loo at any time just go" he tried to whisper "there is always a member of staff sat outside that door" he again ruffled my hair then turned and pointed to a little desk that had been placed just outside the door. Positioned so that whoever sat there could see the full length of the dormitory. "Now little man, don't you worry about anything, just have a good nights sleep . . . we all have a *very* busy day tomorrow". He let me walk the short distance back to my bed alone and, as I climbed back into my still warm bed, I felt safe; safe enough to go to straight back to sleep. The dimmed lights were turned off as I snuggled under the blankets. Leaving only the blue light to illuminate the dormitory and sleep overcame again me almost immediately.

When I woke the following morning I felt disgusted that I had pissed the bed. It seemed as if I was soaked. I felt dirty and angry with myself and tried to dry the sheets by slowly lifting the sheets to allow air to somehow take away the mess I had made. It was stupid of me and I even knew it at the time. It must have been quite early as no one else seemed to be awake but as I quietly made my way to the bathroom I noticed a few eyes peering over blankets but I ignored them. I was not the only child in the bathroom, there were two other children in there and they were both there for the same reason as I. We didn't talk or even acknowledge each other. Avoiding eye contact we just stood at separate sinks washing our bodies. One of the lads started to cry quietly to him self, trying to hide both his shame and his tears, he could hide neither, as the near empty bathroom echoed and enhanced every sound. Then uncle John suddenly appeared and I tried to hide my pyjamas from him by putting them in the sink, he noticed straight away of course and I was trying frantically to give him reason why I was trying to squash my pyjamas into the small sink. But I needn't have bothered, he knew what we were doing and why. He knew that the three little boys had done all they could to avoid wetting the bed, he knew we felt shame: his smile told me all this.

Uncle John didn't say a word at first; he walked in the bathroom whistling a happy but unknown tune. He walked to the showers, turned them on made sure they were warm and took clean towels of a pile in the corner and simply said "come on lads, get yourselves showered ... you'll feel much better" and then, after telling us to put our pyjamas in the washing basket, he smiled and left us alone. I stayed in that shower for ages, washing off the piss and just thinking. The water was wonderful and the smell of soap soon replaced the stench of urine, and I felt a bit of the shame lift. When I came pout of the shower there was a queue of children waiting, all wrapped in clean towels, all waiting to wash of their own shame. On returning to the dormitory the place was a hive of activity, the beds were in the process of being stripped, revealing rubber covers that protected the mattresses from the nightly drenching.

The staff took no notice when I got dressed, they just sung or whistled, or a bit of both, and they were all smiling. It was as if nothing had happened even though at least half of the beds had been soiled, and within a very short time all the beds were back to their spotless condition and, already, a clean pair of pyjamas had been folded neatly and placed on my bed ready for that night.

Breakfast was yet another feast, cornflakes, porridge followed by eggs and sausages, and as much as we could eat. The milk on the cereals was more like cream than milk, and the porridge was topped with a choice of honey or treacle, or a bit of both. We all, once again and without being prompted, cleared the tables. All the children joined in this 'chore' without the slightest protest, I think it was as much in eagerness to get out and play than any other reason. Once the chairs had been stacked and the tables put to one side of the dinning hall we were all asked to sit on the floor, this was to happen every day of the holiday and, when we had said our prayers, we would be told what we would be doing that day. On that first full day we would have a few hours of lessons, all the children groaned at that until, after a deliberate delay, we were told it would be on the beach, then the groaning was replaced by a loud cheer.

Brian Mynott

The rest of that week was as fun filled as the first and on the Sunday we all went to the church in the centre of Morecambe. We travelled on a very old double-decker bus that you entered and exited via a permanently open back door. The smell of old leather will forever remind me of that bus ride, and the ride along the seafront accompanies that memory. It was the height of the holiday season and there seemed to be millions of happy faces lining the route into town, kites were being flown, football games played and sandcastles were being built. I could see small boats far out at sea and the deep blue sky stretched on forever, broken only by a few fluffy white clouds the ever-present seagulls. I didn't know it then of course, but my whole perception of life was being changed, I would only realise this a week later.

The rest of the holiday was just the same as the first, food, fun and loads of both. They staff and the other children had become a kind of family to not only me, but to most of the children staying there. We were all from Bradford, we were all there because we were all from poor families, and we all had a history that we never exchanged. There was no need, even children so young know when they see bad things or have bad things done to them; there was no need to talk about it, and the staff never asked, they didn't need to: they all knew.

The real highlight of the last week occurred about four days prior to the end of the holiday when I woke one morning and realised I had not pissed the bed and I stood at the side of the bed with a broad grin on my face, I had no need to have a shower, no need to feel shame; instead I felt something alien to me, I felt proud and when uncle John came into the dormitory he knew by the silly smile on my face what I had achieved and in an instant I was being hoisted up into the air, and I felt like I was flying both inside and out. The remaining few nights was spent in total dryness, my bed stayed dry.

The holiday seemed to both last forever and end in an instant and on the morning of our departure I would have given anything to stay there, I even thought about running away or hiding in a cupboard until the bus pulled away. But I knew that I had to go home, back to my real family in Bradford and 'the

Just Once, When I was little

villa' and to the mother who didn't care and the father who I no longer knew.

I was not the only one to shed tears that morning, the other children, the staff and even uncle John had to choke back his real emotions. I think if he had cried it would have made things even more difficult and I am sure he knew it, he stayed the all smiling, solid giant of a man he had been throughout the holiday. He must have seen many children come and go and I now realise how hard it must have been for him to see them all return to the life they had known.

Before I went to Morecambe I had become emotionally hardened and had lost the need to shed tears, tears only meant a further beating. But in Morecambe, at the Cinderella Home, on the day the bus pulled away, I cried and cried until my eyes went dry. I think I was catching up.

I enjoyed the train journey back, the staff did their best to keep the children's spirits up, yet all the time I was aware that every field or village we rumbled through was taking me closer to home and my previous life and I couldn't help but feel homesick, not for my family or Bradford, but for Morecambe and uncle John and the rest of the staff and, of course, the seagulls.

When the train pulled into Foster Square station I felt a kind of dread sweep over me; everything seemed darker. The bright sunny, fun filled beaches of Morecambe, where families played and seagulls flew, were now a thousand miles away, replaced with the dark mills of Bradford. Some of the children were happy to see their parents again and ran into their welcome arms, some like me were more than a little reticent about being back in the care of those that didn't care at all.

It wasn't until all the other children had with their families, and I was left alone with the staff, that I realised no one had come to meet me and a feeling that I was to come to know well enveloped me: loneliness.

The staff tried to make excuses for my parents and I remember I got very angry with them for doing so, I called them cruel for bringing me back and told them to leave me alone but aunty Janet pulled me close to her and wouldn't let go until I had calmed down. I hugged her back, telling her I didn't mean what I had said, she told me she knew I didn't mean it. And so I was taken to the taxi rank placed in a shiny black cab and taken home. Aunty Janet, or someone else, must have paid the driver before we set off because I had no money and the driver simply dropped me off outside the backdoor of my home and drove away without even saying goodbye. I bitterly regret to this day that I didn't say a proper goodbye to aunty Janet or the other staff and thank them, I had been in a black mood and never even realised that it was the first time I had been in a taxi and I hadn't even waved goodbye to them.

The changes that had taken place over the previous two weeks were to be made painfully obvious to me, I hadn't realised at all how much I had changed until I pushed the rotten wooden gate open and went into the rubbish filled back yard and opened the door to the stinking toilet. The stench made me want to shut the battered old door but the need to pee overrode the desire to slam it closed. The newspaper, used as toilet paper, was there hanging on a piece of string, the old ill fitting toilet seat still hung over to one side, the brown stains still remained in the bowl and the slime on the walls seemed even wetter.

I opened the back door of my home and went inside and was hit by the stench of the grease and filth in the kitchen. Smells that, before I had gone to Morecambe, I had never even noticed or ignored, I was now acutely aware of. The kitchen was filthy, pots and plates were either in greasy water or remained unwashed, at the side of the sink. I went through the small kitchen into the front room where I found mother watching television. She didn't even say hello, at first I thought she might have been asleep until I saw her tap the ash off the fag she held into the ashtray she had on her lap. I felt both anger and sadness at being home and I wondered why I had even been to Morecambe, what was the point of making me feel so happy, safe and wanted just to dump me back in this shithole.

I didn't even try to talk to mother, she would have only told me to shut up, if she spoke at all. I went upstairs to empty my little suitcase and as I did so I cried again. Everything in that little suitcase reminded me of my holiday, there was sand in the shoes the staff had allowed me to keep, my clean pyjamas were neatly folded and I could smell the Cinderella on them, I could feel the clean sheets, hear the seagulls, smell the sea, hear my friends laughing, see the dormitory and see the blue nightlight. It was all there in that little suitcase but I knew it was all gone now, another child would be in my bed, other children would be playing on 'the hat' and the seagulls would be still flying about looking for their tea and another child would be on that wall watching them: perhaps uncle John had lifted him onto the wall so he could see better.

I fell onto the bed I shared with three of my siblings and cried myself to sleep; even the smell of the piss sodden mattress could not stop drifting off to sleep. I left my holiday clothes in the suitcase; I didn't want to spoil them in that bedroom.

I was home.

My sister awakened me sometime later, and her smiling face at least made me feel a bit welcome. But even that was short lived when she told me how bad things had become following my mother's thieving from our neighbour, my sisters were too young to be prosecuted but my mother was not. She had been arrested on the day I left for Morecambe; this was why father had borrowed my aunt Pat's car, he knew mother was to be arrested so he needed to get into town and back several times that day and it hadn't taken the police long to prove that she had been responsible for nearly all the burglaries in the area over the previous months. Some of the neighbours had wanted to kick her off the Villa there and then and, if it hadn't been for the fear factor that my father held over them, they would have done so without the slightest hesitation.

I was a child then and unaware of the seriousness of what my mother had done, I knew it was wrong, I knew my mother was a thief, both my grandma's had told me often enough that stealing was wrong and it hurt people, but I never expected what happened next.

I fell back into the usual routine of the house, the mountain of chips shared between the children for almost every meal, the struggle to find space to sleep and a return to pissing the bed every night. My father's drunken rages and my mother's ignorance to all things motherly. There was no shame in pissing the bed because no one cared, we would just get out of bed throw back the tatty old blankets and let nature dry the sheets. I got used to, or ignored, the smells that lingered throughout the house and our clothes and I soon stopped brushing my teeth again when my toothbrush disappeared one day and the summer faded away with my siblings and me wondering the streets of the Villa forming our own little gang, the other kids were still banned from associating with us so we made our own fun.

I don't suppose we even noticed when our mother was sent to prison for three months. It made very little difference other than we saw more of our grandmas, and that was no bad thing.

But the net had closed, the rent had gone unpaid for months and we were hated and ignored by our neighbours so it was time for a 'moonlight flit' so in the dead of night we loaded our few belongings onto anything with wheels on and moved yet again.

West Bowling

The only good thing about moving to West Bowling was that I remained at St James' school. The rest of my lifestyle remained much the same; the move had taken the family only a mile or so from Ripley Ville but it was far enough to take us away from the stigma of my mother's thieving ways. Father didn't change his drinking habits and, with mother still locked up, we were still under the care of my wonderful grandmas, and the house itself was very much the same as all the others, same rundown state, damp and dreary. We were used to this type of house; it was no great shock to me so we just carried on as usual. But I had changed in several ways, I knew things could and should have been different. I knew my father should not be spending his wages on beer every night, I knew my mother deserved to be locked up and I also knew she shouldn't have sent my sisters creeping into other people houses. I was becoming angry at the world; my world was on a downhill slide and picking up speed as it went down it. I knew I stunk of piss all the time but when I tried to change things I was mocked by my father and called a 'tosser' for even trying.

I was a child, a small boy in need of at least one parents guidance, but the guidance I was receiving was the wrong kind and I knew it, and I wasn't even a teenager yet.

The anger that was building inside me I had felt before when I belted the boy at Bradford Moor School for trying to bully me; only now it was a deeper type of anger, stronger somehow and I was now much stronger physically. This was to show itself one day at school when I beat the crap out of the 'cock' of the school.

We had just finished our school dinner and I was playing football in the playground with a few of my classmates when I heard a commotion near the school doors. My classmates suddenly stopped kicking the football and were looking at the top of the steps just outside the door that led into the cloakroom. One of our classmates had gone to the toilet during the break and, on his way back, had been stopped by the boy who was acknowledged as the 'cock' of the school. I had never for a second shown the respect the 'hard man' thought he deserved, even though he was a bit taller and in the year above me, he didn't scare me even slightly, my father had beaten the fear of boys my age out of me, the pain a boy could inflict was nothing to what my father often did.

As soon as I realised what was going on a rage filled my whole body and I ran across the playground with only one thought in my mind. The cock of the school was going to get a thumping, and he got one. I ran up the steps and launched myself at the lad knocking him to the floor and before he had the chance to realise what was happening I was landing punch after punch into his face, even when he pleaded for me to stop I didn't, I couldn't the anger I felt was not just generated by him, it was generated by my mother, my father and my life; he just happened to trigger it and, if the teachers had not stopped me, I would not have stopped. It was a sign of things to come, I had found a way to vent all my anger and that fight was to be the first of many.

The teachers were great about it, I was not a bully and they knew it, but I had gone too far when I wouldn't stop when the boy had started to bleed, so I was given extra homework and told to apologise to the ex 'cock' which he readily accepted and, when the teachers had gone, he apologised back when I asked him to. It didn't dawn on me at first that I was now the cock of the school but, to be honest, I wasn't really bothered I had just enjoyed belting another bully.

About the same time I had a pleasant surprise from the church in Ripley Ville. The church had organised a week in

Just Once, When I was little

Malham for the Sunday School Class and, although we no longer lived in the Villa, I qualified because I was still on their books. Fortunately the letter had been opened by one of my grandmas so my father didn't have a chance to ignore it or burn it. And so I was to have another holiday, and again my grandma paid for it.

I hadn't a clue about the Dales let alone the location of them but when my uncle Joss told me they were between Bradford and Morecambe I couldn't wait to get there.

As I waited with my grandma for the coach that would take me and the other children to Malham I was surprised to find that the other children didn't try to isolate me, in retrospect this may well have been due to the fact that I was getting a reputation as a fighter and I was the cock of the local school, but at the time it didn't occur to me as a reason, I just thought they no longer blamed me for the sins of my mother. Maybe they didn't, I will never know.

The coach journey to Malham was fantastic and I felt the same kind of freedom building in me that I felt on the trip to Morecambe. As we travelled through the rolling landscape of the dales I was amazed at the number of sheep that just seemed to wander at will across the hills. There were little farmhouses high in those same hills, isolated and miles from anywhere, and I remember wishing I lived in one of them on my own.

The signposts were counting down the miles to Malham and it was getting closer and, looking at some of the young passengers holding on to sick bags, I knew some of that passengers had found the rolling of the old coach as it travelled along the winding roads and over stomach lifting little bridges, too much to take and were more than ready to get off. They had even refused the pop and crisps that had been offered to them as their faces had turned greener. I had not had the same problem, not only had I eaten my crisps but also a few extra bags that had become available and, when we arrived in Malham some of them had to be helped off the coach.

I was far to busy looking around the little village and river that runs through it to bother with the kids that were sat about trying to stop their world spinning.

Malham is a wonderful little village nestling in the Yorkshire Dales and the hostel we were to spend the following week was only basic but it was right in the middle of the village and only a few yards from the river. There were no seagulls but hundreds of ducks, they seemed to be everywhere and went anywhere they pleased. Incessant quacking filled the air whenever I went near them, especially when I sneaked some bread from the dinner table, but I thought it was brilliant when they all splashed out of the water and charged towards me. I got in to trouble a couple of times for feeding those ducks and ended up washing dishes as a punishment.

The people that looked after us in Malham were not the same as the ones in Morecambe; I don't think they had the same grasp of dealing with children from the bottom of the pile. But they were not unkind in any way but they dealt with bed-wetting quite bad. Many of the children admitted when asked that they wet the bed, me included, but this time we were given a different coloured sleeping bag that was lined with a big black plastic bag. It had never occurred to me, or the other kids that had never been to Malham before, that there were no bedrooms, no dormitory just one big room, a kitchen and several toilets. We were to sleep on the floor, which at the time, I felt was quite an adventure but I soon changed after the first night. It was bloody uncomfortable.

The meals there were once again plentiful, fresh eggs and milk, bacon and enough fresh bread to fill even the hungriest of the children and, of course the ducks. And did we need the food. I have never done so much walking. Mile after mile of open moor land was covered by my feet in all sorts of weather, when it rained we were issued with the same plastic bags that lined the sleeping bags and holes were cut into them so we could pop our heads out. It was a strange site watching thirty odd children walking in a line over the hills with bin liners over their heads, I couldn't help but compare us to the pictures of penguins I had seen in books. And although it was hard work hiking around the hills of Malham and we were all knackered at the end of them, it was also a lot of fun. I wonder what the sheep made of it all?

It was after a few nights sleep that I realised I had not wet the sleeping bag and I was allowed to leave the liner out of the bag, it was a triumph of a kind but I didn't realise at the time what it meant. I now realise that it was because I was happy and away from my father and the sheer stress of living in continual fear of being battered. I was brushing my teeth again, I was feeling clean again and, in a strange way, found it more comfortable sleeping on the wooden floor of the hostel than I did squashed up in the sunken piss sodden bed with my siblings.

My fondest memory of Malham is one of sitting in isolation, normally after our evening meal, on the ancient bridge that spanned the river that ran through the village. I would sit there for at least an hour, just staring at the clear flowing water, watching the ducks waddling around the waters edge. I found a kind of peace sat there that I had never found before; even in Morecambe I had not felt so calm. Perhaps it was the water.

As my stay in Malham came to an end I found that I was once again regretting the fact that I had to go back to a life I didn't want to live. But it wasn't the same as when I was about to leave Morecambe, I was ready for the welcome I would not receive and prepared my self for my life back in Bradford; however there was something I hadn't reckoned on when I returned, my mother had been let out.

Much the same took place when I returned home, however, due to my grandma's efforts, the house didn't stink nearly so bad. My mother though had not changed in the slightest; she was still the same lethargic lump she was before she was sent down. Prison had not changed her at one bit, and in no time at all she was once again taking her daughters for late night walks, and once gain she was caught and sent back to prison. I honestly think she liked it inside; no responsibility and plenty of bed rest would have been a kind of utopia to her.

It was about this time that I noticed a change in my older sister's moods and behaviour. She seldom laughed and had stopped playing out; preferring to remain isolated in her own company and she would often cry for no apparent reason. No longer the feisty redhead, she became more timid every day.

Being nothing more than a little boy, I was not really concerned and I just thought of these changes as a 'girl thing'.

One of my great regrets at the time was when I realised that I was getting too old to remain at St James' School. I was devastated as my life there slowly came to an end. All my old friends and my status as 'cock of the school' all went, and there was nothing I could do about it. My next school, WoodRoyd, was not a patch on St Jimmy's, probably because the school was much bigger than St James' and, also, I was no longer a 'junior' and no longer a 'little boy'. And it wasn't just my age that made me older; in many ways I was no longer a child. My home life and my daily struggle to survive had ensured that I was far more mature than the other kids in my class, even though I often acted stupid. What I hadn't anticipated was the trouble I would attract from the older boys because I had been the cock of St James' and on the very first day at WoodRoyd I was in a fight. One of the older, and much bigger, boys began provoking me as soon as he saw me and, because of him, I was to feel, for the first time, a temper that removed any fear of fighting.

In the queue for the little bottle of milk that all children received in the 60's I had been pushed and shoved by the lad, he had forced his way so that he stood directly behind me, and by the time I reached the end of the line I was well pissed off, but the monitors were watching, and it was my first day at a new school so I let it pass, or rather I tried to.

Picking up my bottle of milk from the top crate I spun round and pushed the lad full in his chest, I was burning inside but strangely in control. The lad regained his composure and stood in front of me and puffed out his chest telling me he would see me at playtime . . . I remember thinking him a childish idiot. Passing the milk to one of the other pupils I spun back round and, in one movement, smacked him full on his nose. It was only one punch but it was well aimed and carried my full weight and he fell to the floor as if a brick had hit him. Within seconds' monitors, prefects and teachers surrounded me but I just shrugged my shoulders and stood calmly waiting to be hauled away. The lad who had caused the trouble would escape any further punishment; but the blood that ran from his nose was punishment enough for me.

I was taken without any warning to the headmaster's office told that the school did not tolerate such behaviour. Then I was told to hold out my hand and given two strokes of the cane. I didn't protest or give the reason of how I was provoked, I just took the punishment, turned and walked out of the office. It had hurt like hell and my hand throbbed, but I would never have shown it, even if the headmaster had used a cricket bat and smashed my hand to bits.

Because of the caning I was late joining my first class at my new school. And I was made to stand for the rest of the lesson as a punishment for my lateness; my second punishment and I had only been at the school an hour. I felt a right twat stood in front of my new classmates. But I just stood there and got my own back by answering most of the questions the teacher put to the class until she eventually told me not to answer any more, so I smiled to myself at my small victory. When playtime came around I knew I would have to face the fallout from the lad I had belted, these things never just go away, but I wasn't afraid, in fact I was looking forward to it. Being forced to stand in front of my new peers in supposed shame had ensured I was in the right mood to take him on again and I was more than ready to fight whoever was waiting for me.

I think there is something in the eyes, or the behaviour, of people that let others know that they should be avoided. Maybe it's the obvious lack of fear or concern of those that oppose them, I don't really know. But there is something and whatever it is; I had it.

When the lesson had finished and I was walking through the huge hall that was used for PE and assembly, amongst other things, all those who saw me stepped out of my way. They all knew that there was to be a fight and didn't want to get involved.

I didn't wait for the lad to find me nor did I look for him, I just went where I wanted when I wanted, all the time the time the anger was building inside me. No one stood with me or even spoke to me. I hadn't been at the school a single day and already I was an outcast, a 'nutter' that must be avoided.

If it hadn't been for his black eye and bright red nose, I wouldn't have recognised the lad I had thumped earlier that day. But there he was walking towards me with his mates and gaining false confidence from them. He didn't want to fight me on his own again; you could see it in his one good eye. He was already in pain from the first thumping and because of that pain he was vulnerable. If he had had any sense at all he would have waited until his nose stopped glowing and both his eyes worked. But he had been shamed by being beaten up by a 'newbie' and he would lose something fare more precious than a bit of blood if he didn't put it right, he would lose his 'street-cred' and thus the only status he had. He had no real option but to fight me again, if you could call the first meeting a fight. I had beaten him easily with one punch and he knew I could do it again and it would hurt even more the next time. The cock of St James' was proving not to be the easy target he had thought I would be.

The fight that followed was my first real fight, I had thumped a few bullies prior to this one, but this was to be the real deal. There was the usual prompting by the other kids in the playground, urging the already bloodied youth to kick the crap out of me, whilst yelling at me that I was now 'for it' telling me that I had been lucky before . . . blah . . . blah bloody blah. Even when I stood in front of the lad and realised he was a good 2 inches taller than me, I didn't feel the slightest hint of nerves. I was still pissed off with him for causing the fight and I was still pissed off at being made to stand in front of the class; and it was this bastards fault. And he was asking me for another fight!

I had never really fought has a child would normally fight. All that shoving and pushing and 'see you at playtime' or 'you hit me first' shit had little appeal to me. If someone wanted to fight you then they shouldn't say they want a fight until they are ready! And never once have I used the phrase *'you hit me first'* to me, that was just plain stupid; however when I was offered this option, I promptly chose it and obliged them by thumping them.

The fight began with the only real weapon the lad had, himself. He threw his whole body at me, trying to use his whole weight to flatten me. He landed on me with a heavy crash driving the wind from my entire body. His fists started beating down on my head and, for a moment, I could not get my breath and struggled to free myself from underneath his body and I started to panic. But his desperate blows to my head served to ignite the aggression that bubbled just inside me and when it surfaced it gave me the strength I needed to push him off. And, taking a much-needed deep breath, I did so and with such force that he fell back into his gang of mates, in turn causing them to stagger back. Something happened when I got to my feet, a feeling that, although I now know the feeling well, was alien to me at the time. It was a feeling of sheer anger in its purest form. I didn't give a shit that they were bigger than me, I didn't care that there were several of them, I didn't care if they beat the crap out of me, in fact I needed the feeling of physical pain I would get from the fight. This was, of course, the anger that I had for my mother, my father and the life I lived and the free school dinners and those pink fucking meal tickets. I was angry at the whole fucked up world and everyone and everything in it.

As I stood there facing those bullies, they knew it had gone too far, they knew that they had picked on the wrong newbie. I no longer just wanted to fight the one lad; I wanted to fight them all, on at once or all together. They all stood looking at each other, confused at what to do next. My whole body seemed to shake and, ignoring any consequence, I just charged the lot of them. Punching and kicking as I did so. Some of the gang simply fled but a few remained, trying desperately to get me on the floor so they could use their boots on me. The punches that they threw either missed or were so weak that they were almost useless. The fight seemed to last for hours when in reality it was probably only a few minutes old but I was beginning to tire and the weight of three or four lads on top of me began to tell. I could feel myself getting weaker but even then I was quite happy to see that a few of the other lads were bloody nosed. The lad who had caused all the mayhem was sitting on the floor nursing his battered nose. It was fresh blood and he was crying because of the pain and the sight of his blubbering only served to enrage me further. The lad, that had been so tough in the queue, was really nothing more than a bully and a cry-baby. I wanted to pull his fucking head off and belt him with it. The sight of him brought a new surge of adrenalin through my tiring body putting fresh energy into my rapidly weakening muscles. But I knew that I couldn't continue much longer; that's when I met my new 'best mate' for the first time.

All at once the weight of began to ease. Hands released their grip and the punches being thrown lessened. The gang seemed to be disappearing one at a time until suddenly I was left dealing with only one, but he soon lost his nerve and walked away. Even the coward on the ground had left the scene and, as I looked around there was only one lad anywhere near me and he was smiling. I didn't know him but I knew he wasn't one of the gang. He seemed to know that I needed a bit of space and time to calm down and backed away from me; still smiling. I was shaking with anger and looking around, checking for any further threat and my fists remained clenched ready to thump whoever was in reach of them. But there was no one, the gang had done a runner.

I had broken the skin on my knuckles and blood ran freely onto the floor and formed dark little puddles. But other than that, a torn shirt, and a few scuffmarks, I was fine. The blood on my clothing was not all my own, there was too much to be from just a grazed knuckles and, as all the lads had run off, I never saw the damage my first real scrap had caused. I felt proud of myself with no shame at all, they had asked for all they had received and I felt as if I could fight the world alone: and I felt that I was doing just that.

The lad who had helped get the gang off me was a brute of a boy. He had huge shoulders that made mine look puny. He wore a leather jacket covered in silver studs and he looked a real rough bastard. But I liked him immediately. His name was Steve and, though he looked like one of the older boys, he was the same age as me and it was also his first day at WoodRoyd; we stood grinning at each other as the adrenalin levels lowered "think its going to be fucking cool here mate" he said with a widening grin. I couldn't help it, I burst into laughter. I laughed so hard, tears ran down my face and even when the teachers eventually turned up I couldn't stop. I can't remember if I got the cane that day, but I probably did. But I had made an amazing friend.

Throughout the next few years Steve and I were to become very close mates, soul buddies even, and we stood by each other no matter what happened. And a lot did happen. Over the following years and through the many fights and personal heartache, Steve never once let me down, even though on several occasions I let him down; and one time, very badly.

Away from school, my world turned as it always had. My siblings and I avoided all contact with our father. He was becoming ever more and more erratic each day, and his moods became increasingly unpredictable. Sometimes he would demand that we stay in the house for when he came home from work yet he would simply eat his tea of egg and chips, and we would sit in total silence watching him. Every so often I am sure I felt father wanted to say something and that he somehow wanted to be the dad he once was, but felt could not get the words out. Maybe this was my childish, wishful thinking at the time. Maybe I was trying too hard to find my 'dad' or rather the man that had been my dad only a few years before. Maybe it was merely the hopes of a lost, desperate and confused young boy.

I think it may be a good point here to write about an average twenty four hours of my life as a child, it may help to understand much of what made me feel so different from the other children.

Bedtime was never an easy time, with eventually eight children crammed into two beds in one bedroom, it was often chaos. We nearly all pissed the bed every night so every morning I would wake up soaked in urine; it was quite normal. Blankets would be laid flat on the floor to dry them, though often these 'blankets' were nothing more than old rags. The beds would, because of the constant drenching of piss, rot allowing broken springs to puncture any limb that came into contact with them. Many nights would be disturbed by an involuntary scream from a child as their skin was punctured. We would try and put newspaper or cardboard between ourselves and the mattress but it seldom worked. Once wet, the paper or cardboard offered no protection and simply turned into a soggy stinking mess. Waking on a morning, it was never difficult to get out of bed as we would all be eager to get out of the mess that we had created, but we would always wait until we heard father slam the door as he left for work before we dare move out of the bedroom. The blankets were seldom, if ever, washed and neither were we, both child and bed were left to dry without help. When we didn't have an indoor toilet, which was the case in almost every house we lived in, there would be a 'piss bucket' available for night-time but with so many children and a drunken father using it, it always overflowed. When it did get emptied, it was inevitable that piss would slosh over the sides as it was carried downstairs eventually making the whole house stink of piss. Breakfast, if that is what you could call it, if or when we got any at all, would be anything that was left from the previous evening. It could be stale bread, stale bread or stale bread, on the very odd occasion a frying pan of tinned tomatoes mixed with a big dollop of fat. We would dip the stale bread into the tasty mixture and then, like animals, scurry into a corner to eat it: when you did get food, you protected it, fighting off siblings that we every bit as hungry me.

All this took place without any assistance from our mother because no sooner had father gone to earn his beer tokens at the scrap yard where he worked, she would go straight back to bed. We seldom saw her on a morning, not that any of the older children wanted to or cared, there was no warmth or fun watching her sit on the sofa scratching her arse. After trying desperately to remove the stench of piss from my body I would get ready for school, sifting through my meagre collection of clothes to find the ones that didn't stink too bad and looked the cleanest. It was a useless exercise as all my clothes were the same, they were all filthy and worn; and they all stunk.

School was more of an escape from my home life than educational. At school I would receive a free bottle of milk every day and the free school dinners meant that I would have at least some good food during the week. At school I could wash before class and play freely in the playground without the fear of disturbing my father. My academic standard was quite high and I remember getting a part in the school play, I played 'Scrooge' a leading part because I was one of the few pupils who could read all the lines. When school was over for the day I would seldom go straight home, there was no need as there would be little chance of a meal and no welcome arms to greet me and ask me about my day. I would often, along with a few of my siblings, 'collect' pop bottles from the back door of the local pub and take them to the corner shop and get the penny deposit on them. It didn't take long to get together enough pennies to get a 'tanners worth of chips' from the chip shop, piled high with crispy scraps and smothered in vinegar and salt. Those chips were often the best meal of the day.

Every day when I did arrive home I would try and protect my school clothes by hiding them and change into even dirtier clothes to play out in. I would play with my brothers and sisters until it got dark or, during the summer months, as late as we dare, not wishing to bump into our father making his way back from the pub or walk in and see him sitting at the table. We had only once ever pushed it too far and got caught and we all got a beating for not being in bed when he got home, we never took the risk again.

Like all siblings, we would argue. But in our case it nearly always ended with a fight and there was always a fight in the house somewhere. This was down to father's belief that the only way to argue was to 'smack the bastards in the face' You never, ever went and asked him to tell someone to stop doing anything to you, he would smack you across the face and then tell the accused to kick the crap out of you for grassing! Fighting was not just a way of life, it was compulsory.

If we had a television we would watch programmes such as Watch with Mother: there was more than a hint of irony because we never even watched anything with mother. I liked The Wooden Tops; in fact I often wished I was part of their pretend family. They never fought, always had food and the children loved their parents. Perhaps, if I am honest, I wished, if not prayed, for a family like theirs. Though it may seem strange now, I wanted to be a Wooden Top, but to me, a child, the family were very real and represented all that I longed for in a family.

But mostly, we didn't have a television, and so most evenings we would roam the streets of Bradford getting up to mischief or taking pop bottles back to the shop after we had nicked them from the back of the local pub.

One thing that now seems quite cruel was that we had all been conditioned to pick up cigarette butts for our parents, and we would often end up with a pocket of half smoked cigarettes. I remember mother eagerly breaking them up for the tobacco and making 'roll-ups' with it. To me and my brothers and sisters; it was all quite normal and I never even noticed the odd stares we must have got as we stuffed tab-ends into our grubby clothes.

If it was a weekend, especially Saturday, we were made to stay in during the afternoon. Father loved to watch the wrestling when he came home from the pub. He also liked to 'wrestle' with his children. But it wasn't fun and it wasn't wrestling. I realised many years ago that it was just a way for father to sexually abuse his children by rubbing himself against them. I remember the grunting sounds my father made, the pain, the stench of beer that seemed to fill the air, and I remember seeing my mother sitting: watching

The days were all very much the same; whether a school day or a weekend, they were the same.

The end of the day was almost always the same, going to bed hungry and sleeping in a stinking, damp, cramped bed with at least three of my siblings. Only occasionally would we get food, a slice of dry bread that I would break up into as many pieces as possible so it would last longer. We would eat this in bed, there was no danger of the mice that infested almost every house we lived in, there was never a crumb wasted.

On her release from prison my mother had quickly returned to her thieving ways. Showing absolutely no remorse or regret for what she had done to that wonderful old bloke on Ripley Ville. It had destroyed his trust in life and his belief in his neighbours, I found out some years later that not long after the incident his old dog died; he became a recluse and died not long after. Maybe it was pure coincidence.

Why my mother chose to pull off her next job, God knows. But she had her daughters steal a crate of lemons from the lock up of the local 'fruit and veg' man. The lemons were of no use whatsoever, but she stole them anyway. We tried to eat them, and though hunger meant we would eat just about anything the lemons were far to sour, so they ended up being thrown away. Everyone knew my mother had had a hand in the theft but the police could not prove she was involved; even though the whole house stank of lemons for weeks.

Both my parents would confuse me throughout my childhood. My mother's disinterest in everything except laying on the sofa or thieving, and my father's delicate aggressive moods, left me constantly confused, bewildered and afraid. But no more so than the surreal night that my father tried to commit suicide by jumping into a shallow beck when we lived at Buttershaw. Why was he asking for help and what for? He cried like a baby that night and yet he hated to see anyone crying or any sign of weakness; yet he was blubbering like a hungry baby. At the time; I hated him for that. Every day he would call me a useless coward, a cheat or a worthless piece of shit; but never explained why I was any of these. Yet it was ok for him: I felt disgust at his display of weakness. It was a childish response; I know that now, but I *was* a child, and it had been beaten into me, almost daily, not to show the kind of weakness being shown by the same man that beat me.

Back at WoodRoyd things calmed down for a bit after my very eventful first day. Steve and I quickly became inseparable. My punishment for fighting was being made to stand in front of my new classmates with my hands on my head. I would have preferred the cane and stood there glaring, staring at anyone that looked at me until they were forced to look away. I must have looked what I was; a rough street kid and many of the lads in the class breathed a sigh of relief when I was told to sit down. The only lad I hadn't stared down was Steve. He was in the same class and I knew by his constant slanted smile that I had found a mate; a true mate.

Steve and I, after the eventful first day at WoodRoyd, became inseparable and would hang out, we were now too old to '*play out*', almost every night after school and also during the school holidays. Steve became a firm friend, not just to me, but also my siblings, especially my older sister. He fancied her like crazy even though she was a year older and seemed much more grown up than him. But he persisted until they became quite close and eventually they started to become an item of sorts; yet she would never let him kiss her. Even a kiss on her cheek was forbidden; she would just about let him hold her hand. But Steve never complained, she was his first 'girlfriend' and, although Steve was as tough as any one I had ever known before, or since, he was very shy and gentle with girls and he struggled even to talk to them. I was the total opposite. I had a cheeky disposition when it came to 'the ladies' and having three sisters gave me plenty of access girls about my age. Like most young boys do when they are entering puberty, I had exaggerated greatly to my few mates when they had asked me '*how far did I go?*' or '*did I touch it?*' I would boast saying '*a long way*' or '*yes . . . I touched it*' when I had absolutely no idea how far I was supposed to '*go*' or even what '*it*' was I was supposed to touch! But my time at West Bowling was running out. I was still only 10 or 11 years old and I had already lived in about twenty different houses, and I would soon live in another one.

The obvious, and inevitable, was not far away, so it wasn't long before the family were dodging the bailiffs again, and we were on the move. I knew that we would be doing another 'moonlight flit' when I saw the two blokes in suits turn up one day as they always did just before we 'flitted' and, true to form, within a few days of their visit we were sneaking out of the house in the middle of the night again. But this time we stayed in the same area and moved only a few streets away so, for once, I kept my circle of friends and began to feel a bit settled for the first time in my life. At the time, new high-rise flats were being built on Manchester Rd near Bradford town centre, and my father had somehow got a job there working on the roofs, and as it was only about half a mile from West Bowling, it meant I would be living near my mates. It also meant that I would be staying at

Just Once, When I was little

WoodRoyd for the foreseeable future, and that didn't make me chuckle.

WoodRoyd wasn't too bad really I suppose, Steve and I were mostly left alone by the school bullies after the fight on the first day and, on the odd occasion when we were confronted, we stood side by side and the school 'hard men' would soon back off. The strange thing was that whilst Steve and I were both rough and tough 'trouble causers' we were also amongst the brightest in our class. We were even told that we could be Prefects if we behaved long enough and stopped fighting. I think the fact that Steve couldn't stop chuckling and that I had asked if we would be paid for being prefects put paid that silly offer. Being a school prefect was not something that I aspired to. In fact I thought that all prefects' were all stuck up bastards so why would want to be one!

I suppose the main reason I didn't like WoodRoyd much was the teachers. Some were out and out bullies and they were often far too eager to wallop you on the back of your head. Even the most trivial of misdemeanours could result a smack or feeling embarrassed after being called stupid or an idiot by the teacher in front of the whole class, or being left in pain following 'the cane' or some other form of physical punishment. A few of the teachers however were ok and would they would, at least, do their job and teach us something. These teachers would not be hassled by Steve and me during lessons, nor would any of our classmates hassle them. But the bullying teachers had little peace from Steve or me. We used to enjoy winding them up and the cane, though painful, was not really a threat and it didn't scare us into behaving.

When, as a young boy, you're getting nearer to puberty, weird things happen to their penis. The thing suddenly develops a mind and autonomy all of its own. As a pubescent young man the thing would pop up without any warning at any time; and anywhere. No more so than when your teacher just happens to be gorgeous, sexy and clever. And the young female teacher that taught geography was all three, and, when she sat on the desk at the front of the class she would *accidentally* show enough of her legs to drive all the young pre-pubescent boys crazy. So much so that if any of the lads had to stand up during her lesson, then they could only to do so leaning on their desk. The teacher seemed to take great delight in making the poor sod, often me, stand up straight and, due to the short-legged baggy school trousers, it was very obvious that biology was in total control as little wigwams protruded from baggy trousers. Those boys that had discovered the joys of masturbation would be the first in to the toilet and break time! These are memories of my time at WoodRoyd, and fond ones though they may be; there are only a few of them. Memories of my time at the school had little influence on my life its teachers, other than the sexy geography teacher, had any real impact. Unlike St James' and Bradford Moor where the teachers really seemed to care about their pupils and influenced the direction my life would take. The only things I found out during my time at WoodRoyd, was that I could fight: and that Steve was a great mate to have. And that little boys dicks developed a mind all of their own

Scots Street

Once again the family would be on the move only this time we moved several miles away from the West Bowling area and even though I would often walk the distance to be with my mates, in particular Steve, it was not the same and, over time, I lost contact with most of them all. Scots Street was a very different to the other houses we had lived in. The house was on three floors and it had two toilets, one inside and one outside. There was also a bathroom with a *real* bath that had running hot water, it was bliss; no more sitting in tin baths in front of the fire having to share the filthy water with seven siblings. Though the house would have once belonged to some middleclass family and would have been quite posh, it was now bordering on derelict and was, as were most of the houses I lived in, due for demolition. But the house was dry and warm and there were plenty of bedrooms and there was no need for the communal piss bucket, and there were plenty of things to do in the area to keep my siblings and I occupied. But I was beginning to realise that much of my life was wrong; and that much of what I considered normal was, in fact, the very opposite.

This was the period in my life, and everything in it, spun violently on its head and my life would change forever. It was the beginning of the total destruction of my family. It was also the time that I finally realised the reason for my sister's dark moods and the emptiness I saw in her eyes. It was also the time that my father totally and utterly destroyed any residual love or respect I may have had left for him and I finally abandoned any hope of finding the dad I had known in Denby Dale. And I finally realised that he would never, could never return.

Scott Street, and the surrounding area of Undercliffe, would have, at one time, been very different to what it was when I lived there. Victorian houses, once the homes of the wealthy, now stood empty. Old terrace houses, that once housed the workers needed for the many mills in the area, were mostly the same. All, though, were waiting for the bulldozers to come and demolish them. In my imagination, I could see the houses in their former glory. I could imagine vividly the people that once lived in these houses. I could see the horse drawn carriages pulling up outside the homes. I could see children playing with their smiling parents in gardens full of flowers. It made me sad to think that their homes would now be flattened and replaced by imposing 'modern' housing. Instead people would now live in high-rise flats in isolation eroding, possibly forever, the sense of community that once existed there. Undercliffe School serviced the whole area and there was a very diverse group of children due, in part, to the influence of the small Asian community that had moved in to the area to work in the factories in the late 50's and early 60's. I would often wonder at the wonderful smell of spices that often filled the whole area. Though I had never eaten any kind of curry or ethnic food and had no idea what the food would taste like, I knew that it would be delicious. I remember that my father's hatred of the Asians was terrible. Often, when he was drunk so it was almost daily, he would stand at the top of the steps outside our front door screaming all kinds of obscenities at any 'Paki' that happened to be anywhere near the house. It didn't matter if they were young or old; even small children would be subjected to my father's screaming.

I had lived in Undercliffe before then, but it must have been only a very brief stay and when I was very young as I remember very little of my previous life there. However considering the amount of times we moved houses during my childhood it is not so strange. Undercliffe road was about a mile long and was very steep and the old vacant Victorian houses, were a magnet for fun and adventure. My siblings and I would spend hours rummaging through the old cellars and attics of these houses; we would find all sorts of rubbish including dozens of gasmasks, some of them for children that had been discarded following the Second World War. I would often just sit alone in these old houses, even after dark, imagining again the families that once lived there. I would make up little stories about these imagined people and pretend that I was part of a rich family that did nothing but play and read stories all day. There was no violence in my imagined home, no hunger, no piss bucket, no fear of my father and I had a mother that cared, a mother that would comb my hair and kiss me goodbye when I left for school and hug me when I returned. As I say, it was pure fantasy, a way of escaping.

Only a few weeks before moving to Scott Street I was told I had to wear glasses to correct a squint in my right eye, and this compounded my misery. I had a weak eye and, in an attempt to correct it, I was made to wear the glasses with the lens of my strong eye covered. Walking about with a sticking plaster over the left eye not only made me clumsy but I also felt like a right prat, and it was to lead to yet another major fight when I went to Undercliffe School; within a week of my first day I was beating the crap out of the school bully. And getting a boiled sweet from the headmaster for doing so

The playground at Undercliffe School was as steep as the road it took its name from. Slanting at an alarming rate from top to bottom made it difficult to run about or play any kind of game on it and even though there were some goal posts painted on a wall at an absurd angle, the ball simply rolled away as soon as we stopped kicking it. With my free spectacles and a patch over one eye, I was a prime target for the bullies. At first they just stood around the playground calling me names. But the name-calling didn't bother me and they knew it didn't, so it wasn't long before one of them decided to do the usual playground pushing. The bell had been rung to call the children back into class and as I made my way past them one of them shoved me so hard I had no choice but to fall down the slope of the school playground. It wasn't the push that triggered the anger; it was the laughter that was coming from all of the other children. Getting up from the tarmac that covered the playground, I felt the same surge of violence begin to surge through my body that I had felt at WoodRoyd when the bully pushed me in the back. And I welcomed the intense feeling. I didn't run towards the boy that had just pushed me, I walked. Throwing my glasses to the floor not giving a shit if they smashed, I looked at the bastard straight in his eyes and held his gaze as I walked towards him. His mates began to push him forward, urging him to *kick my teeth* in, *blacken my eyes, kick my balls in* or make me *beg for mercy*. None of which this boy, or any of his mates, was ever going to achieve.

It was the usual shit. The lad realised I wasn't going to stop my walk towards him and nervously asked me if I wanted a fight. Of course I wanted to fight; I wanted to rip his fucking head off and play football with it. I carried on walking towards him, my temper rising with each step and my eyes fixed on him The playground rules were as simple then as they are today. If you backed down, you were almost certain to end up being thumped anyway and almost as certain of being bullied by him every day. However if you stood your ground and said yes, then the bully would often back down. Unless he was absolutely 100% positive he could beat you, the bully would find some lame excuse to shy off or tell you he would get you *next time*. It was always the same bollocks and I always found all this rather foolish and unnecessary, you either fought or you didn't, there is never really any half way between the two. The bully that reluctantly faced me now, realised that he needn't bother asking me, we were going to fight whether he wanted to back out or not. He must have seen something in my eyes that scared him because he began backing away as I walked towards him, trying to get back among his mates, and I saw fear in his eyes.

In many ways the fight followed the same pattern as the fight I had on my first day at WoodRoyd, a bully had looked at me and saw a smallish, bespectacled scruffy kid. He didn't know me, he didn't know that I was beaten almost daily and had become so used to pain that, unless he hit me with a house brick, I would not even feel any of his blows. Like WoodRoyd, there were several of them and, like WoodRoyd, I felt the now

Just Once, When I was little

familiar surge of adrenalin begin to flood through my body fuelling the anger that was about to be unleashed. The regular beatings I took from my father had removed all fear of boys my own age, and even older boys, and the daily fights I had with my brothers had certainly taught me how to scrap. He would wish he had never picked on *'four eyes'*

I quickly reached the lad and without the slightest hesitation, I punched him full in the face, there was no holding back, I punched him with the force that only rage allows. He was the first lad I had ever knocked out cold. He hit the floor slowly only because his mates were stood behind him and slowed his descent, then, as I expected, his mates found a collective 'courage' and came at me. I lunged for the first one and clung to his head with all my adrenalin-fuelled strength. I was not going to let go of him even though I was taking blows to the back of my head and body but the pain I felt was fuck all by comparison to the beatings my father gave me. Even though I was totally full of rage, I knew that if I let go of the boys head I would be dragged to the floor where they could all stick the boot in. I remember wishing Steve would turn up, but he was miles away at WoodRoyd, so I was on my own.

The lad, whose head I held, was starting to cry, he was begging me to let go. Many of the punches being thrown at me were accidentally landing on him. In fact he probably took more punches than I did and he was bleeding from his nose and his lips were already beginning to swell. But I would still not let go of his head and continued to punch him whenever I got the chance. Eventually the teachers appeared and broke the fight up. But it was not easy for them, I was on another planet and it took several minutes before I let go of the lads, now much bloodied, head. Still screaming with rage and throwing punches wildly, I was dragged to the headmistress's office to await my punishment. As I was being hauled away one of the gang took it upon himself to have one last kick at me and when his boot landed in the small of my back, I went ballistic and fought with the teachers to free myself so I could rip his head off. But it was hopeless so I stopped struggling and went with the teachers. But I did not receive the punishment that I expected. Instead I was to meet a woman that was to have a dramatic, even profound, influence on my life

The headmistress was amazing; I had only seen her previously in morning assembly prayers or from a distance. Yet she knew me; and more importantly she knew about my life and she knew exactly how to deal with me and my temper. She must have known what had taken place, she must have known the amount of abuse I had taken from the school bullies before I responded as I did. She must have known about the pushing and the laughing and she must have known that the cane would have little or no impact on me because she gave me a *boiled sweet* and *asked* me to sit down. I was shocked and sat down wiping the snot and blood across my face with the back of my hand. She was the first adult that had ever asked me about my life at home, she wanted to know everything about my family, how many siblings did I have their ages, how did we manage? The headmistress seemed far more interested in my home life than my fight in the school playground. The fight seemed secondary to her concerns. We sat and talked for what seemed ages and, by the time we had finished, she must have known more about me and the lifestyle of my family than anyone else. Even my nana didn't know many of the things I told the headmistress. I told her of the beatings, the lack of food, the filth I lived in. I think I told her everything. And when I got up to leave; she gave me the bag of boiled sweets, and a hug.

The headmistress caught up with me later that day and told me she had been thinking about me and decided, in her wisdom, that I needed to burn off the anger I held inside. She was probably right. I was told, in a very nice way, to report to the gym teacher after dinner. The head mistress assured me that it was not to receive any kind punishment and that I may even like what I was going to do. After dinner I made my way to the gym hall, I had taken little notice of the snide remarks from some of the pupils as I stood there; I just kept my head down and stared at the highly polished wooden floor. It wasn't fear that had made me keep my head down, it was because the headmistress had been ok and she had asked me to stay away

Just Once, When I was little

from trouble for the rest of the day, so I obliged and behaved, but it wasn't easy.

After a few minutes of looking at the floor my mind had began, as it always did when I stood still and quiet for more than a few minutes, to wonder. I was probably imagining that I was flying across the sky like an RAF pilot in a Spitfire. I would shoot down a German Bomber as it was about to drop its bombs, and I would save thousands of lives. Or I would fight off Red Indians that were attacking a farm and save a family from being scalped. And prove to the world that I was not the coward my father told me every day that I was. What ever fantasy world I was in I must have been in it deep because I jumped alarmingly when my name seemed to boom out from the heavens. It took a good few seconds, and only when my name boomed out louder, and for a second time, that I realised that I was being summoned in to the gym. So, with my heart still racing, I pushed the door to the gym open and walked quickly in to meet another teacher that was to have a profound influence on my life.

The gym teacher was standing in the middle of the huge gym hall. All the usual gym equipment the pupils used daily had been stacked along the far wall. The gym instructor stood with his arms folded across his chest watching two lads lay down a large green gym mat to cover an area big enough for the boxers to train on. He was an imposing figure. He was about the same height as my father, a bent nose and strange shaped ears; and the kind of face that left you in no doubt he was a hard man. His strong accent wasn't local, it seemed to bounce between Geordie and Scottish but I understood him well enough when he bellowed at me to get changed into my shorts and be quick about it. I ran to the changing rooms and did as I was told, or I would have done had I had some shorts and pumps to change in to. As I stood there alone in that changing room, I stared at myself in the large mirror that hung from the wall at the far end of the room. I felt embarrassed at what I saw; I was shamed by my clothes that I was wearing. They were grubby and I could smell the usual piss and grime on them. It did not usually bother me, I was used to the stink, and to me it was all quite normal. Other than my time in Malham and Morecambe, there were very few times I had clean clothes. Even the free school clothing I received annually from the council didn't stay clean for long no matter how hard I tried: they quickly stank of grease, filth and piss. Eventually the gym teacher came looking for me and, at first, he seemed angry at the delay, but he looked at my miserable face and my empty hands and grasped what was wrong. With an understanding smile he walked passed me, ruffling my hair as he went to his small office. After a few minutes he returned and brought with him a pair of shorts and pumps. Without a word he placed them on the bench and then turned and left me to get changed, again, ruffling my hair as he passed me. I felt embarrassed by his kind gesture but no shame, and I quickly changed and hurried back into the gym hall.

As soon as I entered the big room I was told me to run, and to keep running around the improvised boxing ring until I was told to stop. It felt as if I had run for about two weeks and covered several thousand miles before the my new mentor decided I was red-faced enough and shouted for me to stop running. I almost stumbled to a halt. My lungs seemed to swell to extreme new levels as they struggled to take in enough oxygen. My legs were like heavy lumps of jelly and my heart was beating so hard and fast I felt sure the teacher could see it trying to get out of my chest. Before I had recovered I was told to run two more laps, but run them slowly . . . slowly! I could hardly bloody walk slowly let alone *run slowly*, but I forced my legs to move and I completed the final two laps. The instructor simply ruffled my hair and told me to come back the next day after dinner adding, in his distinct accent, that I was fit enough. I did not feel fit *enough*, I felt absolutely fucking knackered.

The following morning my father had gone to work early and mother was still in bed so I was left to rummage, as were my siblings, for some kind of breakfast and, as usual there was nothing, not even a slice of bread. But I was starving and needed food so I did something that, though I understand the reason, I still feel shame for doing. I stole.

I have never liked thieving of any kind and I could never understand how my mother could break in and rob someone's home and steal their things. But on mornings when there was no food and my belly ached from hunger, I started to steal bottles of milk from doorsteps on my way to school and think nothing of it. Sometimes there would be orange juice so I would steal that to sell to the kids at school. I was crap at stealing and my scam soon failed when half the kids at school realised why there was no milk for their cornflakes and no orange juice; and they soon noticed that I was selling or swapping the stuff at school. I denied all knowledge of course, but they knew it was me that was nicking their milk, they just couldn't prove it but they stopped buying the stuff from me so I stole only what I could drink.

That first time I stole milk I was scared to death the rest of the morning. I was convinced that I had a sign over my head declaring in bold letters that I was a *stealer of milk!*

Dinnertime came and went and I was looking forward to my first day as a boxer. I vowed that I would be the best, I would be the fastest, hardest, fighter ever to go to Undercliffe School; that was until my first time in the ring with another lad.

I had washed borrowed the shorts in the sink the night before and, although they were still damp when I put them on, at least they were clean, and I felt quite proud when I put them on in the changing room. The trainer brought in t-shirts for all the young trainee boxers. Suddenly I felt part of a team, I had found new mates. And I would impress them all with my fighting skills . . . or so I thought.

Mixtures of blue and red well-worn t-shirts were passed around and we were told to form two teams; a blue team and a red team and then had to return to the gym floor. Blue has been my favourite colour since the Cinderella Home in Morecambe where, every night in the dormitory, the night-light had been a deep, comforting, blue, so I snatched a blue shirt, and made an enemy in the process.

The lad who I snatched the shirt from was not amused and stared at me all the way back to the gym floor. I told him red suited him, and then I just grinned at him. He was smaller than me and built like a skeleton so I didn't even consider him a threat but I had managed to piss off a *little Tasmanian devil.*

It was inevitable that we would be paired up, and unless you count the pretend ones I had with my brothers that quickly descended into a 'no holds barred' scrap; I had never really boxed in my life before. It seemed the lad had always been a 'blue' and I, by nicking the last blue t-shirt, forced him to be a 'Red' for the day and I could in see his eyes that he wasn't happy about it one bit: but I wasn't bothered: he was a squirt!

A tight fitting leather helmet was pushed forcefully onto my head and huge pair of boxing gloves was pushed roughly onto my fists. I felt a right idiot stood there with my hands dangling by my sides. Each arm seemed to be weighed down by the two sacks of coal. The lad I had nicked the T-shirt from had suddenly started to look anything but a squirt I first thought he was. He looked confident and calm, except when he glaring at me while he bouncing around smacking his own huge gloves together as he did so. But I wasn't worried; I just thought he was a fucking idiot . . . The instructor eventually told everyone to stop running and get ready to fight. I was utterly fed up with running around the gym hall and I was glad to finally get the chance to have a scrap. But it felt strange. Fighting without feeling angry was a new experience to me when he shouted at my bouncing opponent, to 'take it easy with him' I should have realised that I was in trouble.

Standing opposite my pissed off opponent I must have looked a right prat. Oversized gloves, baggy shorts and wearing glove the size of pillows; I did not look, nor feel, like a boxer. But I bounced around, hopping from one foot to the other trying to copy what the lad opposite me was doing. He looked the part far better than I and when the teacher clapped his hands together and shouted 'fight' my opponent flew at me with the speed of a fleeing cat and must have punched me six times before, at last, my instinct kicked in and I threw a punch back. It was my first real attempt at throwing a punch and I missed his head by a yard. And before I could pull my huge gloved hand back to defend my head as I had been taught, he had landed a punch to the side of the head making it jolt to one side. The blow wasn't a hard one but it shook me, and my frustration at not being able to land a punch in response was growing, and it was fuelling my temper. Never before had I felt so hopeless in a fight, the lad in front of me was taking the piss for snatching his shirt and, as I began to look like a fool, and feel like an idiot. I lost the plot.

As my temper took hold, I tried desperately to pull my gloves off but the boxing instructor had tied them securely in place and, no matter how much effort I put into getting the things off my hands; they would not budge. This only made me feel even more foolish and my anger began to grow. When I had fights in playground or in the streets I always felt a sense of calm and had no real sense of fear. Even when I lost my temper, I was always in control to some extent. But on that rubber mat, and on that day, I was to feel for the first time a deep rage that took control of me, and then after the rage had burnt itself out, I would remember nothing, I could only see the results.

I can remember I felt a deep, burning desire to beat the living daylight out of my opponent. I remember screaming inside my head and I can remember starting to move towards him ignoring the punches that were landing on my head and face. And then nothing else until I saw the instructors face appearing out of a kind of mist and staring at me. My name was being called but it seemed distant somehow. As I came back to my senses I realised that I was shaking violently and my face was covered in sweat. I was sat in the teacher's office trying to make sense of what had happened and kept trying to ask the teacher but my mouth would not work, no words would some out. The teacher was squatting in front of me slowly taking the huge gloves off my shaking hands. He was not shouting at me, nor did he seem angry, he was talking calmly and quietly and he had a puzzled, almost fearful look on his rugged face. As the shaking slowed and the last of my senses returned I too must have had a puzzled look on my face because the teacher asked me if I was ok. I told him that I had no idea what had just happened. I remember feeling scared as I tried to recall the last few moment and couldn't; why was there so much fuss, what had I done? As a sense of panic surged through me I began to shake again. With tears stinging my eyes and a thumping headache I was trying desperately to make sense of it all.

The teacher kept talking calmly holding my now gloveless hands as he did so. His accented voice seemed to soothe my fear Eventually I began to make sense of what the instructor was saying to me. As my mind cleared and I started to understand him I worked out he was asking me if I was ok. In his bouncy accent he kept asking me if it had ever happened before. At first I didn't understand what he meant, and then he told me that I had suddenly run at my opponent and laid into him but he assured that the lad was ok. Then he told me I was crying, swearing and screaming while I was doing it and that it took all his strength to pull off my opponent. But I remembered none of it and then suddenly, and against fierce resistance, I started crying again.

Through all the pains I had been through in my short life, I had never before cried like that. Even in the darkest moments, not during, nor after, a beating from my father, had I ever cried with such force. The tears and sobs were coming from somewhere deep inside me. As they came I was remembering my life. Images of my granddad, my nana, of Malham and Morecambe seemed to fight with those of feeling hungry, piss buckets, stinking mattresses and images of my father and the fear I felt whenever he came near me. I could also see the look of rage on my father's face when he was pissed. It was all there, in those tears, the freezing nights, my mother, going to school dressed in stinking rags and feeling ashamed all the time. And with snot running down my chin and deep sobs rattling from my mouth, the gym teacher sat there and listened to me swearing loudly between each sob. I cursed and cursed everyone and everything I knew, even some of those I loved.

I now realise of course that the show of intense emotion was understandable. I lived in a world that, for the most part, did not make sense. I was just a kid trying to survive in a world of confusion and privation. Searching for a father that no longer existed and wanting mother that cared, a mother that cuddled me, a mother that read me stories, and a mother that loved me. I just wanted what other kids had; I didn't want my life, I wanted to be anyone else but me.

Just Once, When I was little

The lad who had been my opponent came into the office after the instructor had asked if it was ok so I took a few deep breaths and agreed. Again, I cannot remember the lads name; however I have a vague memory of what he looked like. He was smaller than me and looked too soft for a boxer. I remember feeling surprised at the time that he had caused me so much trouble. He looked like butter wouldn't melt in his mouth yet he had landed a good few punches before my world turned red. He asked me if I was ok, I simply apologised. Feeling the urge to cry rush over me again I looked at the floor. I couldn't any more to him. I knew that if I said another word I would turn, once again, into a sobbing wreck and my pride would not, could not, allow that to happen. I was not a coward.

I wasn't kicked out of the boxing team; in fact I became very much part of the team. The 'coach' as I was now instructed to call the teacher, taught me various moves. How to defend and when to attack and how to bounce around the ring like the lad I had lost my temper with. He also taught me that I should never *ever* to lose that temper in the ring. And he took a lot of time teaching me how to keep it under control. He did this by having some of the other lads tease me until my blood boiled then, when I reached boiling point, he would pick me up and stick me in the ring with one of the older and better fighters, telling me to fight them. Although I would let my temper lose, I was bloody useless at first. I seldom landed a decent punch and my opponents would simply bounce around the ring until I stooped fighting and screamed abuse in frustration. The coach would then step in and hold me by the arms until I calmed down. Within two or three weeks I had learned to control my temper and worked out that, in a boxing ring, it worked against me. Then I really started to learn the art of boxing. I began to feel confident and started to land a few good punches and began to enjoy myself. And I realised that I had, at last, found in the coach someone that seemed to understand the confusion I felt and the anger it caused. I went on to fight for the school and, between the boxing and the choir singing, the feeling that I was part of something, that I '*belonged*' grew stronger. I felt proud of myself and happy with life: at least away from home. It was a feeling that I had not experienced since Morecambe and Uncle John. But it was not to last.

I thought I was tough, I thought I could handle whatever crap life threw at me. But I was wrong. During my life thus far I had witnessed, and all too often been a victim of, levels of violence that no child should endure. I had lived in filth and squalor. I had slept in beds that were so worn that springs cut into my flesh. I had survived on free school dinners and stolen milk. I had slept in piss sodden beds so cold that I couldn't stop shaking. I had been pinned down as my father rubbed himself against me. I had felt fear and terror so often that it became my normality. But none of it had prepared me for the sheer and utter violence that was awaiting me. Nothing could have.

Initially, I hated moving to Scott Street. Leaving my mates in West Bowling had hurt. Once again I had to fight new battles with most of the lads in the new area and listen to people chatter about the 'scruffy' family that had moved in to the area. It was something I could never get used to; I hated being the centre of gossip, even though what the gossips were saying was true. But in many other ways Undercliffe was to be a paradise for me and my siblings and, after only a few days in my new home, I decided I was going to enjoy my new neighbourhood. Plenty of old houses to play in and explore and the odd bit of scrap lead or copper to weigh in at the local scrap yard meant that, occasionally, I had a few pennies in my pocket and I was beginning to enjoy parts of life. At home things were much the same but there was a different atmosphere developing that was becoming even more oppressive than the constant feeling of terror I felt in my father's presence. From the summer's day on my father's shoulders when I was little more than a baby, I had never known any kindness from him. He had shown me nothing but violence and hatred. He had screamed at me that I was a coward every time I cried when he beat me. He would scream and beat me harder when I begged him to stop. He would make me watch him eat, taking pleasure in watching me salivate. And now he was. Though still sadistic at times, there were periods when he was almost a dad again. This was very confusing to me. Suddenly there was food on the table, even though it was nothing more than a plate of chips, it was food. And he also started 'playing' with his children more. The weekly 'wrestling' games were happening almost daily and, even though the pain father inflicted during this 'playtime' was immense, you dare not refuse. There was not an option. More often than not mother would sit and watch her husband twist and bend her children, never complaining, never asking father to stop, never telling him he was going too far. In fact, the look on her face was not one of concern for her children, it was one of enjoyment. These games were almost always 'played' with the children wearing only underwear, often only a vest. Father would twist little arms and bend little legs and then lie on the top of his victim for what seemed ages until he got his breath back. I can still smell the beer on his breath and the grunting noises he would make as he pinned me to the floor, pushing my face on to the stinking, sticky excuse for a carpet.

I was a young lad, streetwise in the ways of violence and survival but naïve as to what was really taking place. My older sister, however, was the opposite. Made a thief by our mother; and a victim by our father, she knew exactly what was happening.

My older sister was becoming ever more estranged from her siblings; she would no longer play out with or get involved with any of our pranks. I didn't know what was wrong with her. Why was she always sad? I just thought she was being miserable like girls tended to be. But I was so wrong, she wasn't miserable because she was a girl, there was another reason. And I was about to find out what was wrong; because it was going to happen to me.

Not long after we had moved to Scott Street my father had started taking his sons on camping trips. Every few weeks we would load up his old, grey Austin van and head out to the moors that sprawl around Bradford and Howarth, pitching our tent miles from anywhere and, I must admit, for a time I felt like I had got part my dad back. He didn't drink while we were away for weekends and he seemed less angry. Although father was still very unpredictable and he wasn't exactly funny, loving or kind, but he seemed a far cry from the monster he had become over the years. We would cook breakfast on a little camping stove; we would even have a rare treat of bacon and beans cooked together in the same frying pan, and they tasted glorious. Crows would squawk above our heads and sheep or cows would stand looking curiously at the strangers gathered around a tent in the middle of their field cooking breakfast.

Those memories of playing with my brothers on Howarth Moor are good memories that stand out from the bleakness that was to follow. Those camping trips were to be the last really happy memories of my childhood. However for a long time the memory was blemished, father was not being nice, nor had he morphed into a caring parent. He was turning into a different kind of brutal monster and though I wasn't to know it then; but it was the beginning of the end for my family.

I had often witnessed my father intimidating people. Old men, young men, women, children, it made no difference to my father who he scared the shit out of. And one day I was to witness firsthand, not only this intimidation but also the sheer violence that he was capable of; and it scared the shit out of me. While I was playing in Barkerend School playground, riding a bike that I had borrowed from a mate, I was riding like a 'bat out of hell' on the smooth tarmac surface. I was so caught up in the feeling of freedom that I wasn't looking where I was going when I accidently ran over a little girl breaking her leg. The little Asian girl had run out of a toilet block and, although I had managed to slow down before I hit her, the force of the impact was still enough to send her flying. I was mortified at what had happened, she was screaming in pain and her leg was unnaturally bent below her knee. I knew her leg was broken, and I was looking desperately for a grown up to come and help me when the little girls older sister came rushing out of the same toilet block. I tried the best I could to explain what had happened but the older girl would not listen. The little girl was in too much pain to care how it had happened so in a state of panic and stupidity I picked the little girl up and carried her the short distance to her house. The girl didn't live far, her house was almost directly opposite my own, but in the few minutes it took to carry her there she must have alerted half of Bradford with her screaming. I was confused and scared as people stopped and stared. Some shouted to put her down, others just looked at me. But no one took her off me, no one took control, no one helped me.

The little girl's older sister ran on ahead of us to get help from her father, and I knew that that meant I would be in trouble. And I was not wrong.

The little girl's father came tearing out of his house as I approached carrying his broken daughter in my arms. My head was already awash with the sound of the little girl's screams of pain, and so I panicked when her father began screaming as well. Putting the girl quickly, but as gently as I could, on the pavement, I turned and ran as fast as I could towards my own home. Running so fast I didn't notice my father until I bounced off him. But he took no notice of me as I lay at his feet expecting a beating; but he was too busy watching the little girl's angry father striding over the street towards me, hurling abuse and threats as he did so. He never made it to our battered front gate. Father's hatred of Asians came flooding to the surface. Father didn't care what I had done or even if it was accident or not, nor did he care about the little girl's broken leg. Father saw only the 'paki' coming towards him and father didn't give a shit about the rights or wrongs of it, he went into fight mode and raced towards the oncoming man.

My father hit the little girl's father so hard I thought he must surely have killed him and I stood both amazed and afraid in equal measures at the sound of my father's fist slamming into the mans face. The man seemed to lift off of his feet and smashed against my father's van and then dropped to the floor. He lay still on the floor and looked like a rag doll and I knew that he was almost unconscious. I couldn't believe the sheer rage my father was in. His eyes bulged and his face was a deep purple as he screamed curses at the man started to come round. My father reached down and dragged the man back to his feet; father was screaming obscenities at him as he threw him back against the van. Blood was already bubbling from the man's mouth and nose. The anger the girl's father had shown as he strode across the street had gone, replaced by fear and confusion as my father continued his attack. I had seen, and been the victim of, my father's anger many times, but I had never witnessed such violence before. The van was being rocked back and forth with the weight of both men. Blood was on the man's shirt, running freely from his nose and mouth. He didn't want to continue he kept begging my father to stop. I felt sorry for the man and I was tempted to plead with my father to stop, but I dare not, I was already scared at what my father was going to do when he had finished with the man who was struggling to stay on his feet. He would surely blame me and then all his anger would turn in my direction. I started to shake uncontrollably and I could not control my bladder and, because of the utter feeling of dread, I pissed myself.

The scene was surreal; my father was beating up the man that was, without any doubt in my mind, about to wallop me, yet I now felt sorry for him. The little girl, whose leg I had broke, was screaming in pain and terror as she watched her dad being beaten senseless, I stood rooted to the spot. I was terrified and piss was running freely down my legs and I struggled with my fear, fighting the urge to run away.

My whole world was there in front of me, it was my life; there in that street was everything I knew, there was nothing there but violence.

Eventually both the police and the ambulance turned up, the ambulance driver gave me a serious telling off for picking up the girl and running with her, I quietly told him to fuck off. I had had enough and the driver was trying to bollock me for doing something I knew nothing about. I didn't know what the fuck to do; I had never run a little girl over before, and being shouted at for it really pissed me off. I was a kid. I had never seen a broken leg before let alone been responsible for breaking one and I certainly didn't know that I should have just left her there and got help. The bloke my father beat up would not press charges; maybe it was that my father had told him he would batter him twice as hard and set him on fire if he did. Whatever the reason my father did not get arrested and, by the time the police and the ambulance people pulled away my father had calmed down and, other than bragging about the punches he had landed, he said nothing more to me about it. In fact he seemed quite pleased with me. But I couldn't stop my body shaking nor get the feeling of shame out of my mind. The little girl's dad had every right to be pissed off with me and I probably deserved a wallop; he didn't deserve the battering he received from my father.

For weeks after, every time I looked out of the window of my house the little girl seemed to be there staring back at me. I could not escape her and the bright white pot that covered the full length of her broken leg was a constant reminder of what I had done. Her father wouldn't speak to me; in fact he would not even look at me. I wanted to say sorry. I wanted to tell him that I didn't mean to hurt his daughter, and tell him that she just ran in front of me, but I didn't get the chance. I think he was more scared of my father than he was angry with me. So I kept feeling guilty and stopped looking out of the window.

Mother's thieving was yet again to cause problems; she had her own 'MO' and was well known to the local police and the beat bobby was always calling in. I remember one day the police came to search the house and they went in to every room and looked in to every box and cupboard, even pulling back the stinking bedclothes and looking under the beds. That experience could not have been very pleasant for the officers and I can only imagine what they thought of the piss soaked mattresses and sunken beds. When they found what they were looking for my mother was arrested in front of her family. The officers had told her that if she told them where she had hidden the loot they would not have arrested her at home, they said they would have taken her to the local nick to do it and save her and her children the embarrassment. But mother didn't care about her children, she just hoped that the police would not discover her hiding place, but they did and so they put handcuffs on her and took her away. Watching mother being walked down the path in handcuffs escorted by two coppers in full view of the neighbours filled me full of shame. A deep urge to run overwhelmed me; so I ran out of the house. I remember I ran passed the cops has they placed my mother into the back of a car and I caught a glimpse of my mothers face and saw she was smiling. I felt disgusted and ashamed and suddenly I started to cry. My life was fucked up. I had a father that terrified me and a mother that seemed to enjoy being locked up. I started to run has fast as I could, and kept running until my lungs nearly burst. The next memory is of sitting in the middle of a room in one of the big old derelict houses feeling angry, confused and ashamed. I felt totally alone in my misery and wanted to stay there in that old house forever. Looking round the room and seeing peeling wallpaper, damp walls and broken windows, I realised that, although it was derelict, the house was still far better than the one I lived in. The place I called home was a shithole that stank off piss, grease and filth. It was not a home full of laughter and love; it was full of fear and privation Anger continued to grow within me, I couldn't stop the growing feelings of rage and disgust I felt at the person I was becoming. Why wasn't I like other kids, why did no one love me, why did my father hate me so much? Everyone else lived 'normal' lives and lived in 'normal' houses. My own life was as shitty has the house I lived in and I didn't want it anymore. Sitting on that floor, sobbing from deep inside my young soul I did something that shocked me; not at the time, but afterwards. I caused my self pain. In sheer desperation to ease my emotional agony; I bit my finger so hard that I tore through to the bone. I remember screaming in pain. And it felt wonderful. For a few glorious moments I felt only physical pain; and the images of my life briefly left me. I had, for some reason, bitten the index finger of my left hand throbbed and blood ran freely out of the holes left by my teeth. From that day on I would bite that finger every time my self-loathing and anger became too much to bear. I bit my finger so often and so hard that, eventually, the skin thickened and I lost all feeling in it.

    Later that day two detectives called to interview my sisters for their part in the theft. Although they were both still too young to be arrested my sisters still had to make a statement; but it didn't really bother them, they had become used to it. But while they were in the house the two coppers caused uproar when they ended up covered in the caterpillars my siblings and I had been collecting all that day.

We had collected a bowl full of the little green things, why we had done this I had no idea, it was probably just one of those daft things children do during school holidays, but collect them we had, by the thousand. The detectives were ok, they didn't shout at my sisters and my father didn't seem to give a shit; he stayed quiet and just sat at the back of the room drinking tea and belching. It was when one of the officers asked what was in the bowl that was suspiciously covered up at the back of the room when we all started to giggle. The copper didn't believe us when we told him what they were, he was sure that whatever my mother had stolen was in the bowl, so when he asked if he could have a look we obliged and, either by design or accident, when he took the bowl and plonked it on his knee it tipped over spilling the wriggling caterpillars as he removed the cloth that had been covering the bowl. The little things were all over him within seconds and he stood up as if his arse had burst into flames, swearing loudly as he did so. I was amazed to see the big burly police officer scream as if ferrets were attacking his balls. No one in the room, other than the officer with an obvious phobia of caterpillars, could stop laughing. Even his mate couldn't stop himself. It was a surreal moment in my life. My mother was back in jail, my finger was still bleeding from the self inflicted bite and I was still shaking from my emotional meltdown. I should have been at *least* upset a little bit! But I couldn't give a shit; I was too busy laughing at one of the cops that had locked her up! Even my father laughed. But it was rare to her my father laugh, and it scared me. Life was dealing me some strange cards. In one day I had screamed and sobbed; felt shame and anger and laughed so hard my stomach hurt . . .

My boxing was going well enough. I had learned to control my temper in the ring and I was turning out to be a decent fighter. No longer did I fight in the playground and no longer did bullies try to intimidate or pick on me, except for one, a real 'hard nut' who thought he could beat anybody in the school and claimed he was the 'cock of Undercliffe'. The fuck he was; and I longed to tangle with him but I knew the coach would be pissed off if I thumped him. But it was proving difficult to avoid the shithead. The lad almost daily asked me if I wanted a scrap and he must have seen it has a weakness that I didn't accept and he would smirk as I walked away. This was strange to me; I had never been challenged so calmly to a fight before. But he had seen how I had flattened one of his sycophantic mates and must have felt I was a challenge in some way to his lofty position as 'cock of the school' I had been cock of St James and had earned the respect of the teachers by stopping the bullying; but this lad had not fought me, or anyone else as far as I knew, so his claim was unearned and in his head only. He must have thought I declined because I was afraid of him and I had simply accepted him as the better fighter. Or he maybe just thought of me as a soft touch that got lucky which, being smaller than most in my class and being a skinny scruffy kid wearing wire framed classes with an eye patch; I suppose I looked the part.

I continued to decline his daily offer, ignoring the taunts and the nudges and remembering the lessons about restraint from the gym about control. But eventually the taunts and childish nudges began to piss me off and he began to get under my skin. Then one day after a bad night at home, father had locked me in the loft again and so I had had no sleep and was sore from the battering I received for daring to ask why. As I walked through the school assembly hall that day I was pissed off and looking to vent when the lad try to stop me and would not let me pass him. We were almost dancing at one point as I tried to pass him and he moved to block my move each time and within a few heartbeats I had had enough and so I pushed him hard to one side. The lad slammed into the wall and I was just about to batter him when the boxing coach appeared as if from nowhere. The coach had been watching things develop from the other side of the hall and had waited until the last minute to step between the 'cock' and me; then, in his rough accent, he asked if we wanted a fight. Of course we did, I wanted to beat the crap out of the lad and he wanted to prove that I couldn't; so things needed to be settled, and the coach knew just the right place to sort it all out: in the boxing ring. So it was arranged for later that day after dinner.

The coach told me that I should avoid eating too much food at dinner time saying it would slow me down. I didn't tell him

Just Once, When I was little

that the dinner at school was the only real food I would be eating that day, or any other day for that matter. I didn't tell him about the loft or that I hadn't slept or eaten since the day before; even though I had 'acquired' two bottles of milk, I was starving, but I think he understood the reason for my reluctance at agreeing to this and, after a moments pause, he told me if I won my fight he would give me half of his own lunch; plus his pudding. The worst part of the day was sitting at the dinner table with only a few scraps on my plate and not allowing my self a pudding. I was starving hungry and most thought I was sick though some thought I was afraid to fight the school hard man. I was neither of course, and I watched with a smile on my face as my opponent tucked into a full dinner followed by a big, fat, stodgy pudding. All the time he was watching me, smirking, no doubt thinking that I was scared of him; I suppose I helped him to think that I was by avoiding his stare and looking sheepish. But inside, I was burning with rage and wanted to punch the arrogant look of his smug face.

Just after dinner I made my way to the gym to meet the coach, and he had erected the ring making a far better job of it than when we trained and, for once, it looked like a real boxing ring. I did my usual work out and ran around the hall for five minutes then did a bit of skipping to warm up and by the time my opponent turned up I actually felt like a boxer. Blustering noisily into the gym with about six of his mates the bully started to take his shirt off; the coach bellowed at him to shut his gob and get changed in the changing room. My opponent started to chuckle. The coach threw a pair of gloves at him and knocked the smirk off his face by striding towards him asking if he thought this all a big joke. The bully stopped smiling and hastily backed away and, almost running, made his way to the changing room. He did not look so cocky then, and when he had to ask to borrow some shorts and pumps, I couldn't help but smile to myself. The coach gave him some shorts alright, that were bright green and far too big, and when came out of the changing room and tried to put the boxing gloves on I struggled not to burst out laughing. The lad looked a fool; he had no idea about boxing even though he had boasted about being the 'cock of the school'.

He reminded me of me when I first put the heavy leather gloves on and I knew the effect my dancing around the ring smacking my own gloves together would be having on him, so I danced and bounced around like a mini madman, slamming my gloves together as hard as I could, the sound echoing off the gym walls. My opponent looked lost as he walked onto the makeshift ring, all his bravado had left him, but the coach kept talking to me telling me not to be fooled, he warned me my opponent was a big lad and if he could land a punch on my head then he could hurt me. He was telling me to stay out of his reach and to attack when his arms became heavy and his guard was down. With the wise words of my coach ringing in my ears and the confidence of a 9 year old, I bounced to the centre of the ring and waited for my opponent. He looked a sorry state, his arms already looked heavy and he walked slowly to meet me, his mates were shouting encouragement, but I don't think he was too impressed with them. And then, as he walked towards me, I saw the first hint of fear in his eyes and I knew then that I would win.

I had missed my dinner, normally the only real meal of my day, for a fight that never really took place. Within thirty seconds of the fight starting, and after only being thumped a couple of times on the side of his head, my opponent backed off saying he had had enough; he was almost crying as he struggled to get his gloves off. Some hard guy!

My mother was once again in prison. I have no idea how long she had been sent down for, and I doubt I really cared because whenever mother was locked up my wonderful nana called in almost every day to take care of us. Nana made sure we had breakfast and clean clothes every day and even father's temper seemed to calm down when Nana was visiting—Nana may have been only 4 ft 8 inch in her shoes, but she never showed the slightest fear of my brutal father. However my older sister seemed to take my mother's incarceration badly, she was already becoming increasingly withdrawn and would often cry at the slightest thing. Then one morning my sister was so poorly that Nana called the doctor out to see her. The doctor gave my sister some pills and told her to stay off school. Father was well pissed off with Nana for calling the doctor and though, in his anger, he kicked the crap out of me, he didn't say a thing to Nana.

Father's moods were becoming ever more bi-polar and very difficult to predict. One minute he would be 'wrestling' with his children and then, within minutes, would turn suddenly turn violent slamming his fist into the wall or door or child. So it was with mixed emotions when father decided to take up camping; but I didn't have a choice in the matter, if father wanted to go camping then that was that.

Father had either bought, borrowed or stole a big old grey van and decided to take all but the youngest kids camping for the weekend. The van was a battered rusty thing that filthy, rusty and stank of petrol both inside and out. We spent hours cleaning all the old rubbish out of the back of it and did our best to wash the crap off the outside. Father appeared to be in a good mood and he even laughed a few at our mucky faces as we scrubbed and polished. It was a hopeless cause and the only difference was that the van was now a clean battered wreck! But it would do and so we loaded the tent and other stuff in to the back and found places to sit for the long journey. I felt quite happy as we pulled away from Scott Street, I was fighting for a comfy place in the back of the van as it rattled loudly on the cobbled streets until we turned on to the smooth tarmac on the main road. It was a bright glorious sunny day and father had opened both front windows of the van causing a wind to swirl about in the back keeping those in the back cool and also keeping the stench of petrol at bay. The overloaded, battered, van struggled to cope with many of the hills during the long drive through the countryside to the campsite my father had chosen. The site was a little village high in the Yorkshire Dales called Sedbergh. It seemed to take forever to get there, but my father stopped the van several times during the journey and let us all out of the van to stretch our legs and so he could piss in the hedge. It must have baffled the sheep on those high hills when we pulled up and a load screaming kids jumped out of the van. All that is except for my sister she seemed petrified and simply sat there with her legs pulled up to her chest resting her head on her knees. I didn't really give her too much thought as we ran about chasing the sheep. I felt free. Father was in a good mood and mother was locked up. Life felt good that day: but it didn't last long. My camping holiday to Sedbergh would send my world crashing. As crap as my life was I had assumed that it could not get any worse. Lack of food, love, security, continuity and frequent beatings and psychological abuse and become my 'norm' and in many ways, I had accepted my life. But it was to become so much worse. My father's camping trip was little more than a reason to share a bed with his children.

When we eventually pulled up at the campsite, the bloke in charge said we couldn't stop there because they didn't allow 'vans like that' on the site. My father stormed towards the man and quickly persuaded him that it would be better if he allowed us to stay for a few days, and so we unloaded the van and made camp. It didn't take long; we all helped, and within an hour we had created our own little three-tent village that stood out from all the others. The tents stood out because they were all mucky old stained tents that would have been bright white at one time, but none of us cared. As a family we were used to being stared at and, silently, mocked, and so we made even more noise just to piss people off.

A few hundred yards from where we had pitched the tent there was a wonderful river that carried crystal clear water straight from the surrounding hills. It was blistering hot and I was still sweaty from the long stifling drive in the battered old van so it wasn't long before I had stripped down to my underpants and paddled in; splashing about exploring under every rock looking for fish. The water was bloody freezing at first and total contrast to the hot summer's day and took my breath away as I waded deeper away from the bank and the water reached my bollocks. My shivering body soon got used to the cold but it took a while to get used to the strong current and more than once the force of it nearly pulled by sagging underwear off; but I didn't care, I felt free, happy and alive. I kept seeing little creatures' dash between the smooth rocks that covered the riverbed and put my hands into the water and turned one over. It took some doing but eventually I managed to move the large rounded boulder and found a fresh water crayfish trying desperately to find somewhere to hide. Having never seen a crayfish before I wasn't sure if the little animals were dangerous so, having cornered the creature, I cautiously tried to pick it up but it scurried away at lightening speed making me jump and I fell on my arse in the panic; the sudden emersion into the freezing water to my breath away. I spent an age trying to catch the little creature but eventually gave up and looked for something else to occupy my time. About 20 yards downstream there was a bridge and, as the crayfish didn't seem to want to be caught, I went to investigate. Out of the warm sunshine and a few yards under the bridge, the temperature dropped dramatically and I soon began to shiver. It was then that I heard my sister scream loudly and I looked towards the tents just in time to see my father storming angrily out of the tent I knew my older sister was in; seeing my father so angry I wondered what my sister had done to spoil the good mood and anger my father and I remember feeling annoyed at her for spoiling the day. I was a child and knew no better; and I had no idea what was really wrong with my sister, but I would soon know the truth and I would soon know the fear she was feeling.

For tea that evening father took the van and went to the village a chip shop. I remember sitting outside the tents eating chips with scraps making 'chip butties' out of thick fresh bread smothered in butter and drinking tea from an old jam jar. The sun started to set behind one of the high hills that surrounded the village and all seemed well with the world. Father was reasonably sober my belly was full. If it had not been for the constant sobs coming from my sister who had remained in the tent; it would have been a perfect end to the day. I kept expecting father to scream at my sister to tell her to shut up but for some reason he didn't; he just let her continue to cry.

After our tea we all played football, including father, until it got quite late. We were having a wonderful time, my sister seemed to be recovering from the beating I thought she had received earlier but and she stayed at the front of the tent. She didn't even eat her share of the chips so we shared them out among the rest of the kids. It was then that father dropped the bombshell that he was going to the pub. All the children looked

Brian Mynott

at each other, we knew that he would get drunk and we all knew what that meant, or at least we thought we knew. As the grey van pulled out of the campsite we all knew that it would be a very different father that would return. And he would utterly destroy my world.

There was a large shower block on the site many of our fellow campers were making their way there to shower and toilet before sitting outside their tents relaxing in the warm evening air or going to bed. Since my holiday in Morecambe I had at least tried to keep myself clean and the ever present stink of piss at bay; but I was the only one of the siblings to bother showering, they didn't seem to care. I knew we had not brought any no soap or towels but I wanted to use the shower so off I went alone. The shower block was quite busy but I didn't have to wait long before a cubicle came free, and it was worth the wait. On the floor was a small piece of soap that someone had either discarded or forgot. It was Imperial Leather, the same soap that I had used in Morecambe and the smell of it brought many wonderful memories flooding back to me. I stayed in that shower until someone lost patience and knocked loudly on the cubicle door. So I pissed on the shower floor and stormed out naked. One bloke suggested I used the sink next time. I told him to fuck himself and stared at him; daring him to have a swing at me. He just shook his head and mumbled a few incoherent words and, pushing passed me, strode into the shower cubicle. I smiled when saw him put his feet into the little puddle I had left him. Has he closed the door and turned on the shower, I noticed that he had placed his towel on the bench that ran the full length of the wall; it was folded all nice and neat next to his clothes. I didn't even look round to see who was watching, I just I picked it up the man's towel and dried myself with it; folded it neatly and placed it back on the bench. I walked out of the shower block with a smile on my face. I was dry, clean and confident the bloke in the shower would not like the skid marks I had left on his towel.

Walking back to the tent in the warm evening breeze, I was fascinated by the surrounding countryside and the noises that filled the air. I could hear sheep bleating on the hillsides and cows mooing in the fields. The entire world seemed at peace as I walked slowly towards the riverbank to watch the water as it cascaded around the rocks and disappeared under the bridge. Sitting on the riverbank watching the sun slowly disappear behind a hill, I was at peace with myself and the world. Even the bleakness of Bradford seemed too distant to trouble me. But at the back of my mind I knew that my father would be returning soon and that he would be drunk. I can remember wishing that he, my father, would crash the van and die and that I could sit on the bank of the river forever. I wanted time to stand still.

I sat there for a long time then I realised that father would be returning from the pub so reluctantly stood up and headed back to the tent. I wanted to be asleep, or at least pretending to be, before father returned. I didn't want to annoy him in any way so I hurried my step and, in my haste, almost fell into the tent nearly squashing my younger brother as I stumbled through the tent flap. It was then I realised that, because I had been to the shower block and sat by the river, I was the last kid into the tent and I would have to sleep next to my father. The thought terrified me for some reason. There would be no way any of my brothers or sisters would trade places, no amount of persuasion or pleading would change their minds not even when I threatened to piss on them.

I couldn't sleep and the noises from the hillsides that only a few hours ago I had found so wonderful, now seemed nightmarish. With every sound I expected my father to burst in to the tent and fill the place with the stench of beer. By the time he did arrive I was petrified when I realised that I would be sleeping next to my father and I knew that the slightest noise or disturbance would make him angry and trigger a beating. He hadn't fooled me with his pretend good mood; I had seen him leave the tent after he had beaten my sister for no apparent reason, so I knew it would be no different for me. My father didn't so much enter the tent as fall in through the flaps almost bringing the tent down as he drunkenly tried to stop himself falling. Even though father had crash landed on to my siblings they, like me, did not utter a sound in either pain or protest; they, like me, dare not make a sound, preferring to cling to the childish belief that our father thought we were asleep. He was a heavy man my father; packed with muscle and an ever expanding beer gut. Father must have caused more pain as he wriggled trying to regain his feet, not caring where or on whom he stood on or dug his knees into. As he was struggling to stand father kept muttering something as he did so, something that I couldn't make out, it was as if he didn't even realise where he was, I could only make out the odd swearword as he continued his drunken struggle in the confines of the tent. Struggling and swearing he took off his clothes, threw them around the tent and then fell down at my side. Struggling to get him self comfortable, father didn't care who or what he shoved out of the way, he finally settled of sorts and I cringed when he put his arm over me feeling his weight against my back. The tent soon stunk of stale beer and farts and I was relieved when he started to snore and turn away from me releasing me from his grip. I kept as far away from him as the tent and my siblings would allow. I didn't want him near me, I didn't want to touch him, I didn't want to smell his stinking beer drenched breath and I even thought about sneaking out and sleeping in the shower block, or down by the river, but I dare not move in case I woke him. As I lay there listening to the deep guttural snoring of my father, I felt nothing but fear. No love. No pride. No feeling of security. The weight of my father's arm was almost unbearable and I felt suffocated: but still I dare not move. I lay there in the darkness of the tent breathing in the stale stench of booze and farts until the days travelling and playing finally caught up with me and sleep took me away from reality.

   I tried to scream but my mouth was covered. I couldn't breathe and tried to resist the powerful force that was pushing my face hard into floor of the tent. I could hear grunting. I could smell stale beer and cigarette smoke. I could feel my body being twisted painfully. Someone was kneeling on my leg and the pain seared through my body. Why didn't my father wake up? Why didn't my brothers and sisters help me? Was I asleep? Was I having a nightmare? Was this really happening? Pain: Suffocating: Fear: Terror: Confusion. And then a new unbelievable agony surged through my whole body. I tried desperately to scream but my face was forced even harder into the floor. I tried to get up, to run away, but I could not move. The pain was unbearable and I started to cry. Silent sobs tried to escape but couldn't. then it all stopped.

I heard my father grunt and felt his weight lift from my body. I wanted to cry, to scream, to run, to breathe clean air... but I dare not, could not, do anything. I lay trembling with fear, biting a pillow to stifle the screams that the pain was forcing out of my mouth.

I remember thinking about Morecambe and Uncle John, I wanted my nana. I wanted someone, anyone, just to hold me and make me feel secure and loved. I felt alone, vulnerable and utterly terrified. I was a boy, a child in a tent with a man that hated me. My father had finished with me and simply pushed me away; squashing me against my older brother. I felt used, filthy, dirty, unclean and desperate.

My father had done what he had wanted and simply turned over and fell asleep. There have been many times since that night that I wished I had murdered him. I should have slit my father's throat with his own knife. He always had a sharp knife and I knew that he had one in the van. But I was a child, I was terrified and confused so I just lay there, bleeding and crying until father fell asleep.

I waited and waited until he had been snoring for at least half an hour before I dare move. But when I thought that my father was in a deep sleep, I tried to move but I couldn't. Even the slightest movement sent spikes of pain searing through my backside and into my stomach; but I stifled my scream; I had to get out of that tent and away from him and the stench that lingered around him. It took every ounce of my strength to pull myself away from my father. The pain was so intense that I almost fainted as I climbed carefully over my brothers. My whole body was trembling and I felt weak and I remember silently screaming to myself not to fall on my father. I doubt that my siblings were asleep; they would do as I would have done, pretend to be asleep. They must have heard or felt what my father had done. But I do not blame them for doing nothing;

if it had been happened to one of them, I would almost certainly done the same.

As I pushed back the tent flaps and escaped from the stench of the tent I started to cry. I remember falling to the ground and pulling up tufts of damp grass and rubbing it all over my face and head. I wanted to scream at the top of my voice but I dare not. I could feel the freshness of the night, and I could at last smell the cleanness of the air and breathed in as deep as I could. The river still rumbled along, filling the night with a low rumbling sound. Only a few hours before I had been fascinated by the sounds smells and peacefulness of the surrounding hillside; but it had all lost its magic now. It had all changed, as had my life. I couldn't walk, I could only crawl, I wanted only to be clean, I wanted to remove the mess that was oozing from my bottom and running down my bare legs. I lay on the grass for some time trying to make sense of what had happened. The attack had seemed to take hours, but in reality it was probably no more than a few minutes. It seems almost unbelievable now that I didn't realise that my father had raped me; I didn't even know what rape was, and I remember thinking it was a strange type of beating and, naively, I didn't know what the mess was mixed with the blood that seeped from my bottom. I tried to wipe the mess with a clump of grass and the smell of my own shit was overwhelming. I had to wash myself; I had to remove the mess. I started to cry, alone outside the tent I felt lower than I had ever felt before, I felt totally and utterly vulnerable. Why. Why. Why. I kept whispering the words when I wanted to scream them aloud; but the deep fear of my father forced me to cry and scream in almost total silence.

The shower block lights were still on so I slowly made my way over to it. I couldn't stand, even to try sent a surge of violent pain surging through my whole body but I wanted desperately to wash the filth and the stink of my father off my body and get it clean again. I wanted to wash what had happened away. So I crawled like a dog across the grass, slowly inching my way towards the lights, fighting the urge to scream every time I moved. But I had to get clean, I had to wash the filth off, I had to wash away what had happened.

The grass was damp and, whether because of shock or pain, I started to feel the chill of the night air. I was wearing only a small tatty vest and tried desperately to cover the rest of my body with it, but it was stupid and fruitless to try and only caused more pain so I gave up trying.

After what seemed an eternity I eventually reached the shower block. I sat for several minutes outside the door listening for any noise of people inside. I was aware that I was all but naked. I was aware that I stank of my own shit. I was aware that something bad had happened; and I was aware I was on my own.

When I eventually entered the shower block the place was silent and empty and looked far bigger than when I had gone there for a shower earlier that evening. Every sound echoed back off the walls and when I let the door go it slammed in to its frame, sounding like an explosion as it crashed shut. I froze, I was sure I must have woken the whole camp, including my father. But after a few minutes nobody came and the quietness returned. I made my way slowly to the nearest shower using the tiled walls to support me; as I did so I passed a large cracked mirror that hung from the ceiling and almost reaching the floor. Stopping to look at my reflection I didn't recognise the boy that looked back at me. Blood, grass and snot covered most of my face and my mouth was swollen due to the immense pressure my father had used to keep me from screaming. The upper half of my small vest was dark red with my blood. Looking at the blood on my face and chest, the mixture of shit and blood on my legs; I felt as I looked: pathetic. I couldn't stop the feeling of emptiness from overwhelming me and I started to cry again. I wanted to scream. I wanted to scream so loud that I would wake the whole fucking world up. But I dare not; it would have woken the monster that was my father. So I screamed silently and I spit blood onto the mirror.

Even though I tried desperately to open the shower cubicle door quietly, the door creaked and screamed in protest as I pulled it open. All the time I was expecting my father to come charging through the door and in to the shower block and beat me again. I was terrified and my heart raced at every sound and I started to shake, a terrible shaking that I couldn't control, and it took all my strength to move; but I desperately wanted to wash my body and, with trembling hands I eventually managed to pull the door open and crawl into the shower. Falling against the wall I lay on my side, tucked my knees under my chin and sobbed. Then suddenly I didn't care that the tiled cubicle was freezing; and I no longer cared who heard me crying. I had had enough.

It was sometime before I could stand, and blood was still dribbling between my legs and it had started to a crust on my cold skin. The shaking had calmed down a bit and I began to feel the cold more so I struggled to my feet to turn the shower on. The sudden impact of the cold water when I turned the tap took my breath away. Moving my body to avoid the water made me cry out in pain; and I began to cry again. I thought the water was never going to warm, but it did eventually and the feeling of the warm clean water running down my body was wonderful. I stood there just letting the water cascade over my head run down my body taking the filth away. Feeling the blood and shit being washed from my body and watching the white shower tiles turn a mucky brown colour and then watching the stained water disappear down the drain helped a little. But the feelings of fear and confusion that were running through my mind did not wash away with the filth. Those feelings and the memory of what had taken place did not go down the drain and dissipate with the water; they stayed with me. As steam filled the cubicle and condensed on the glass door memories of my short life seemed to flood my mind. And I just cried at the unbidden recollections and decided that I didn't have a 'life' like other kids; I existed in a totally different world.

I must have fallen asleep in the shower because when I finally left the building I could see the dawn beginning to appear; changing the colour of the sky and taking away the darkness of the night but not the horror of it. I could see the tent where my life had changed and it all seemed so surreal. Birds were noisily welcoming the new day, sheep were bleating on the hillside, the river still rumbled along and the day promised to be just as sunny as the previous one. But it all seemed so different, the magic that I had felt the day before had vanished with the night that had passed. The birds were just noisy, the sheep would be dead and eaten someday soon and the river was just boring and pointless. The first noises of movement came from the tents. People would soon be up and about preparing for the coming day. Some would go for long walks in the surrounding hills, some would walk into the village, and some would stay on site and play football, swim in the river or just sit and relax. What would I do? I knew I had to move away from the toilet block, I was almost naked and shivering in the dawn chill but I did not want to walk the short distance to the tent. I did not want to smell the stale beer and the stench of my father's constant farting. I did not want to be near my father, my brothers, sisters, I desperately wanted to be alone. But I had no option, I had no choice, I had to go back to my life.

Much of the pain had eased, but the pain from my bottom was still there. It was still intense and increased every time I tried to walk upright, so I walked bent over hoping that the toilet tissue I had trapped between the cheeks of my bottom would stop any more blood from escaping and trickling down my legs. The shower had cleansed my body, but it hadn't made me feel any cleaner. But slowly I had half waked half crawled until I reached the tent. I still felt filthy and I stood outside the tent shaking with fear and dreading entering the dark stinking world inside. Eventually I entered the tent and the stench inside those canvas walls made me wrench and pull back. The tent stunk of stale beer and farts. The usual smell of fresh urine from the children's bed paled in comparison. Taking a deep breath I re-entered the tent; only this time on all fours; all the time I was terrified that I would disturb my father; I knew that, although I had withstood countless beatings and was almost used to the pain, I would not have survived another.

My father didn't move; he lay on his back naked. As I crept slowly over my siblings I couldn't help hurting them as my knees dug into them; and even though I must have caused them considerable pain they didn't complain, they knew something terrible had happened. They must have had a terror filled night sleeping in the tent with our father feeling dread every time he moved. Looking at my father caused me to shake uncontrollably. Even though he was deeply asleep his face had a look of evil and I knew that I could not and would not sleep next to him again; even if he beat me to death for refusing. After silently crawling once again over my siblings, I wedged myself between the tent wall and one of my brothers, keeping as far away from my father as the tent would allow. I was still shaking, trying to make sense of it all and failing, the welcome warmth of blankets and the feeling of security I got from having people between my father and I, I eventually fell asleep. I didn't want to fall asleep and I tried hard not to, but both physically and emotionally I was exhausted and, as the rest of the campsite started another day in Sedbergh, I finally, unwillingly, fell asleep. When I woke up the tent was empty but the stench of filth filled the air; I remember thinking I had dreamt the events of the night before, but the thought only lasted a brief moment, the pain in my body told me the truth.

The first thing I did was to check the tissue that I had put in place to stop any blood leaking from my bottom. There was a trace but it was not much but when I moved my legs to stand the pain was intense. Once again I stifled the screams that threatened to escape from my mouth. The bedclothes, although they were scattered across the floor, were still in the tent and I could see the bloodstain where I had laid at the side of my father. There were several dark bloody marks smeared on the side of the tent and I knew I must have made them. In my mind it was still happening, I could feel the pressure, the pain, the smell, the power of my father's hand pushing my face into the grubby pillow. And I felt the urge to flee the confines of the tent and escape into the fresh air. It was as if the tent walls were crushing me and squeezing the air from my lungs. I struggled to breathe and I crawled quickly on all fours towards the tent flaps. Pushing them open I desperately gulped air into my lungs and breathed deeply until I stopped shaking and the panic subsided. As I looked out across the campsite there was no sign of my father or the rest of my family; I could see only other campers carrying on with their holiday. And again I cried.

Eventually my family returned from where ever they had been. My older sister who hadn't really spoken to anyone for months walked towards me, indicating with a slight movement of her head for me to go in to the tent that was being used for both storing our equipment and where father made sure she slept alone. She looked back at the rest of the family to check that no one was watching, especially our father, but he was busy thumping my older brother attracting everyone's attention so, quickly, my sister pushed me into the tent. It took a few minutes for her to settle and calm her obvious fear. Then my sister started talking, for the first time in years I spoke to my sister; or rather she spoke to me. She told me she knew what had happened, she knew how I felt, she knew that I felt alone, and she knew that I had spent half of the night in the shower. She knew everything, but she didn't say how she knew. My sister held both my hands in hers and looked into my eyes and I could see only sadness in them; then she started to shake, then we both started to cry.

When we heard father bellowing at one of the other children we knew he had finished beating our older brother and would wonder where we were. After one last cuddle we wiped our faces in an attempt to hide the redness of our eyes the tent; I was still in pain and my sister helped me to stand. Holding hands we lifted the tent flap back and went back out into the sunshine to face the world and our father.

When father saw my sister and I together coming away from the tent he went crazy. He strode angrily across the grass towards us. I held my sister's hand tighter as he drew near. Grabbing my sister roughly by her arm, he dragged her away slapping her about her head as he did so. He kept screaming at her as he hit her *"what were you two talking about . . . what have you been doing in that fucking tent"* his face was red with anger and his swearing and shouting increased when my sister started to cry. Pulling my sister about like a rag doll my father threw her from side to side. I wanted to be brave and shout at my father to stop, I wanted to run over and kick him. But I didn't, I dare not move. Instead I started to shake again. People stopped what they were doing and stared at the scene that was erupting in front of them; but not a single person said anything or tried to stop my father;

they all just stood there, silent, watching. Maybe it was fear that stopped them; my father was a powerful man; a violent man that could turn any argument in to a fight. But to stand and do nothing as they did while a young girl was being beaten so viciously was, to me, pure cowardice.

Watching my father beat my sister so mercilessly I was shaking uncontrollably. I was terrified waiting for my father to stop hitting my sister knowing he would then turn his anger on me. But he didn't, he stopped beating my sister and threw her onto the ground like a rag doll then started to walk towards the tents, but just as I expected him to grab me, he walked straight passed me. Father didn't do anything to me; in fact he was acting as if I wasn't even there, he didn't shout or look at me; he totally ignored me as if I didn't even exist. This made me feel both relieved and terrified. It was totally alien for my father not to beat me, though it was not unusual for him to delay the punishment, he enjoyed the psychological torture that this would produce in his children.

Father remained in a foul mood all day and as the day turned to evening and people started to use the shower and the younger children were being put to bed, I was seriously considering running away. I knew that I could not live through another night like the previous one. Then, for some reason, father suddenly decided we were going home. I nearly cried with relief. Within minutes father had started to angrily pull the tents down. He didn't care about folding them, he simply threw them and everything else, including his children, into the back of the van; and from start to finish it took less than half an hour to load the battered old van. As soon as the van had been loaded father screamed at us to shut up and not say another word; revving the old engine loudly the van roared out of the campsite and within minutes we were driving through the winding lanes pulling away from Sedbergh. The surge of relief I felt at not having to spend another night in that tent with my father was immense. Even though all the children had been forced to sit in the back of the van because father had forbid anyone to sit in the front with him while we bounced around in the back; I couldn't stop smiling. My older sister held my hand throughout the long journey back to Bradford and, at one point, even fell asleep leaning against my shoulder. I remember she kept twitching and muttering to herself as she slept, it was as if she was trying to cry but couldn't.

As we bounced our way back to Bradford I kept thinking that once we got home things would return to 'normal', that everything would be ok. But I was so very wrong; nothing would ever be the same again, and my life was about to become dramatically, violently, worse.

When we eventually arrived back at Scott Street, father was still in a violent mood and screamed at everyone to get the van unloaded; everyone except me that is; father was still ignoring me and hadn't said a word to me since the night before. Once the van had been emptied all the children were ordered to get in the house and get to bed. No supper, no cuddles, no reminiscing about our camping trip just a stark order from our father. A few days after we had returned strange thing happened to my father that, even though I was still so young, I felt had happened on purpose, as some kind of punishment for the bad things my father had done. Maybe it was my lovely granddad that had died a few years before who was the cause of what to my father. One afternoon father was climbing the stairs that led from the kitchen in the basement to the room on the first floor; as usual he was slamming his feet down on each step: he did this to scare his children. The old wooden stairs were quite steep and creaked with each step we took no matter how quiet we tried to be or lightly we placed our feet; as father made his way up them suddenly a great lump of plaster dropped from the ceiling onto his head. It floored him. Cutting a large gash in his scalp and knocking the sense out of him; if he had been a few steps higher, the resulting injury would have been far worse as another, heavier, piece of plaster that had fallen in front of him had a lump of cement attached to it that was so heavy it smashed the step it landed on. Looking at my father as he lay on the stairs with blood gushing from his head I felt no pity at all. If anything, I wished him dead. And I remember smiling inside.

Father's temper became even more unpredictable after the near miss. And the bandage that covered most of his head made him look a right prat didn't help. He knew he looked stupid even though no one dare tell him; he knew. When he spoke to me it was always aggressively. He would suddenly shout at me to sit down, or stand up, or get to bed, or shut up. It wasn't this that was strange; he had shouted at me for most of my life. It was that he had stopped hitting me. And when you are walloped at least once a day, it becomes normal and you miss it. Not in a nice way; but you miss it. One thing was very obvious; he could not stand the sight of me or me being around him or even the same room.

One night it particular remains vivid and painful in my memory. It was a night when one of my rotten teeth eventually caused me so much pain that I cried out during the night. I had tried to cry quietly but the abscess in my mouth was throbbing so much that I couldn't stifle my sobs enough and it woke my father. Within minutes of my first unbidden cry of pain my father burst through the bedroom door cursing as he did so. And dragging me from the pile of children that I shared a bed with he suspended me in mid-air by my hair. Holding me securely in his powerful hands he then began to squeeze my whole head. My feet searched desperately for something to take the weight of my body. I tried to grab my father's arms but he screamed at me to let go, so I quickly released my grip. As the pressure on my head became intense I thought I was going to die and I almost surrendered at one point. I felt I had had enough of it all. I could feel no pain; even my tooth had stopped hurting. And all resistance to life began to leave me. I stopped struggling and surrendered. My life was shit and I couldn't find one reason that would prompt me to struggle again. I have never sought death, even during the darkest days. But I had had enough. Then suddenly I was on the bedroom floor gasping for breath and my father stood over me breathless.

It was my older sister's scream that caused my father to let me fall to the floor with a bump. She had screamed so loudly that my father was stunned momentarily. But he hadn't finished with me. Dragging me violently across the bedroom floor by my arm my father almost whispered in a cruel voice that he would make sure he didn't have to listen to me *'fucking whimpering all night'* The pain in my gums had simply stopped, as did all other feelings in my body. I thought that he would kill me, was he going to throw me down the steps? Was he going to throw me of the roof? Was he going to strangle me or squash my head? I pissed my self as the fear built from deep inside me, I couldn't stop it no matter how hard I tried, and my urine splashed onto the bedroom floor as I was being dragged across it. A few drops must have landed on my father. He went crazy kicking me violently as he dragged me. Calling me a *dirty little bastard* with almost every violent step he took.

The house had an attic of sorts; in reality it was nothing more than a loft with a poorly made set of wooden steps leading up to it. My father threw me up those steps, pushing me violently in front of him. I scrambled to keep ahead of him and didn't stop until I had pushed back wooden hatch and dived through it in to the attic, moving quickly away from the opening to avoid my father's grasping arms. When he pushed his head through the hole, the light from the landing shining behind his head made him look like a demon. His eyes seemed empty and he smiled that evil smile of his. I could hear him screaming at me that I was to sleep in the attic until my toothache had gone, even if it took a week. His voice almost squeaked he was that angry and it was said with such venom that I was glad when he shut the hatch and his head had disappeared. He wasn't going to kill me after all, but when he turned the landing light off leaving me alone in the pitch-black attic, I wished that he had.

The respite from father's beatings had been short-lived, lasting little over a week, and it was that break that probably lulled me into a false sense of security and the courage to cry and landed me in the attic.

The night I spent in the attic reinforced my deep fear of the dark. I had sat hunched up all night on a wooden beam not daring to move. I was petrified of the many strange noises that filled the darkness. Mice seemed to be everywhere, I couldn't see the furry rodents, I could only hear them and several times I felt one run over my bare feet. Mice, rats, bugs didn't bother me, I had lived in houses that were overrun with them but there was a strange scratching sound that sounded as if something was crawling about on the roof and it terrified me. I didn't know what the fuck it was and my young imagination ran wild with the monster that it could have been. I stayed there all night, not wanting nor daring to move until slivers of daylight seeped through the tiles of the roof and I was totally certain my father had gone to work. It was only when I was absolutely convinced that it had been his car that I heard driving off that I opened the hatch and made my way slowly down the wooden stairs. I was thirsty, cold, stiff and hungry. The beating from my father, and my overnight imprisonment in the loft, had not even got rid of my toothache, plus now I had bruises and bumps all over my aching body.

I wanted-needed a cuddle, I stood at the foot of the stairs in my vest desperately needing someone to hold me and take all my pain, both physical and emotional, away and tell me it would all be ok. I wanted my mother to be that person. But as I went into the kitchen and saw my mother sitting at the table smoking, she didn't even acknowledge my presence. It was as if nothing had happened. There was no breakfast, there seldom was, there was no loving embrace, no concern for about my toothache or the many other bruises and swellings that covered my body, so I turned around and went to the bedroom. For once not caring about the smell of piss that seemed to cling to all my clothes, I just put on the clothes that I had worn for several days.

My father had almost ignored me since Sedbergh; he hadn't even looked at me. But I was once again back on his radar, and now his violence against me knew no bounds.

The episode of the attic was only the start of the violence he would now aim at me and I would spend most of my time hiding from his anger. This seemed to suit both my father and my self. He didn't ask anyone where I was or what I was doing and my siblings knew not to mention my name. My boxing career was, like anything else that allowed me to develop friendships, short lived. It wasn't that the coach didn't do his very best to understand me. He would spend much of the training sessions talking to me and trying to get me to control my aggression. But he could not; in fact my anger grew steadily worse, I wanted to fight, I wanted to feel pain and prove to everyone that I wasn't the coward my father screamed every day that I was. No sooner had I entered the ring and the fight would be stopped. My anger always too near to the surface and I would quickly lose control of it; even when training I would often go too far and fly into a rage without the slightest provocation. Eventually the coach had no option than to boot me out of the team. I was gutted, but I knew it was my fault, I was becoming a very angry boy and every day images and feelings of the rape would come unbidden in to my mind. I could not escape the images. Day or night, asleep or awake the memories of that night were always there; and all I could do was get angry, it was all I had.

My sister was the only person that seemed to understand me and for a while we became quite close again. I didn't know then why I had become so close to my sister but she wouldn't speak to anyone else and I began to feel a bond that was not there before. It was just the little things that she did; she would hold my hand; something she had not done since we were toddlers. She would smile and give me a knowing look and I was tempted many times to tell what had happened in Sedbergh but I felt scared: how do you begin to describe what my father had done and the pain that I felt? I didn't know it then but she was feeling the same confusion and fear, my sister was only a year older than me, we were little more than toddlers. Although we shared the same secret only my sister seemed to know what it was.

Lidget Green

The family were on the move again, this time without our mother, she was still locked up somewhere and I didn't really care where she was or how long she would be gone for. I certainly didn't miss her. We moved to the other side of Bradford this time to an area called Lidget Green, a place that I can't really remember much about as we only lived there a few months. The only memorable highlight of living there was when my father was run over by some blokes in a car as he left the local pub one evening. It seemed he had pissed a bloke off by not paying for a car my father had been driving around for several weeks and claimed as his own. He was supposed to pay for it; he didn't so he was run over; simple justice. My father ended up with a broken leg and a broken arm and many bruises; but when he came out of hospital he just sat in the front room every day and night for several weeks watching television and ordering everybody about. Fetch this, fetch that, turn the television on or turn it off. Even though he was immobile and in pain no one would dare refuse him. He would lash out with his walking stick if he even thought you were considering disobedience. I had not the slightest bit of pity for him and I enjoyed watching him struggle and cry out in pain. And I prayed every day that he would never recover in fact I ask God several times to make the bastard worse.

One other memory from Lidget Green is of the Salvation Army Band marching down the road in front of our house. I loved to watch the band and the people that followed it.

Everyone dressed in their best clothes and smiling, they reminded me of Ripley Ville and the churchgoers there. The band members all wore smart uniforms and belted out tunes with their trumpets and drums, the whole area responded to the music and everybody seemed happy.

Because of my father's injuries he was off work and the sick pay he received was not enough to support a family of eight children and two adults ten. Although it would have gone a lot further had my father not bought so much booze from the local off-licence? Hunger, never far away, again became a problem so I went back to nicking bottles of milk on the way to my new school, I always seemed to be going to a 'new school' Princeville. I carried on my boxing there for a while but the coach was useless, all he did was have us running around like headless chickens and doing very little sparring or real boxing, so I quit, and told the coach why I had quit and that must have pissed him off because I found myself kicked out of all the other sports. But we didn't stay at Lidget Green very long, maybe six months or so, so I didn't really care about the coach or his school. One memory of Princeville was the 'gold stars' they gave all the pupils at the start of every week; the idea being that if you lost all your gold stars during the week then you were 'disciplined' during Monday assembly in front of the whole school. Most weeks I had lost my stars by Wednesday so I was nearly always on stage Monday. Princeville wasn't a bad school really it was just that none of the teachers seemed even try to understand me and so I was in constant conflict with them.

Hampden Place

When we moved again, yet again, it was back to the West Bowling area so I was at least back among some my old mates, including my best mate Steve. We had no sooner unpacked than I was round at his house waiting for him to come home from school, I hadn't seen him for over a year and when I did meet him, Steve, had changed, if anything Steve looked even bigger and harder. We were soon up to our old tricks again. Steve still drooled over my older sister and, I think, she was pleased to see him again. But she still wouldn't let him kiss her or even hold her hand. But Steve and I were a two-man team and we promised each other that no matter where we moved to in the future we would still be best mates and meet up one a week. It was a solemn promise and one we kept for many years.

That first night back in West Bowling found Steve and me back to normal. Within in a few hours we were fighting the local lads. It hadn't taken much to start the fight, the usual childish '*what you looking at*' but it was enough, it was what I desperately needed; but I didn't fight with the same passion as before, I was now much worse. I now fought with a deep anger that showed during the fight. I didn't seem to care when I was hit, in fact it seemed to spur me on, making me ever more aggressive with each blow that landed. And I became worse. Within a few days of being back with my best mate all I wanted to do was fight and I would start a fight without any provocation and I wouldn't stop even when they pleaded to that they had had enough. Steve often had to pull me away telling me to calm down and

I would often cry after a fight. I had changed, I didn't just want to fight and inflict pain; I wanted to *feel* pain. Even the hardest fight couldn't slake my deep and desperate need to feel pain and I started to do something that even to an adult would be scary; but to the young boy that I was, it terrified me. After a fight I would shake and cry uncontrollably, I would stand and scream at the top of my voice. The sounds often didn't make sense to anyone, including me, and I would just stand there with tears flooding down my face and the only way I could stop the emotional explosion and regain control was to create even more pain, pain that was sharp, violent and extreme, extreme enough to stop the images that would not leave my brain, and I would stub a cigarette out on the palm of my hand. I would make the end of the cigarette glow until it glowed: then I would stub it out on the palm of my left hand. And I would laugh and scream as I did it. It wasn't the pain of the burn that made me scream; it was something deep inside me that I felt was trapped and needed to get out but couldn't and the only release I knew was pain, physical searing pain that I controlled. Even the blisters that quickly covered the burn would take weeks to heal has I continually picked at them to make them bleed; not wanting them to heal.

Something had changed inside me, I felt angry all the time. Even when I felt happy I could still feel the anger lingering below the surface of my skull, ready to explode. Often I would start to laugh but then I would start to cry, and then scream and I would run as fast as I could and find somewhere I could burn my hand and take away the emotional agony that came with the anger. I was a fast runner, far quicker than Steve but he would always try to catch me. Steve never once caught me in time to stop me screwing the cigarette violently into my hand; and though Steve took a lot of shit from me for interrupting my personal moment of self-hatred, not once did he show any anger towards me. And as I calmed down and shaking and the sobbing took control over my body, Steve would put his thick arm over my shoulder until I stopped.

I should have told Steve; I should have cried with him, I should have told him everything, about the rape, but not just once in Sedbergh. I should have told him about the times my father had 'wrestled' with me, how he had sat me on his knee while he satisfied his lust. I was growing up. I was beginning to understand what my father had really been doing for as long as I could remember. I should have told Steve it all. He was my best mate, a true friend and I know he would have just listened, and he would have cried with me.

My life was about to change dramatically; and not for the better. My family would be broken up forever and we would never again share a bed, a meal or play together. We would become estranged.

In many ways I was entering a new stage of my life. My life in Leeds road, Ripley Ville, Cinderella, Malham, the violence, was all about to become memories that I would try deliberately to bury. Good people, bad people, the people that hated me, the people that loved me. I would bury them all. But not before my father had finally tried to kill me.

The night that was to be the start of the next stage of my life came at the end of a very normal day. I had been out with Steve; we were few months away from being teenagers so we were now getting too old and mature to 'play out'. Nothing out of the usual had taken place; we had just walked about 'hanging tough' and fighting like pubescent teenager boys tend to do and then we had gone home and, not wanting to sit with my mother, I went to bed.

It was late in the evening when my father returned from the pub and, when I heard the door smash open and crash against the inner wall, I knew someone was in trouble and when I heard him scream that he was going to '*kill the little bastard*' I knew without any doubt that it was me: I was the *little bastard*' he was going to kill. My brain raced in an attempt to work out what the fuck I had done, I could think of nothing that would so enrage my father so much. He was furious and I could hear furniture being thrown about, I could hear him screaming over and over again that he was going to "*kill the little bastard*" I resigned myself to my fate and, as my bowels turned to water and my stomach tightened to a knot, I waited for the beating that inevitable.

Just Once, When I was little

Since Sedbergh and the short, blissful, few weeks my father had ignored me, and I had a few brief weeks of nervous peace. Now he turned his attention to me with a vengeance and he had gone out of his was to land a fist at every opportunity. He didn't need a reason; he just needed me to be near him. And now somehow I had given him the excuse he needed to *really beat his guilt* out of me. For I know now that the reason for what was to follow was his own guilt.

My father stopped banging around downstairs and, after a few seconds of deafening silence, the first heavy footstep thumped on the first of the steps that led to the two floors above and I began to feel true fear grip me. I knew that I was in danger; I knew that night that there was something about my father's temper and rage that different—there was evil in his voice and my entire body shook. The terror that I felt filled the whole bedroom and I remember watching the tatty bedcovers shake as my siblings hid under the filthy blanket, each filled with their own terror. There was nothing I could do. It was as pointless to hide as it was to plead for mercy. My father was going to beat me; but had I known the depth of the beating I was about to receive I would have jumped through the bedroom window and smashed my body into the rubbish strewn garden below.

I remember looking around the dismal piss stinking bedroom, staring at the torn hanging wallpaper. I remember the piss bucket was nearly full. An acceptance of my fate seemed to have calmed me. I had been beaten before. I had been kicked, punched and even spit on by my father so often that it had become normal, almost routine. But the anger in my father's voice was different, stronger, fiercer and more violent than I had ever felt before and I knew that the beating would be bad. And it was.

After the loud thump of my father's boot on the step, it seemed an eternity of silence before I heard him moving about downstairs. I felt desperately alone and totally vulnerable; but even through the feelings of dread and terror I felt, I also felt anger at my mother. Why didn't she tell my father, plead with my father, beg my father, or even offer her own life to make him stop what he was about to do, and the anger and hurt increased because I knew she wouldn't anything, I knew that she would just sit there and let it happen. It's what she always did. Then I heard father's heavy footsteps; he was heading towards the stairs again: and terror gripped me.

The downstairs door suddenly burst open and my father screamed my name, his voice cut through me tightening my bowels and for a moment I didn't respond, I was frozen in the grip of fear. His voice grew louder as he repeated my name and reached fever pitch when I hadn't responded. Father screamed a warning that if he had to come up and get me then he would throw me down the fucking stairs; I didn't doubt him for a second. My voice would not, could not carry, my mouth had dried so much in such a short time that I couldn't utter a single word. Father started to slam his feet on the steps pretending that he was coming to throw mw down the stair. Panic gripped me and I dived for the bedroom door and, at last, I found enough spit to allow me to tell father that I was sorry, and that I was coming. As I made my way down the stairs I kept repeating *sorry dad; sorry dad; sorry dad*. I was shaking; crying, and as I forced my legs to carry me to my beating, I left a trail of piss on each step.

When I reached the bottom of the stairs I opened the door as slowly as my shaking hand would allow, I so desperately did not want to open that door. Every nerve, every sense in my body screamed at me to leave it shut, run back up the stairs and jump out of a window. But I dare not do what my senses screamed at me to do; I dare not run, I knew that he would catch me and that it would be far worse in the end. But now, as I look back, I don't think it could have been worse.

As soon as I opened the door a few inches my father bellowed at the top of his voice to "*get in here . . . you thieving little bastard*". He was almost on his feet as he screamed at me and then he jabbed his finger pointing at the floor in front of his feet. I had seen him do this many times. Not only to me but to all his children, it was his signal to stand in front of him and receive a punch or a slap. But this time he looked lost in his rage. His eyes bulged and were full of hate and so intense that I knew my fears were right: I was not going to get a simple 'slap' or a punch. All I could do was repeat the words *sorry dad, I'm sorry dad* I didn't know why I should be saying sorry, I must have said the words a hundred times but I had no idea what I had done; but my pitiful pleading was the only defence that I had against the monster I stood shaking in front of him knowing that it was totally futile.

Father was pissed, and as I scurried towards the spot he was pointing at for me to stand, the stench of stale beer was overwhelming. As I stood shaking in front of him my father stared at me with disgust as well as anger in his eyes; he must have seen the terror he had created in mine. I tried desperately to look calm and to stop the tears that were threatening to spill down my face; but I couldn't and as I blinked tears flooded down my cheeks and snot ran freely from my nose. That brought the first slap. As the back of his fist landed on the side of my head I felt my legs weaken and I struggled to remain standing. I remember seeing him smile. On the table was a plate of chips, piled high with two eggs perched on top. I remember feeling hungry. I was terrified, shaking with fear and about to be beaten and yet I could feel my mouth fill with saliva at the smell and the sight of the food. My father saw me look at the food and threw a chip at me, and when it fell to the filthy floor he ordered me to pick it up; I didn't hesitate I picked it up and, not bothering to brush off the muck that that had clung to the chips greasy surface, I ate it. It wasn't hunger that made me eat that filthy chip, it was fear and that fear was building as my father rocked back and forth smiling without taking his eyes off me. He screamed at me to keep looking at him. He would not allow me to look away and I saw that the emptiness, coldness in his eyes had replaced the hate that I had first seen in them.

I no longer recognised the animal that sat smiling in front of me. He was no longer my father, he didn't even seem human. And he wasn't looking at a little boy anymore. He wasn't looking at his son, and resemblance to the dad I knew in Denby Dale had gone, the stranger that sat in front of me had only hatred in his eyes, an animal that liked to inflict pain for the sheer pleasure of it.

I was forced to stand in front of him as he ate his supper; all the time staring at me his gaze never leaving my face. He ate his chips slowly, knowing that hidden in my terror was a gnawing hunger that I could not control and he smiled every time I swallowed the saliva the smell of the food produced. As his plate emptied of food I knew that when he had eaten the last chip he would attack. I wanted to piss, I wanted to empty my bowels on the floor where I stood, and all the time the child inside me was dying. After that night I would never be a child gain. Father saw me shaking as he wiped a slice of bread across the plate until there wasn't a trace of food left on it. My father smiled at me, the cruel smile he was so fond of and I heard him utter the name he often called me even though he almost whispered '*coward*' And I admit, I felt like one

My father pushed the empty plate to one side and I watched my mother, she had been released a few weeks before, calmly take the plate in to the tiny kitchen, shutting the door behind her. I was alone. My mother had once again turned her back on me and I was left alone with a man I no longer knew, a stranger, a wild eyed animal that was going to batter me. At first my father spoke in that quiet yet threatening tone that he often used when he was about to use his fists. I would rather he shouted than use that tone, it held a dark threat that was more fearsome than any screaming he could do. His slurred words baffled me and I couldn't understand most of the utterances that slobbered out of his mouth. He sensed this and suddenly thumped me in the stomach then screamed at me to stand up straight and slapped me across the face when I couldn't. He told me I was a *soft piece of shit*, screaming at me so close that I could smell the beer on his breath and feel his spit land on my face. He kept telling me I was a *coward* and I wanted to scream at him that I wasn't, I wanted to tell him that I could, and did fight and that I always won. But I knew better, nothing I would say or do would alter what was about to happen, so I kept my mouth shut. He continued to speak slowly, as if I was hard of hearing or a baby, and he exaggerated each drunken word, but at least I could now understand him.

He had been in the *Listers Arms* that night, a pub on Manchester Road that he had been his 'local' for many years, and one of the neighbours had told him that he had seen me climbing out of a neighbour's small kitchen window carrying some stuff. My father told me all this in a slurred and exaggerated almost matter of fact way. Then father said something that has remained with me throughout my life and, in many ways, caused more emotional pain that the physical pain that I would endure that night.

Father smiled his sick smile and, almost whispered, to me that if I told the truth and admitted what I had done then he would ground me for a week but not beat me and I could go back to bed. *All I had to do was tell him the truth.* I knew it was just one of his games but I was trapped in world of confusion and clung to a possible escape route. *If I told my father a lie and told him I did it then I would just be grounded; however if I told him the truth and tell him I hadn't done it, then he would beat the crap out of me!* How can an 11 year old lad make a decision, or even make sense of what was happening. So, standing in front of him shaking with fear I told my father a lie; I told him it had been me and that I was sorry and started to cry. *I'm sorry dad. I'm sorry dad; I'm sorry dad . . . .*

My father suddenly exploded in a rage and smashed me in the face with his fist. The force was so severe that I was knocked across the room and into the sofa. My father continued his attack and came screaming at me and, grabbing my hair, dragged me off the sofa. I tried to cling to one of the cushions but it was useless it just came away with me still holding it. His fists were pounding in to my back and I had never felt such force. My arms, my legs, my head were being pummelled but I had managed to keep my face buried in the cushion. My nose was broken; I could feel the bone move and the blood rush out of both my nostrils. The pain throughout my body was increasing with each blow my father inflicted upon it and I began to weaken. Not just physical but emotional; all feelings seemed to be leaving me. The wind had been beaten out of my lungs. Blood was running down the back of my throat and I was losing consciousness. The cushion I was clinging to fell from my hands when my father threw me back onto the sofa I landed so hard that the sofa went over backwards trapping me underneath, for a brief moment I felt secure. My father had fallen against the television and was untangling himself and, in his drunken stupor, he was struggling and, if it was possible, getting even angrier in his frustration. Pain racked my body and I knew that I could not take much more. Noticing the stairs door was open I did something that I had never done before, I ran away from my father. The pains surging through my body was intense but fear induced adrenalin forced it to the back of my mind, numbing both emotional and physical pain.

Pushing the sofa just far enough so I could escape, I took a painful deep breath and ran the few feet to the stair's door and bolted up the steps. My father was screaming and swearing demanding that I get back in front of him, he was calling me a coward and a piece of shit and that he was going to kill me; but I wasn't taking any notice. My heart was near to bursting and my back and ribs hurt terribly but panic eased all the pain. I had to get away from him somehow, and every nerve in my body pushed me to the limit to achieve it. I made it to the top of the stairs in a matter of seconds and the panic increased as I looked at the bedroom window and, if father had been closer, I would have jumped through it. But then I remembered the attic and the skylight that led to the roof and ran up the second set of steps that led to the damp room at the top of the house where my sisters slept.

My drunken father struggled to follow me up any of the stairs and I had reached my sisters bedroom at the top of the house in the attic well before he had taken even a few steps. I stood in my sisters' bedroom shaking; blood was all over my face and body. My nose was misshapen and already great bruises were starting to appear all over my body. I was crying for someone, anyone, to help me, my sisters could do nothing, they were as scared as I was, I still remember the fear that I saw in their eyes that night. They lay there huddled together and I felt ashamed that I had run in to their bedroom but I was terrified and it was the only route of escape that I had.

The only way out of the attic for me was via the skylight; the wood was rotten and the thing almost fell to pieces when I pushed hard to open it; but it wouldn't move and in blind panic I started to smash the glass. After only one smack the whole thing opened with a crash. I climbed through just as my father staggered up the stairs and into girls the bedroom. I had only just managed to get my legs through and scramble away from the opening when my father's head appeared. He tried desperately to grab my legs but I just moved further away from the window each time he tried. It didn't concern me at that moment that I was on a roof in the rain about 30 feet above the back garden; it certainly didn't bother my father because when he couldn't get his bulk through the window, he started throwing things at me to knock me off. Pillows, the piss bucket and even the girls' shoes; anything that was not fastened down father threw out of that window to dislodge me. Eventually my father ran out of things to throw at me and packed in trying to knock me off the roof. He warned me that I would die when he caught me, he told me slammed the skylight shut, locking me on the outside, I could hear him screaming at my sisters telling them he would kill them if they let me back in: but my father's bellowing and violence had, at last, been heard by someone other than a mother that did nothing. And At last, that someone did something and called the police.

Not only did the police turn up but also the fire brigade and an ambulance. The whole of Hampden Place suddenly seemed filled with noise and lights. I couldn't see much from where I had scrambled on the roof and I dare not move closer to the edge or climb nearer to the top; I was shaking so much that knew that if I moved an inch I would slide down the damp slates and off the edge to my certain death. Suddenly the skylight slowly opened and bloke's head popped through. He spoke gently telling me he was a fireman and that I was ok and not to move. I remember nodding; my throat was so dry and tight with fear that I couldn't utter a sound. The fireman told me that his mates were going to put a ladder against the gutter and for me to stay calm and still; but I could not stop shaking and crying and when the ladder thumped against roof I almost lost what little grip I had and slip a few inches towards the edge. The ladder rattled has a fireman made his way to the gutter and even though I knew that they had come to save me I was scared shitless when another fireman's head appeared over the edge of the roof. I remember that the new fireman was whistling and this seemed to calm me. The man was only a few feet away from me and, in between whistling his tune; he told me I was going nowhere other than back through the skylight. The thought terrified me. My father would kill me, he would throw me off the roof or beat me to death if I put so much as a toe through the skylight; and for a few seconds I was more afraid of going back into the house than I was of falling off the roof! The fireman with his head still poking through the skylight must have known why I was on the roof and, and why I was so terrified. Speaking in a reassuring voice he told me that no one was going to hurt me and that I was safe then he coaxed me towards the skylight, assuring me that if I slipped his mate would catch me. He spoke with such confidence that I couldn't help but trust him. Slowly I shuffled towards the skylight and only a terrifying moment later I felt the fireman's hand grab mine. Then everything goes blank in my mind. I have no memory of climbing back through the skylight or making my way through the house or even seeing or hearing my father; the next thing I remember was being helped into an ambulance. The ambulance took me to hospital, I was wrapped in a blanket and one of the crew sat with me checking my bruises and trying to calm me down. I remember he put his arm over my shoulders and spoke to me in the same tone as the fireman that had coaxed me off the roof. The feeling of security, or maybe because I just needed to, I started to cry. The tears than ran down my face mixed with the snot, but the ambulance man didn't seem to care as I buried my face in his smart uniform.

At some point during the journey in the ambulance I told that my mother was following in another car. And I remember I suddenly stopped crying and sitting away from my carer. I went into an emotional void. The mere thought of my mother seemed to separate me from reality. I refused any attempt by the ambulance man to pull me back, I think I even started to fight him off, screaming at him to let me go and go fuck him self.

Within minutes of the ambulance delivering me to casualty, a department of the hospital I knew very well, my mother turned up, all tears and caring, trying to hug me. I just stood there cringing with both disgust and pain as she slobbered all over me. The 'perfect mother' was just in time to tell the police what had happened. She told the police that I had been seen climbing out of the window of a neighbour and my father had only slapped me and the rest of the damage was done to my face, and the furniture, when I went crazy and ran to the roof falling up the steps several times as I did so. The lying bitch was up to her old tricks. She told unconvinced police officers that I was *always fighting and coming home with bruises* and that my father was *trying his hardest to get me to behave'* Not only did she, as always, defend my father but, as usual, turned her back on her own child. As soon as the police left the room my mother almost pushed me away. She spit on a tissue to wipe some of my blood off of her arm. Prior that night I had had no real feelings for my mother but after that night, I felt only disgust for her. And later, much later, in my life, I would realise something else about my mother that intensified that disgust to a new, much higher level.

While I was still at the hospital a social worker came to see me while I was having my nose straightened and my bottom lip stitched up. I could not speak because I had gauze stuck up my nose and my mouth was numb, so my mother repeated her lies to the social worker repeating how I was '*always fighting and getting in to mischief*' she stood there, lying, talking utter balls as if I wasn't even there. One word from my mother could have put a stop to all the violence and abuse, yet once again she said nothing, she just smiled as she told her well practised lies.

My life was again about to change and nothing would ever be the same for my family. In the following days my father's life would be utterly destroyed: as would the lives of all of my family. And also the lives of many others

A few days after I had been released from the hospital, and I was waiting for the inevitable thumping that I would receive from my father that was yet to happen, perhaps he was waiting for my face to heal before he punched it again, my mother was arrested. She had been arrested for getting the boyfriend of my younger sister to climb in through a kitchen window and open the front door of a neighbour's house. The police had recognised mother's MO immediately. Of course mother denied knowing anything about it, she cried her usual 'crocodile tears' and pleaded her innocence. When it came to dramatic acting, mother was brilliant and should have won, at least, one Oscar. But the coppers were neither fooled nor put off by her pleading and, anyway the young lad involved had confessed and told his dad all about it and his dad had then told the police. So mother was off to prison again. I can't recall who told me or how I found out about the house my mother had robbed. But I do remember feeling totally and utterly let down by my mother. Even all the beatings, the abuse, the filth and possibly even the sexual abuse, did not hurt me as much as finding out that it had been my mother that was the reason I had been beaten, she had been the reason I had clung to the roof as my father tried to knock me off, she had been the reason. *I had been blamed, found guilty and punished for a crime I did not commit; I had been beaten half to death and chased on to the roof where I had cried out in terror as my father tried his best to knock me off. I had pissed myself and lost control of my bowels through fear. And my mother had made me tell a lie that haunts me still to this day.*

My mother had known the truth from the start and because she had robbed the house next door and yet she had simply turned her back and hidden in the kitchen and allowed her son to take the blame and to be beaten without the slightest remorse or concern for him.

I often wonder what my mother felt as she stood alone in the kitchen listening to her son beg for mercy from her husband. Did she cry; did she feel guilt when she heard me scream out in pain? Or did she smile as I unwittingly took the blame for her crime. Strange as it may seem to others, but I often, and for years after, imagined that she had cried for me. Even knowing that I was lying to myself, it still somehow helped me to hang on even pretend affection. Maybe I could have understood if she had hidden in the kitchen because of fear for her own life. But aren't mums supposed to protect their children: no matter what consequence to themselves? But mother had no excuse later, when the police were at the house and she was safe, she could have told the police then and not just told them about the assault on me that night and what had really taken place, but she could also have told them about the repeated rape of my older sister. She may not have known about my father raping me in Sedbergh; but she *MUST* have known about my sister, she must have heard her scream, she must have noticed a drunken man staggering from her bed in the middle of the night. And she must have known what father was really doing when he sat one of his children on his knee rubbing himself against them. Or the '*wrestling*' games he like to play every weekend. She must have recognised the movements as sexual, yet not once did she say or do anything to stop it happening.

Because of the burglary that mother had 'encouraged' my mate to commit, she was locked up again. I can't remember how long she had been sent down for, but it didn't matter because by the time mother was released my whole world had turned up side down.

With my mother safely locked up in prison it was left to nana to look after her eight grandchildren children and although I know she loved each one of her daughter's offspring, I also knew she hated the contact it forced her to have with my father. Although it had always been obvious that she hated my father. I didn't know why. But I realised some time later that she had suspected, or maybe even known, for some time what my father had been doing to his children, that he had been abusing them for years. But because mother always covered for him Nana could do nothing, but while mother was sat in a prison cell somewhere, Nana got the chance and the evidence she had been waiting.

The night I took a beating for the crime that my mother had committed proved too much for my elder sister. She would not go to school, she would not wash, talk or do anything and she would sit crying for hours at a time and when she wasn't crying my sister would withdraw into a world of her own where no one could reach her. Then one night, during the early days of my mother's latest visit to prison, my father ordered my sister sleep with him, he told her she needed to keep warm and she would be all right; then, like a blinding light, I realised what my father was really up to. My mind flashed back to Sedbergh and the night my father had raped me. I suddenly remembered the words that my father had drunkenly whispered, slobbering in my ear as he started to rape me "it's *cold in here . . . . I will get you warmed up . . . . you'll be ok . . . .*" And I knew that's what he was using my sister for, that why she was always so quiet, that's why she had stopped playing out and the reason she would not let Steve hold her hand or kiss her. My head felt like it was going to explode. Nothing in my world made sense. I made a silent vow that I would kill my father as soon as I was big enough. That I would rip his throat out, I would stab him in his eyes, I would burn him in his bed along with my mother. But I wouldn't get the chance. Father's depraved world was about to come crashing down around him.

The morning of my father's arrest began like any other morning, children rummaging for any kind of food and, if need be, fighting for whatever was found. I had passed my 11 plus exams and had won a place at Fairfax Grammar School and I was fiercely protective of my uniform and, like all the other mornings, I did my best to make sure it was as clean as it could be and I was polishing my well worn black shoes with grease and soot when my elder sister appeared and stood, half naked, quietly at the foot of the stairs. There were tears running down her face and she was sobbing, no one could understand the words she was trying to utter between her deep sobs. She couldn't stop sobbing and she was shaking, she looked so lost, so scared. I knew she had had enough, the night she had spent keeping father 'warm' had, at last broken her will to go on. We were all staring at my sister, my other siblings were confused but knew what was wrong; I knew what father had done to her. I knew how he had 'kept my sister warm'

My older brother moved towards my sister to comfort her, but she backed away from him and her fear seemed to increase as he got closer to her. My sister looked a pathetic sight, she was only a year older than me, but as she stood there terrified and shaking, she looked much younger. Since Sedbergh my sister and I had become quite close, we had a silent understanding and I knew I was the only person my sister would allow near her so I went to her and held her hands while she sobbed. At first she wouldn't allow me to cuddle her and struggled against me; but her resistance didn't last and we hugged each other. As I held her close I could feel my sister trembling and I could hear her shallow breathing. It felt strange to be hugged and to hug someone; showing or seeking affection was not something that any of my family was used to displaying. It had been beaten out of the children. If we felt pain, emotional or physical, we had been conditioned to ignore it, only cowards felt pain and only sniffling babies cried.

As we hugged and cried I think we both knew that it could not continue and that father had to be stopped. My sister almost whispered to me between sobs that she could take no more. But neither of us knew what to do, we were children under the total control of our brutal father and the thought of him finding out we had told terrified us, so we decided to ask the only person in the world that either of us could really trust what we should do. So, using the few coppers I had acquired by taking pop bottles back to the local shop, together we walked to the phone box just around the corner to make the call that would change our world. I remember our siblings begging us not to tell Nana, they pleaded with my sister and I saying father would kill us all if he found out. They were right of course, father would be beyond angry and the beating my sister and I would be lucky to survive the beating we would receive. When we reached the phone box it was empty but it must have been at least five minutes before I plucked up enough courage to open the door then another five minutes before I picked up the heavy telephone to make the call.

I dialled the number and hesitated a few seconds before I pushed the coin, as soon as I heard Nana's quiet voice I started to cry and found I could talk so I passed the phone to my sister.

The call lasted no more than 30 seconds, my sister told my Nana what had happened and then she told Nana about me. That was it. Nana told us to go home, not go to school and to wait for her: Nana was on her way.

When she arrived in a taxi a short time later Nana didn't even give us all her usual cuddle and kisses, instead she immediately took my sister upstairs. I had never heard my Nana shout at anyone about anything before that day, all she ever did was smile and cuddle us. But that morning she was so furious she swore aloud screaming *'the bastard'* every few minutes. Even though I knew every swear word going, thanks to my parents, I was totally shocked to hear Nana using them! I didn't think she even knew such words. Nana came back down the stairs and she looked a different woman, tears filled her eyes and there was anger in her voice. Nana tried to hide both emotions from her grandchildren, but we all knew that she was struggling to deal with what was happening. My sister stayed upstairs and my Nana told us not to go near her then, after giving me a big cuddle and asking me very quietly if it was true, Nana squeezed me has hard as her she could and, wiping tears from her eyes, she went to phone the police.

I remember, before Nana set off to the phone box to make the fateful call, she gave my younger sister some money to go to the corner shop and get some bread, butter and jam and told my older brother to wash some cups and make a cup of tea for everyone. I think Nana knew what was about to happen to her grandchildren; that it was going to be a very long day and, Nana being Nana, she wanted to make sure we had some jam and bread inside us. It would be the last meal I would ever share with all my siblings.

When the police arrived there was suddenly utter chaos in the house. Police, ambulance drivers, and people in suits filled the house. All of them asking questions, but with eight chattering children to interview it would have taken some time for them to get to me. Then my older sister told one of the officers about Sedbergh and the night my father raped me so all attention was suddenly turned to me and my blood ran cold when I was asked about that night. They wanted know why my face was bandaged and about the many bruises that were showing on my arms and legs. When they asked if I had any more bruises I took my shirt off to show them my chest and my back. A female officer gasped when she saw the mass of deep purple bruises that still covered my skin. They wanted to know every detail of how I had got them. At last I was not only being allowed to talk about what had really happened but, more importantly I was being believed. Gently a police man sat beside me I was then asked in a quiet, patient voice about the night in Sedbergh and what my father had done. Where I was touched, what had my father done to me and, as I told the officer all the details the memories became ever more vivid, the shower block, the pain, the filth, the isolation, the hopelessness, and the pain. It became so real that I could once gain smell the stale beer on father's breath, I could feel the force of my father's strong hand as he pushed my face into the grubby pillow. For a moment in my mind I *was* back in Sedbergh. I felt a great pressure inside to flee, to scream and though I tried desperately to keep the feelings hidden from the strangers that had invaded my home. My father had beaten into me that to cry or seek pity was cowardly, that to show any kind of feelings of sadness, was a weakness. He had done a good job. But inside my head was screaming in confusion as I fought the memories that were suddenly flooding back. Suddenly, like a breached emotional dam, all the pent up emotions crashed through skull and I could not hold back the tears and anger; I remember suddenly screaming like an animal. The police officer that had been talking so gently and patiently to me didn't even flinch, she just kept hold of me tightly until I calmed down. She kept her arms around me and I remember suddenly stopping crying and screaming, a strange calm had descended over me. It was as if all the confusion and madness of that morning had lifted, it hadn't of course; I had simply shut down my emotions as I had in the past when things failed to make sense. I looked around at the people that had invaded our shithole of a home and I could see the look of disgust they failed to hide on their faces as they searched about the house. What they must have thought of the piss bucket and stinking bedrooms I can only guess. But I no longer gave a fuck what they thought or what they did. I was in some kind of emotional void; a place where happiness and sadness didn't exist. The only emotion I felt was one of deep loneliness

When the woman officer had finished talking to me another officer, a big rough looking copper, asked me, in a fake caring voice, to go with him to the police station so they could 'have a quiet chat' to me about what had happened. I didn't give a shit, but my legs felt strange so I slowly got up from where I was sitting and, although I felt extremely calm, when I tried to stand my legs would not support me. My legs would not stop shaking and I felt weak enough to faint; my mind was struggling to make sense of what was happening to me. I remember being almost carried out of the house and placed in a big black car and driven away from my family, my home, my normality. In a dream like state, I was driven from one hell straight into another one, a hell

The drive to the police station didn't take long, I remember people staring at me through the windows of the car as we drove past. It was worse when the police cars stopped at traffic lights, some people even put their faces close to the windows so they could get a better look at the 'thief' sat in the back seat, and I remember feeling shame. I don't why I felt so ashamed, or why I hid my face from them. But I did. Only a few hours before I would have stuck two fingers up at the lot of them, or screamed abuse at the nosy bastards. But I was already losing all sense of my self. I felt weak, physically and emotionally I felt drained, empty of any will to resist what was happening to me.

The big copper back at Hampton Place had lied. It was not a 'quiet word' at the police station, it was an interrogation and there was little or no compassion from any of the officers in the nick. It was the start of a nightmare, full of noise and confusion and fear. I was asked over and over again and again to re-live that night and each time I cried my way through the answers. I was then asked to sign the statement and go with a doctor that arrived to examine me. The doctor was a tall, skinny uncaring elderly man wearing a white coat and, other than saying a quick hello and gesturing for me to stand up; he didn't really speak to me. As I stood I felt as if I would fall over. My head seemed to spin. I felt alone, isolated and afraid. I didn't want this shit; I wanted to go home.

There were no words of comfort from doctor, no kind words assuring me that I would be ok, nothing, he either didn't care or hadn't noticed that I was clinging to a chair to steady myself. He didn't see the tears running down my face or see that I was shaking. He simply took me by my arm and almost dragged me to a medical room where he told me to remove my clothes and get on a table and curl into a ball. As I climbed on to the table fear was building deep inside me. The doctor was making things many times worse as he clattered instruments into bowls—then he slammed a cupboard door shut making me jump. Only the day before I would have sworn at him, told him to fuck off, I certainly wouldn't have stripped naked, climbed onto the table and curled into a ball—but I was broken and accepting my fate. Tears were running down my face as I silently cried and said and did nothing. But the worst was to come. Without any warning I felt his cold hands fumbling around my backside, I tensed as I felt his fingers probing. Then with no warning, no calming words of assurance he pushed his fingers deep inside my bottom. Inside I screamed and I tensed at the invasion. Images of Sedbergh flashed through my mind. I remember screaming, not loudly, but the doctor carried on as if I was nothing more than a piece of meat. I felt his fingers turn inside me, I felt sick and the bright white room began to spin. I felt his fingers being withdrawn causing more pain. But at least the examination was over. But there was still not a word from the doctor just another loud clattering sound as an instrument landed in a metal bowl then took off his gloves, washed his hands; wrote something down, and then left me in the room all alone. I hadn't moved and I lay there almost naked with only a small white towel to hide behind. I felt the loneliest person on the planet, where were my family, why was I still here. I was a little boy and I just needed someone to hold me and tell me I was ok, that I was going home soon and every thing would be alright. Even if the police couldn't tell me I was going home; one of them could have at least sat with me; cuddled me, held me until I stopped crying. But no one came, no one held me, no one cared. I can't remember how long I was left in that fucking room alone but it seemed like an eternity.

My bottom hurt and the lubricant the doctor had used was seeping out of my backside leaving shitty goo that I didn't even attempt to clean. I'd had enough. It was as if I had been raped all over again. Some one, eventually, brought a blanket in for me explaining as they passed it to me that a woman would be coming to take pick me up to take me somewhere safe. In my mind I screamed silently *"who was coming to pick me up: where the fuck was somewhere safe*? I didn't want *picking up;* I didn't want to go *somewhere safe* I wanted to go home. Home was a stinking hovel that offered only fear and hunger, violence and filth. But it was *home* and it was my normality and I wanted nothing more than to be there. I started to cry. Sobbing deeply I felt snot mingle with the tears, goo still seeped out of my arse so I wiped the mess on the blanket. The last thing I remember about being in the examination room was pulling the blanket over my head as I tried to block out and hide from all that was happening to me...

Then the shouting started

I recognised my father's booming voice immediately. The swearing, the growling, the crashing of furniture and, strange as it may now seem, I started to smile. In my mind I thought, hoped, prayed that my father had come to save me. That I would be going home. But I was wrong of course.

Why the police chose to drag my father through the main room in full view of me I still can't and will never understand, perhaps it was an oversight, perhaps they thought that seeing my father being brought down would help me in some way. But it didn't and seeing my father again certainly didn't help me; in fact it only added to the fear and confusion I was already feeling. As I heard the booming voice of my father protesting his innocence then, as they came in to view, I watched the police drag him across the station floor. all my hatred I had held for my father left me and I felt a great surge of love for him and I wanted to protect him and I screamed for the police to let him go, I screamed that I was lying. I was crying, sobbing as I pleaded them to listen to me. And when they wouldn't I screamed at them, calling them all bastards and then I tried to reach my father by pushing my way through the crowd of police that were pinning my father to the floor. I didn't get far, after a only a few feet an officer picked me up and took me screaming back into the examination room. The door was closed behind me and the officer then stood at the door keeping me in there and blocking my view.

After all the evil that my father had done, after all the beatings, and the suffering he caused, I would have done or said anything to stop the police hurting him that day. I just wanted to go home; I wanted them to leave my dad alone. And I hated everyone, my sister, my Nana, my mother . . . everyone.

Father was eventually dragged away and taken to another room, probably a cell and, after he had gone, I calmed down enough to be given the first food and drink I had had that day. I was handed a big white plastic mug that was covered in scratches. In that mug was the strongest looking tea I'd ever seen and it tasted just as it looked, but it was still welcome. In reality I had eaten nothing since the previous days meagre offering at teatime and my stomach rumbled when I was handed a sandwich that was at least a day old smothered in jam and forgot my desperate state as I wolfed the food down, it was dry and stale: but I had eaten worse, much worse. When I had finished a policewoman came and sat next to me, she was the kindest person I had seen in that shitty place and I started to feel a little better. But then it all became a swirl of emotional pain when I asked her if I could go home. I could see the pain in the copper's eyes when she told me that a person had arrived and I was to be taken to a children's home. I cried like a baby. I didn't want to go to a fucking 'children's home' I wanted to go home and go out with Steve and my mates, I wanted to sleep in that piss soaked bed and fight with my siblings, I didn't want my life to change, I wanted it all back. But I couldn't stop what was happening. My life *had* changed direction and it would never, could never, be the same again.

The reason that I, and all my siblings, had been taken in to care was because our mother was still in the nick, and our Nana worked fulltime so there was no one willing to be a surrogate parent to eight emotionally damaged children. The fact that no one else wanted anything to do with us didn't help my feelings of loneliness. I found out later that many people simply wouldn't believe what my father had done, and later I was even being called a liar by my father's friends and my paternal grandmother. They all thought he was *a really great bloke that just liked a drink* and that, with so many kids to control, he *had to keep them disciplined* . . . blind, ignorant idiots But what they thought didn't really matter; it was the fact that they *chose* to ignore or even consider the truth that hurt.

The person arrived to take me away. It was a middle aged woman and she seemed to be in a rush to get things over with so, with little thought to my feelings, she took my hand, not in a nice way, and almost marched me out of the police station and on to the noisy, bustling streets of Bradford. The woman must have sensed that I was ready to run and she slid her hand in a quick movement and grabbed my wrist. And I would have run, but I knew I would not break her hold so I resigned myself to whatever was going to happen. I was to be taken to a place of safety, away from everything I knew and wanted. But I was not going to a place of safety, I was being taken to a place that would very nearly break me; a place that was to make my life even more miserable.

When the car carrying me to the children's home pulled away from the police station I began to panic. I felt like a trapped rat and I was desperately trying to open the door to get out, I was frantic to escape and return home. At that time I was unaware that my siblings had been scattered all over Bradford in various children's homes; none knowing where the others were. After a few miles the driver pulled up sharply and the driver grabbed my arm, pulling me with force towards her. The woman told me she had had enough of me and shouted, almost screaming in my face, telling me that if I didn't sit still and shut up then she would shove me in the boot of the car, I told her to fuck off and turned my anger on her. For the next few minutes I kicked and scratched at her trying to free myself from her grasp and make my escape. But I couldn't break her tight hold. Eventually she lost her temper and hit me, not hard, and nothing by comparison to my father's beatings but enough to shock me back to reality. I stopped kicking and screaming but I continued to tell her to fuck off every time she tried to speak to me. It would be wrong to say the driver was a bad woman, she could have responded better I suppose but, even though I had every reason to react and behave has I did, I must have driven her crazy by the time she hit me. When we arrived at the 'place of safety' I stared in awe at the big old house where I was to stay. I recognised it immediately. It was in Bradford Moor, just a few hundred yards from the house where the family had lived on Leeds Road and right next door to my old school. This gave me dual feelings, I felt a kind of comfort at being somewhere I knew, and somewhere I had lived only a few months before.

A trolley bus passed, the inside bright in the darkening evening, and I could see the people inside. Were they going home? Would they be sat with their families watching television? I felt jealous, angry, hurt, alone but the overwhelming feeling was sadness. The day had lasted forever. I had woken that morning in a stinking pissed reeking bed surrounded by my brothers and sisters. Everything was as it should have been. Then my sister had come down the stairs and we had made that fateful phone call. And now everything in my world was upside down.

As I sat in the car looking at the house that was my place of safety, I realised the woman driver was talking to me . . . *"when you get in here . . . blah fucking blah . . . they won't stand for any of your nonsense . . . blah fucking blah . . . don't you try run or I'll have you locked up . . . blah fucking blah . . .* I was only half listening to words I didn't want to hear and I stared at the woman and I could sense that she wanted to slap me again. She wanted rid of me, get me out of her car and out of her life. I felt like shouting *"you're going home you old bag, I'm staying here . . . you don't care, go home and have your tea and then fucking choke to death . . ."* and I said the words, but only in my head.

The woman told me that someone from inside the house would come out and make sure I didn't run away. Keeping one hand on my arm the woman tapped on the steering wheel. She

Brian Mynott

didn't look at me, she was far more interested in looking at her watch every 30 seconds or so. As we sat there my mind wandered and I remembered my time living only a few hundred yards down the road towards Bradford town centre. It all seemed so real to me, as if I could just get out of the car and go home. I could see my old school, Bradford Moor, and I could remember the fight in the queue for the school dinners. I could relive in great detail the accident when we pushed the scrap car into a wall and I remembered my younger sister's green hair. But it was all in the past now, it had all gone. Both my parents were either in prison or locked up in the local nick. Life had shown me many times that if things could get worse, then they would, and I knew that they had when I was marched away from the car and into the home.

The next thing I remember is entering a dim office and being told to stand in front of a big polished desk behind which sat a fat woman. The woman didn't look at me at first but the woman that had brought me coughed to get her attention.

"*You will call me matron . . . you will stand up straight when I talk to you . . . blah fucking blah*" The matron was talking to me but I could only make out a few words. The goo from my arse had clung to my trousers and had started to smell, or I had just noticed it, and, in the confines of the matron's office, it wasn't long before those near me got a good niff of it, the stench contrasting with the smell of polish that had filled the room. After what seemed an age, the matron finished telling me the thousands of rules that ensured the smooth running of *her* home, concluding my induction with the immortal words "*I will NOT tolerate any nonsense . . . blah fucking blah . . .*

The school uniform that I put on that morning, before the chaos of my father's arrest, was now not only stinking of shit but also looking decidedly shabby, even by my low standards, I looked like a street urchin. The looked me up and down and took great pains to ensure I knew that she didn't approve of '*little scruffs*' and assured me that I would be taught to look after my clothes better while I was in her care. I was never in that woman's care, I was under her control and she had no fucking idea how every day was a battle for me just to keep the few clothes I had anything like clean. And, again, I spoke words only in my head, telling her to fuck herself: but she must have seen something in my eyes because she asked me very stern faced if I had something to say. I didn't even respond. That was that, the woman that had brought me handed over a file and, without even looking at me, turned and left. I was told to wait outside matron's office; I think more because of the stinking clothes than any other reason because I heard a window being opened as I closed the door behind me. The only thing I remember about standing outside matron's office was the smell of polish, it was a smell I had always liked for some reason, and it seemed to be every where.

The children's home still stands to this day, but it's an office block now, though I doubt that the office workers that work there now know the buildings history and the misery that the people who worked there in the 60's caused the children. I drove past it recently and it still, in my mind, looks like something from a horror film. All that was missing was thunder and lighting and a bat flying round the chimney.

The matron knew what I had been through, she must have read my files, yet throughout my time there I was made to feel that somehow it had been my fault, as if I was responsible for my life. The matron had not the slightest empathy towards me, or any of the children in the home for that matter, she never smiled and she always looked angry at the world, and it was inevitable that we would clash, and we did. But it was not until I had reached rock bottom did I fight back.

My first day, and night, at the children's home is a bit of a blur and I cannot recall anything about the first 12 hours, maybe it was because it was so late and also that I was both emotionally and physically knackered, but all I really remember is the matron, her office and being given a cup of milky, lukewarm tea and a single slice of cold toast. I remember going to bed, it was a small dormitory of only six beds. The bed sheets were crisp and clean, but there was no blue light, it was not The Cinderella in Morecambe. Then I cried myself to sleep with my face buried in the pillow; I remember my first morning and the reaction

I got when it was discovered that I had pissed the bed. And I remember the punishment for my 'crime' to this day.

When I woke that first morning I soon realised that I had pissed the bed, my pyjamas and the sheets were soaked. I was embarrassed but I didn't think I would be in any real trouble, but I was wrong. As I got out of bed, I slowly I took my first real look at the dormitory in the daylight, the six beds in two rows of three. Two of the beds were empty and neat and tidy. The top covers were pulled so tight on those two beds that they looked like coloured cardboard. I could hear the sound of the cutlery and plates clattering and assumed it must be the breakfast table being prepared, and I felt hungry enough to eat two breakfasts.

With my nerves and my emotions stretched to snapping point I got out of bed as quietly as I could, I did not want to draw attention to the fact that I had wet my bed. I thought that it would be like Cinderella that a kindly member of staff would tell me not to worry and they would quietly take the soiled sheets away without fuss, but I was very wrong. As I stood at the side of my bed trying to pull back the blankets to remove the sheets the dormitory door swung open and a woman walked in clapping her hands and shouting '*come on . . . get up*" and in the same loud voice told all the '*bed wetters*' to stand at the side of their beds. There were two other lads who got out of their beds and stood with their arms by their sides, shamefaced they stared at the floor. I just stood looking gormless wondering what to do and what would happen next and what happened next was the final humiliating straw and it broke me, and it would take years to recover from that morning.

The woman stormed over to my bed and pulled back my blankets with tremendous force and reminding me that only *dirty, lazy children wet the bed*, the woman threw the all my sheets and blankets in to the middle of the dormitory, all the other lads, the ones that had not pissed the bed, just lay in their beds grinning. The three 'dirty, lazy' boys were then told to remove our wet pyjamas and get to the bathroom. We were told to remove the pyjamas in the middle of the dorm and in full view of everyone, including the woman. Only a few days before I would have told the woman to fuck off and, probably, thrown the piss soaked sheets at her, but I could not, I felt weak, alone and scared and beaten. Almost all the fight had gone out of me and the only shred of resistance I offered was a weak effort. I simply stood there making not movement at taking my pyjamas off, but the woman only needed to take a step towards me for me to capitulate. So I quickly removed my pyjamas and stood with the other two lads by of the pile of bedclothes where the woman had ordered to stand. I tried to cover my private parts with my hands, but this just made the other lads, still in their beds, burst out laughing, and it was several long seconds before the woman told them to shut up. She had allowed them to ridicule the three of us just long enough to cause maximum embarrassment to the *'three dirty little boys'* before we were ordered to pick up the soiled white sheets and follow her to the bathroom.

In less than 24 hours I had lost my family, been dragged around a police station, watched my father being dragged through that same building, and a doctor had pushed his fingers up my arse. My whole life had crashed, but as I walked naked to the bathroom it took the last of my stubbornness to stop myself from crying, I didn't care how wretched or violent my previous life had been, I wanted it back, but I was powerless to do anything.

We followed the woman, like the scared kids we were, to the bathroom, walking along a wide corridor covering our bodies with our damp bed sheets, I felt, as I must have looked, pathetic. When we reached the bathroom I expected to be made to take a shower, but there wasn't one, there was only two large baths to one side of the room with a row of sinks running on the opposite wall. We were told to stand against a wall, even though there was a bench nearby, until she had run the bath. It didn't take her long and she stopped the tap when the water was only a few inches deep. When she was satisfied that the water wasn't warm the woman ordered one of the other lads to get in and when he had slowly lowered himself in to the cool water, she threw his wet sheets in with him and told him to wash them. I watched as the lad, he was a couple of years younger than me, shivered with a combination of shame and the coolness of the water. The lad cried quietly, but I could tell he was used to it; this must have been a regular greeting to his day. The woman took no notice of the lad's tears; she just stood at the side of the bath with her arms folded across her chest telling him to hurry up. The lad in the bath rubbed soap on his soiled sheets and then washed them as best he could: he sat silently sobbing as he did so. This was repeated with the other lad and then it was my turn. The now cold water was a filthy grey colour, scum floated on the top of it but that didn't bother me. I had shared a tin bath with my siblings in water just as cold and even dirtier. I think it pissed the woman off that I didn't cry or protest in some way. I wasn't being stubborn or hard-faced: I was simply used to it: but the matron wasn't to know and I did nothing to change her mind. But something inside me had changed, I was simply accepting things, I wouldn't, or couldn't, fight back. Even when a lad, a few years younger than me bumped into me, as we were marched to the bathroom, it was no accident; I knew he had done it to test me. But I backed down and stuttered that I was sorry; at the same time making myself a target for the house bully.

After washing the sheets and being made to apologise to everyone for 'spoiling their morning' the 'bed wetters' were marched off for a breakfast of cold toast and milky tepid tea. It was the breakfast for bed wetters. If you didn't piss the bed you could have hot tea, cornflakes followed by hot toast and jam. The idiots could have offered me whatever food they wanted and it wouldn't have stopped me pissing the bed: you can't beat, bribe or threaten a child into stopping bed wetting. You would have thought that people looking after troubled children would know that little gem of wisdom!

It seemed that the Home had a policy towards bedwetting that included total embarrassment as part of the punishment. No child was exempt; no matter what trauma the child may have witnessed or experienced, in the staffs' eyes nothing could not justify pissing the bed. The same zero tolerance policy applied to all areas of discipline. Not only psychological punishment, but also physical punishment and the staff would not baulk at slapping a child for the slightest misdemeanour.

Other punishment included being denied food, polishing floors or, and although I didn't mind it and didn't consider it a punishment, standing outside in the far corner of the garden no matter what the weather.

My first day at the home is a blur of confusion and fear. After the previous day's emotional and physical rollercoaster, I think my brain just couldn't make sense of it all and gave up trying to.

I, of course, pissed the bed the next night and the one after that and the one after that. It wasn't as if I tried not to, I tries desperately to keep the sheets dry; staying awake until the early hours did nothing, not drinking for most of the afternoon and evening had the same effect. Nothing I did or didn't do seemed to work. So every morning was a cold bath, cold toast and milky tepid tea.

For the first few days I was kept a prisoner in the home. No phone calls, visits or letters from the outside world. My old clothes, including my school uniform were taken from me and, as the matron so considerately put it, destroyed. I was given second-hand clothes that didn't fit. Some items were too big and some too small only the socks fit me.

Not being allowed out of the home really got to me. It was not until I went to church on the Sunday after I arrived that I saw, and realised, that the world outside still existed. And it hurt like nothing else I had known. As we walked, I was escorted, to the church, we passed many of the places that I had played with my brothers and sister only months before. I was lost in the memories of the happy hours I had spent with them when I felt my foot being kicked from under me. I hit the ground with my elbow and pain shot through me as blood ran from a small but deep cut caused by the impact. As I lay on the ground rubbing the fresh cut on my elbow, I started to swear but was cut short by my escort and told not to use such language. Some fucking escort! My escort, was a big fat bastard of a man that reminded me of my father when he looked at me with cruel anger in his eyes. He screamed at me to get off the floor; but it wasn't my escort that pulled my attention, it was the house bully that stood smirking behind him that I stared at. Laying there I felt empty, ashamed, alone, sad and afraid. I hated my self, hated being me. I lay on the floor like a shaking puppy, too scared to move. I remember looking at those that had gathered round me and my escort. They were all laughing, sneering at the pathetic boy that lay defeated on the hard ground. And my shame deepened when I realised I was crying and then realised that the laughter was louder because of my tears

My memories of that home are not fixed and the images and incidents merge in to one big miserable nightmare. The bullying grew worse by the day and I never did get used to the morning cold baths. Even going to school offered no respite for me. The local media had made sure that everyone in Bradford knew about what had happened to me and, as a result, every day, if not every minute, of my daily life, I was an object of curiosity. Teachers, parents, pupils all wanted to see the boy that had been raped by his father. I was avoided by some, ignored by others and bullied by most. I had made it easier for them; I had stopped fighting back. I was empty inside and missed my family, my home, and my friends. I was still too young to see the reality of it all. I was full of pain and desperate to see, to touch any of my family, even my father: even my mother.

One day when I was out in the corner of the garden of the children's home enjoying the solitude, the lad that had been constantly bullying me appeared with two of his mates. I felt my gut tighten. I knew immediately that they didn't want to chat and the fear I felt must have shown on my face as they swaggered towards me. They started by calling me names and asking if I had enjoyed my father's dick in me, when I didn't respond they started to push me—calling me names that only a month or so before I would have exploded with rage and ripped into them. But I didn't; I couldn't. And I couldn't stop my self from crying. The sight of my tears only encouraged the attackers and they started to punch and kick me. It wasn't the pain that forced me to curl into a ball on the ground and cry, I had felt and dealt with much worse, and hardly felt it, I was crying because I was angry, angry with me not them. I felt ashamed of myself. I heard the bullies' laughter increase and felt my clothes getting damper. They were laughing, calling me a *'piss-bedder'* and I realised I was being pissed on. I curled into a tighter ball and cried as I became soaked in piss—and did nothing.

That night, as I lay in bed ashamed of my tears and feeling utterly beaten, my mind raced with thoughts of what had happened, and I thoughts of escape. The day had been one of the worst of my short life thus far and I felt I could take no more. When the bullies had finished pissing on me and, after a few more kicks that I hardly felt, they left me alone, laughing as they walked away. I then sat in the corner of the garden curled up in a ball. I had started thinking about running away then, but I drenched in piss and my legs wouldn't stop shaking and knew I wouldn't get far. When I eventually got to my feet I almost staggered through the back door of the home: *my place of safety*. I wanted to get out of my piss drenched clothes and tears and snot ran down my face. I must have looked as pathetic as I felt; with my legs still shaking and my heart broken, I staggered across the garden towards the bleak looking house; as I reached it I fumbled on a step and lurched forward and almost fell through the door causing it to slam against a table. The noise it made ensuring that all eyes were turned on me, the staff, the bullies and the matron, and her eyes were fierce when she looked at me. The matron smiled at me, not a nice warm smile, but a sinister smile: like the one my father could turn my bowels to liquid with. Then the sniggering started . . . then the laughing. The matron allowed the mocking to continue for a few long seconds then she stopped smiling and spun round and glared at the sniggering crowd. Her glare had an immediate effect and there was silence. Then I felt the full force of her anger. To the utter joy of the bully the matron grab my arm and started to shake me, until the stink of the fresh piss on my clothes reached her flaring nostrils. A look of complete disgust cut across her face and she pushed me away from her as if I was a piece of shit she had suddenly discovered on her fingers. I don't know if I fell, tripped or was pushed, but I remember lying on the floor crying with the matron standing over me ordering me to the bathroom. But I couldn't move. I wasn't being stubborn or brave. I was broken. I can't remember how long I was on the floor but I remember the laughing. I remember the bully, my nemesis, standing behind the matron smirking as he pretended that he was pissing on the matrons back. I thought then that I would beat the shit out of him one day. But on that day I was a beaten little boy living in a world of strangers; strangers that for some reason seemed to hate me, so all I could do, all I wanted to do was to find somewhere quiet and cry.

Sitting in the bath that evening, with the matron stood arms folded watching every tear fall from my eyes, I felt a deep loneliness, an emptiness that left me feeling nothing. Later, when I had stopped crying, I vowed to myself that I would never cry again, I would of course, but not during the rest of my time there.

One morning I shocked the matron by not pissing the bed, don't know how or why I hadn't and no one was more surprised than me that my bed sheets were bone dry. Matron insisted that it was that she was finally instilling some discipline into me. I doubted it, but I didn't really care and it was the first morning I ate my breakfast with the rest of the kids.

Of course the next night I pissed the bed again so it was back to the cold bath, that by now, no longer caused me any embarrassment. I was becoming immune to the constant name-calling and my father's fists had hardened me to pain so I spent my time wandering around the home or sitting alone in the garden locked in my own mind. I did not daydream of wonderful things or even terrifying moments from my past. Instead I thought of as little as I could. Because to think about anything hurt too much; I was empty of all emotion, so I tried desperately not to think. But things were about to change, after what seemed like a thousand years of living with strangers, I was told that I would be allowed to meet my nana.

One morning as I sat it the tepid water of the bath the matron told me that she had some good news for me. And it seemed to stick in her throat when she told me that I would be allowed to see my nana; but she made sure that I knew it was not her decision. My heart leapt and for the first time in that shithole: I smiled; then I found my quiet spot in the garden and cried; like a little boy should.

The morning of the day that I was to meet my nana was very different from the norm for me. Even though I had pissed the bed I was not ordered to the bath with my sheets, instead they were taken from me to be washed and I was allowed to take a warm bath after I had had my breakfast with the other children. Following breakfast I was told to return to the dorm to get changed and the tatty hand-me-down, clothes were exchanged for new everything, new shoes, shirt, trousers and even new socks. My hair was trimmed and groomed until it shone and stuck to my head. All this was to me without affection. The new clothes were thrown on to my bed and my head was yanked and twisted as a pair of chrome hair clippers roughly pulled at my shaggy hair; almost pulling the hair out rather than cutting it.

I took it all without a whimper, I was used to the pain the clippers caused, my father had cut my hair with similar brutality quite often and, although the new smell of them made me breathe deeply, I didn't really give a shit. All I wanted was to see my nana as soon as I could.

I recall getting dressed and feeling clean and smart and, except for my hair that looked like it had been painted on, I knew that nana would be pleased to see me so clean and tidy. But nana would not know the truth of it; nana would not see that my head throbbed due to the smart hair cut, nor would she know that being dressed smart was not how I dressed every day.

I was to meet my nana in a park, I was to be escorted and watched over and, if I tried to run away or talk too much about the home then I would be brought straight back and see no one else: ever. These are, almost verbatim, the words the matron said to me as I stood waiting for transport to take me to the meeting with my nana. The matron stood, arms folded and foot tapping, as she scowled the words at me. I knew she was not happy seeing me standing there; or maybe she was afraid. The woman had made my life more miserable than it already had been. I had been ripped from away from my life, forced apart from my siblings, had suffered rape and violence throughout my short life. Yet all she seemed to care about was beating what little was left of me, out of me. Maybe she saw the spark in my eye that I felt in my stomach. Even the thought of seeing my nana had reminded me of a life away from my 'place of safety' and the hope it brought me.

I cannot recall the drive to meet my nana, I only remember getting out of a car and walking through the park with my hand being held too tight. I walked past the play area where I had, only a few months before, played with my siblings. I walked past a pond, past shrubs and neat cut lawns and I noticed more than ever before the families that seemed to be everywhere. There were children playing with each other, screaming as they chased about the grass playing games. There were mums and dads looking after them, laughing with their children, they were enjoying life. And I felt sick to the bottom of my gut with jealousy. I envied them and their happiness, their 'togetherness' highlighting the chasm between their lives and my own. Then I saw nana and started to cry even before she saw me.

Nana still hadn't seen me as I wriggled out of the grasp of my escort almost pulling him over in my eagerness to reach my nana's arms and feel the warmth of a loving hug. My escort screamed at me to get back, but though I heard the words I ignored them and ran towards my nana picking up speed as she turned in response to my escort screaming my name. Her smile was wonderful, warm and as I reached her my tears became sobs, deep sobs that made it difficult for me to breathe so much so that it took a while for nana to clam me down.

Wiping the snot and tears gently from my face with her hankie and shushing as she did so, nana kept looking me over as if checking if I was broken anywhere. I was broken, though not where she or anyone else could see it. Satisfied that I was all in one piece and unharmed she took my shaking hand and we walked to a bench near the pond, sitting in the shade she pulled me close and started to tell me about what was happening in the outside world. My escort caught up and came a bit too close and started to bollock me for running off; but he soon shut his gob when he received a quick glaring look from my nana. As soon as the man had moved far enough away nana began to tell me all that had happened. My father was on remand in

Wakefield waiting to go to trial but she told me I wouldn't have to go to court because he had pleaded guilty. This didn't impress my nana, she said that he had done it so he would get a smaller sentence, but I struggled to understand what was happening, I didn't understand all the legal stuff. But strange as it may seem to others even now, the mention of my father almost made me cry. I missed him.

Nana went on and told me, as she stroked my hair and fussed over me, that my siblings were in various homes throughout Bradford and that she had been to see most of them already. Nana told me that they were ok but they, like me, wanted to go home; nana also told me that my older brother, her first grandchild, was not in home and that he had stayed with her since the arrest. I felt a surge of anger, jealousy run through me and I only just managed to stop my mouth saying things that nana didn't deserve. It was only a small thing really, but it hurt me for years to think that I, and most of my siblings, had suffered while our older brother was with nana, safe, secure and happy. I was having trouble dealing with this when nana told me that mother was to be released to look after us. It was the one and only time I ever swore in front of nana. With a surge of emotion that was neither happiness nor anger, I stood up and swore . . . a lot. Mother being released was both good and bad news. On the one hand, it meant I would be released from my 'place of safety' and going home and that brought a broad grin to my face, but it also meant that my mother would be there. And that thought quickly took the smile off my face.

The meeting with nana seemed to only last a few minutes but in reality it had lasted for almost an hour, and my heart ached when it became obvious I had to go back to the home. As I hugged nana goodbye I felt like begging her to take me with her, I wanted to cry and never let her go, but did neither. I knew I couldn't go with nana, and I knew it would hurt her too much to see me cry. Nana hugged me close and I could smell her flowery perfume *"be brave love . . . it wont be much longer . . . I love you"* it wasn't me that cried, it was nana, she tried to hide the tears and keep her voice level. But she failed at both and I'm sure that had I cried with her we would have both just collapsed into floods of them. So I was brave, I didn't cry and, as I thought about the place I was to be returned to, I became angry and promised myself I had had enough. I would be bullied no more.

When I arrived back at the home the evening meal was almost over and the matron took delight in telling me that I would have to wait for supper and that I was to go straight to the dorm and get changed before I ruined my clothes. I did two things. One, I smiled at the matron knowing I had three bars of chocolate my nana had sneaked into my pocket and two, one of the smaller bullies tried to trip me up as I turned to go, I simply jumped over his outstretched foot and smiled at him saying tough as I did so.

The meeting with my nana had reminded me that I had a life, of sorts, outside the shithole, and had also reminded of who I was. And it would be a very different boy than the one they had all become so used to bullying. And they would find out very soon.

Later that evening, after a supper of cold toast and tepid cocoa, I was waiting to go the bathroom. As always there was a small queue of pushing and shoving boys waiting to get ready for bed and it was in that queue that I finally fought back. After weeks of endless bullying from staff and children alike, I began to stick up for myself.

One of the lads in the queue had been more of a nuisance than a bully, he was not the worst by some distance but he had laughed with the rest when I had been pissed on or made to sit naked with my piss soaked bed sheets, so when he saw me and said he could smell piss, I felt a surge of anger flood into me, and I felt the power it gave me. The boy nipped his nose pretending to gip at the imaginary stench, confident that I would do nothing and he soaked up the giggles and back slapping that his antics brought him. I glared at him until he stopped laughing and let go of his nose. Then I took a few steps forward and thumped him, a quick clean punch that connected with his now vacant nose. Then there was silence as those in the queue stood slack jawed. I didn't say anything, didn't look at anyone; I just walked

Just Once, When I was little

passed them all in to the bathroom, ignoring the boy as he sat on the floor with blood running down his chin.

Later as I lay in my bed I heard the shuffling of sheets being pushed back followed by naked feet slapping on the floor. Then there was an hand grabbing my hair and a fist trying to land on my face; but it was dark and the punches missed or landed harmlessly on the blankets. I soon realised that it was my nemesis, the bully that had humiliated since day one; but his blows didn't hurt in the slightest and I remember being surprised at my lack of fear as I waited for the bully to finish his pitiful attack. My intention was to batter him as soon as he stopped; but one of the staff put a stop to it all when she bounded into the dorm and dragged my attacker away from my bed. I watched all this happen in a state of total calm. No anger or desire for revenge filled me; in fact I smiled when the staff member left the room and the bully assured me he was going to rip my balls off and make me eat them . . . blah fucking blah.

The following day must have been a Saturday because I was playing football on the local field when I finally snapped. After all the crap I had been through, I had been pissed on, made to sit naked in front of everyone, constantly bullied and I had even been spit on. All this I took while I was in a state of utter despair; my only reaction was to cry and sink into a deeper depression, and yet all it took was a single word to drag me back to the boy I really was. We all have a point when we will react, a point when we will defend ourselves, and that day, the bully found my point of no return, and he wished he hadn't.

We had been playing football for about ten minutes and I had already been upended several times and sent flying onto the muddy pitch. This had caused a lot of sniggering and name calling, all aimed at me. But each time I was knocked down, I just got back up and smiled and carried on playing; and it was driving the bullies crazy, then my nemesis must have flipped because he suddenly charged about 10 yards and flattened me. The impact knocked the wind out of my lungs and I must have travelled three times my body length through the mud. Smiling at his mates he stood over me with his arms bent. He was showing everyone watching his muscles and I thought he was going to put his foot on me as if I was a wild beast he had shot; then he changed his mind and bent down asking me if I liked being pissed on, did I enjoy cold baths. I smiled. He stood up. Then he called me a coward. Then I almost launched myself to my feet. The words were repeating in my head but in the voice of my father. My nemesis didn't know what hit him.

As my feet touched the muddy ground I was already landing punches into his face. I was screaming with the rage that had built up over weeks, months of abuse and, as my nemesis went down, I couldn't stop. The bully curled up in a ball and screamed for me to stop, but I had lost all sense of reason and continued punching him as he lay on the ground. My father voice echoing in my head *you fucking coward—piece of shit—useless—coward—coward—coward—coward* . . . I wanted to kill that boy, I wanted to hurt him until he screamed in agony . . . but it wasn't him I wanted to kill, it was my father; in my mind it was *him* it was *his* face that I was punching with every ounce of my strength. I came back to reality when I felt a blow to my left side but it didn't stop me or even slow me down, I kept on punching the face of my father . . . *I am not a fucking coward* . . . I kept repeating the words with every punch that smashed in to the boys face. Then I felt another blow to my left side and this time it hurt and got my attention and I reacted to the sudden surge of pain when a sudden surge of adrenalin flooded my brain. And I exploded All I can remember is seeing one of the bully's mates leaning over me trying to drag me off as another kicked me in my ribs. I remember hitting the boy that was trying to drag me off, but I didn't thump him, I head butted him ramming the top of my head in to his face and he fell away holding his mouth and nose. Then I leapt to my feet, I was full of a burning rage and hatred for the world and I wanted to fight everyone in it. I wanted to beat them all to death, The boy that was kicking me in the ribs saw the sheer anger in my eyes and ran away as I went for him; but I was rooted to the spot in my anger, so I punched the boy nearest to me in the face instead, I was about to turn my attention back to the bully as he sobbed pathetically on the ground, but before I could batter him to a pulp I was overwhelmed by staff and dragged away.

And I wasn't easy to drag; I kicked and punched, scratched and elbowed calling them all bastards. I felt a few slaps but I think they would have needed hit me with a brick and knock me out to stop me. I remember screaming at one of them *"is that the best you can do . . . go on hit me . . . bastard . . ."* but I was lost in a world of anger and hate and utter confusion. My brain was spinning with images of my past life and none of them were nice. But I remember also feeling a great release has all the hurt and the anger, months of it, years of it, was finally let loose.

Then I remember nothing until I was stood in front of the matron some time later. I was shaking and tears ran down my face, but they were not tears of fear or sadness, they were tears of anger. I remember feeling hands gripping my shoulders and arms. Then I remember being on my knees sobbing and wiping snot and blood across my face. I knew that I had taken a few solid blows; yet I felt no pain, well no physical pain anyway. Then I remember the matron screeching words that I knew would change everything *". . . home tomorrow . . . good job you're going home tomorrow . . . remand home . . ."* the words, at first, didn't make sense though they were plain enough. Going home, did I still have a 'home'? Did I still have a family? As I slowly returned to reality and my anger waned, the pressure of hands holding me relaxed enough for me to stand, though I was still shaking and finding it hard to breathe, I interrupted the matron as she bleated on and on. The matron was not used to anyone talking unless spoken to and I remember the look of sheer anger that I had interrupted her. Through tears, blood and snot I asked her *what the fuck she was on about.* This got me a firm slap to the back of my head and I retaliated by instantly kicking my booted foot out backwards. I don't know who I caught, but I felt the impact and then I the hands grabbed my shoulders again, forcing me to the floor. I kicked and screamed, not because I wanted to fight, I just wanted the screaming matron to repeat the words and explain. But she didn't, instead she screamed at whoever was holding me to get me out of her sight.

I didn't have any tea or supper that night and I was ignored by the staff and feared by the other boys in the home; and it drove me crazy that I didn't know what was happening. The bully, now ex bully, kept well out of my way as he tried to hide his bruised face from me, but he couldn't, and when I did see the mess I had made, I smiled at him. It was a genuine smile, I had enjoyed battering the big headed twat, I had enjoyed releasing all the anger that he had helped to store up. I had enjoyed the power it had given me; and the feeling of pure freedom of pain it brought.

I didn't sleep that night, not even for a minute. For one, I couldn't get the words of the matron out of my head "*. . . home tomorrow . . . good job you're going home tomorrow . . . remand home . . .*" and I wished more than once that I had listened and not kicked out, and the other reason was that I knew that the bully was laying awake and I knew that he would want to get his revenge and, like all bullies, he would do it while I slept. Because I hadn't slept I hadn't pissed the bed. I lay there wide eyed but tired and hungry; and pissed the bed.

I refused to stand and strip, I refused to take the bed sheets off and take them to the bathroom. I was expecting to be surrounded by staff and forced to comply. But none of it happened. Other than being told to go to the bathroom and get a wash, I was ignored by everyone. No bath just a wash! My brain spun as I tried to make sense of it all. Was I going home? it was a thought that both filled me with terror and happiness.

After I had washed, under the watchful eye of a staff member, I was marched to the dinning room for breakfast. I was alone at the table and still being ignored even when my breakfast was carelessly plonked in front of me and I, probably, would have pushed the porridge away had my stomach not demanded that I eat it. I ate the toast and loaded the first slice with as much butter and jam as I could fit on the bread. This pissed the staff member off so the butter and jam were removed. I didn't respond, I just scraped some off the first slice and carried on. Then the dinning room door burst open and the matron strode in carrying a bundle. Dropping the bundle on the empty chair next to me she told me to finish my breakfast and go to the dorm and get changed. I remember leaning over to look at the bundle and could see that it was made up of clothes; and by the smell of them they were new clothes. Then the matron did something that brought my temper flooding back. She sniffed me. I realise now that she was checking to ensure that I didn't smell of piss, but even so she could have been discreet. But she wasn't and I stood up so fast the chair I was sitting on flew back and hit the wall. The matron backed away and a male staff member stood in front of her as I screamed at her to fuck off, I called her a sick old fat cow and would have kicked her if I had got near enough. Instead I was dragged off to the dorm screaming and kicking; only calming down when I was pushed into the room and the door clattered shut after me, then a few minutes later the door opened again and the bundle was thrown onto a bed near the door; as it landed it came apart revealing a full set of brand new clothes, then I knew I was either going to court or going home. I remember sitting on the bed looking at the crisp new clothes, then I started to cry. A huge part of me didn't want to go 'home' even thinking about Hampton Place made me feel scared: I could not imagine the place without my father. My mind would simply not allow it. Every room in that shithole held bad memories for me; even the roof. And every room would hold the smell of him. The tears that I cried were not because of sadness, they were tears of fear as I finally made sense of the words the matron screamed at me the day before. And I remember feeling the terror that only my father could fill me with start to build as I fought the images of what he would do to me if he was there: waiting for me.

    I must have sat on the bed too long because one of the staff opened the door and screamed at me to get dressed '*NOW*' and then the door slammed shut before I could tell them to fuck off.

    I didn't hurry, I could no longer be bullied by them and they knew it, and no matter how loud they shouted or slammed doors, they knew I couldn't give a shit. I finally finished putting on the smart new clothes, including brand new shoes, the feel and smell of them eased my fear and sadness a bit, enough for me to take a last look round the dormitory. Then I remembered my first morning there, I remembered standing naked while everyone laughed. And I became angry again and walked along the two lines of beds and pulled all the blankets off and threw them in a pile on the floor. I remember I was going to piss on them but the door opened and a booming voice told me to move my arse, the male staff member looked at the pile of blankets and sheets muttered something then looked at me with disgust in his eyes. The pillow hit the door has he shut it.

I wasn't escorted to the matron's office, no one wanted to be near me and, when I passed the TV room where the rest of the boys sat there were a few words of abuse . . . *the pissy arse is leaving . . . go on fuck off . . . blah fucking blah* they were all hard again, but when I stopped at the door and glared in, none would look at me.

When I entered the matron's office I didn't stand in front of her desk, bolt upright with my arms by my side as was usual, instead I stayed near the door and refused to move an inch. Matron's face was full of thunder and hate and it was all aimed at me, but I no longer gave a shit about her or her staff. Standing there all defiant had really got to the matron and she probably thought that I was a hard, arrogant little boy with little or no feelings, and I suppose that's what I intended to look like. But inside I was scared and shaking; I couldn't make sense of what was happening. Only the day before I had been playing football, finally lost the plot and accessed a temper I didn't know I had and I had fought all comers with it, and I was bruised and aching all over as a result and, yet only 24 hours later I was standing in matron's office listening to her telling me I was going home that day. And I remember feeling an overwhelming urge to cry, to scream, to rip the face off the matron, to destroy the home and everyone and everything in it replace my feelings of fear. Then I noticed a woman, a much younger woman than the matron, sitting quietly in the corner; a woman I would never forget and I still owe so much.

The young woman didn't say anything at first, she simply sat quietly watching and listening to the matron berate me for being a *stubborn, bad little boy that would do nothing but cause trouble and no matter how she tried she could do nothing with him* . . . The young woman also heard me scream back at the matron, that she had done a fucking lot *to* me; and the young woman then saw the matron lose her composure. The matron slammed her hands down on the desk in front of her as she shouted at the young woman to get me out of her sight. The young woman smiled at me, just a small grin really, but it was enough to let me know that she understood what was happening. Perhaps she had been to the home before. The matron stood up and handed my files over to the woman without looking at her; she was too busy staring at me. I may not recall all the words verbatim from that day, but I remember the look on the matron's face as if it was only a few days ago and I am sure she would have loved to have slapped me!

The young woman came and stood by my side and I remember she was not much taller than me; but she was nonetheless a tough cookie. Just as we were about to leave the matron started to say she had one more thing to say to me; the young woman simply asked her if it was anything to do with my future and, when the matron said no, the young woman said that I didn't want to hear it. I could have kissed her.

As we were walking down the path away from the home every emotion my young body knew surged through me. Except one. Anger, fear, sadness, and feelings of loss, loneliness, confusion and emotions that even today I cannot name. But I felt no love for any one. I was going home, to the loving care of my mother. My mother; the woman that had sat and watched, *scratching* herself between her legs as my father raped, abused and beat her children. They were sending me home to her. And then I stopped, turned and screamed abuse at the house and everyone in it, at the faces staring at me, some laughing, some contorted with anger as they shouted words that I couldn't hear. I started to run back towards the house but two male members of staff blocked my way. I was 11 years old, a little boy, terrified of life. And all anyone wanted to do was hurt me. Except, that is, the young woman.

She didn't scream at me, she didn't shout and tell me to stop; she didn't threaten to have me locked up in a remand home. Instead she put her hand on my shoulder and almost whispered that it was time to go; and that simple act of kindness triggered something inside me that made me feel like I should have felt. Suddenly I was a little boy again and I felt a deep longing to be held, protected and loved and so I turned around and almost fell as I reached my arms out: longing for her to cuddle me.

I am not a religious man, though I often wish I was, but I will call the young woman *my angel* because, at that moment in my life, she was.

My 'Angel' put her arms around me and pulled me tight against her chest. She didn't care about the snot that ran down my face and on to her clothes. She didn't care that I was squeezing the breath out of her. She didn't care about the swear words that I couldn't stop screaming out of mouth nor did she care who was watching. She only cared about me. Me. I remember, at one point, trying to pull away when my anger started to replace the longing to be hugged; but she clung on to me and squeezed me even tighter until the anger slowly subsided again.

I cannot remember how long my Angel and I stood there hugging, but I know it was not until I had finished crying *and I let go* of my angel that we slowly came apart. With one final surge of anger I turned and faced the house and screamed at the matron has she stood at the window of her office staring out at me, she shook her head and turned her back to me. I carried on swearing and cursing even when she had disappeared into the darkness of her office. Then *my angel* took hold of my hand and we turned back towards her car, has we were walking she told me that she had been to my home at Hampton Place and met my mother. We stopped walking and stared at each other; she knew what she was taking me *home* to, she knew what my life had been like, and what I'd been through, and she knew what my life was going to be like when I was returned to my mother. She hugged me, and I could see clearly the sadness in her eyes. She could do no more for me; but, though I didn't realise it then, she had done so much more than I think, like me, she realised. My *Angel* had shown me that someone did care, and, over the following years, I would remember the kindness she gave freely and the warmth I felt has she held on to me, even when I dribbled snot all over her clothes. The 'Matron' had not only failed with me, she had made things profoundly worse. If you look at the definition of matron it reads thus: *a woman who has charge of the domestic affairs of a hospital, prison, or other institution.*

She was not fit to be in charge of any of them. I had entered that home, my place of safety, a terrified little boy that needed to be understood. I needed warmth and security, I needed people like Uncle John from the Cinderella in Morecambe to show me that the world was not totally cruel and my perception of normality, of wrong and right, was wrong. But I got none of it. What I received instead was daily psychological and physical abuse that pushed me until I discovered something in me that I didn't know was there; and that something offered me the only protection from the outside world I knew, something that would allow me to bury my memories and emotion. And that something was pure aggression. I think that, at some point during my last day there, I had made a subconscious decision that I would never allow my self to depend on anyone for love, I would never allow anyone close to me again and I would rely on no one for anything.

Pulling away from that home I started to shake, and then I started to cry. But the tears, I remember, were different from the deep angry sobs that had been created by anger and confusion, the tears were the just the tears of a sad little boy. Which ever way I looked in my life I was fucked. My father was in prison. My mother had been released from prison. And I was going home. I had nothing in my life that could make me smile and, when the car turned into Hampton Place, all that had happened there flashed, unbidden, into my mind. I was convinced that my father would be standing there or just coming home from the pub pissed. My brain would not accept that he was not there and, as strange has it may seem now, for a brief moment, I wanted him to be there.

Walking up the passage towards the house, the familiar stench of the outside toilet started to reach my nostrils. The smell of shit, piss and rotting waste seemed much stronger after my time away from it, my sense of smell had been used to the smell of the Home, bleach, disinfectant and cheap polish. And, after standing outside for several minutes to bring some kind of calm to myself, I opened the door. The smell stopped me breathing when the stench of filth, grease, piss, sweat and shit hit my nostrils. Then I saw my mother sitting on the same sofa that I had taken refuge under when my father had tried to batter me to death. She was smoking a cigarette, watching a television that wasn't the same one that was there the day my father was arrested; it was a much newer one mother was staring at. She hardly seemed to notice that anyone had come into the house let alone her own son, a son she hadn't seen for months, a son that was an emotional wreck. Nothing had changed, the stench of filth was everywhere, and mother was sat on her arse watching the fucking television. Even now, I feel some of the hurt, and the sense of confusion, I felt then. All those years ago I stood in front of a woman I hated; a woman that I had shown me little or no affection throughout my life; was my mum. Standing there I desperately wanted to run to her, to hold her, for her to cry with me as we hugged. But I knew in my heart that it was not worth even trying; and I knew that it would hurt even more to be pushed away. So I stood there, my eyes and heart aching, watching mother staring back at me with a lost, confused look in her eyes, cigarette smoke bellowing slowly out of her mouth, something died inside me as I finally accepted what I had known, but denied, throughout my life: my mother did not love me. But it wasn't this hurtful realisation that killed a part of me, it was the realisation that, though I hated my mother due to years of neglect and covering for my father, I also loved her, needed her. But the futility of loving her hit me like a brick. I had survived the violence of my father, withstood all the beatings he daily inflicted on me, I had survived the trauma of the children's home. Yet the pain I felt standing there in front my mother was a different kind of pain and I would have gone through a dozen, a hundred, of my father's savage beatings than the empty, gut chilling pain I was feeling.

 I turned away from my mother's empty gaze and looked at the wonderful woman that had brought me home; she was staring at the floor slowly shaking her head, when she looked up I could see that she was struggling to retain the tears that filled her eyes. She knew I needed my mum and that I longed to be loved by her, she knew that when she left I would be at the mercy of a woman that had given birth to eight children yet had been a mother to none of them.

The woman got up from the stinking sofa and held her hand out to me telling me she had to go and, gesturing to me with a slight movement of her head to walk her to her car, I looked once more at my mother and then reached out and took the woman's hand. I remember her hand feeling very soft and the gentle, her skin was as smooth as silk. It felt strange holding a person hand, it was not something I was used to and, as we manoeuvred our way out of the stinking room, it was getting ever harder to stop myself from begging the woman to take me away from the terrible memories that the house still held for me; and a mother that didn't give a fuck about me.

I don't remember much more about the day I returned 'home' I only remember being out on the streets after 'My Angel' had gone. I remember looking for my old mates, walking the streets in the smog of Bradford, and not finding them. I remember sitting on a swing at the local park and it was raining. I remember sitting alone on a wall, crying. I remember feeling totally, utterly, desolate. And I remember hearing Steve's voice calling out my name. My only *true* friend had found me. But I remember feeling great sadness that he had; and even thought about running away from Steve. I remember feeling that I didn't want anyone, or need anyone to be close to. I, instead, wanted to run to the moors that surround Howarth and live in a field for the rest of my life and see no one ever again. People hurt me, no matter who they were. People left me whenever I grew to love and need them. They left me: they always left me. And the urge to run grew ever deeper with every hurried step Steve took towards me.

"Brian, my mate, it is you, fucking hell, what they done to your hair . . . fucking hell mate" I hadn't given in to the powerful urge to run and Steve nearly lifted me clear off the wall where I sat in my misery. I wish to this day that I had returned his happiness at our reunion, but I couldn't; inside I was an emotional, confused, mess and I wanted to punch Steve has he ruffled my hair and threw me about like a rag doll. Steve just saw his mate, his buddy that had disappeared one day and his face beamed with happiness. Then Steve's happiness drained from his face when he saw the anger that was in my eyes as I pushed him

away. I can still see the pain and hurt I on his face as I did so. We were both so young, so very young, and Steve had only heard rumours about what had gone on and the real reason my father had been arrested, he didn't know what to door what to say to me when he realised that what he had heard were not rumours, they were the exaggerated truth.

We sat on park wall for several hours, long after Steve should have been home and in bed. We didn't talk much; Steve kept asking me what had happened but I remember the terrible thoughts that filled my mind and the shaking they caused. So I kept looking at the wet pavement, the miserable dank Bradford night matched my misery. Many of the old street gas lamps had been replaced by tall electric lights, but all that seemed to do was highlight the constant drizzle that swirled about them.

Steve, at last, decided that he had to go home; his mum would have been worried sick. Even though Steve was a tough bastard and very street wise, he would never defy his mum. His mum was the total opposite to my own mother; doting after her two sons in every way a mum should, but she was as firm as iron when it came to discipline. But Steve had repeatedly reassured me that she would understand when he got home and explained why he was so late. I think he still expected a wallop, but his mum's wallops were not like my father's fists, Steve would shrug it off as usual, and he would probably smile at his mum's attempt to inflict pain on her growing son.

I began to talk to Steve about the home and all that I had been through, I remember talking fast and loud, a feeling of sadness and anger rising as I recalled the loneliness I felt. I remember Steve putting his arm around me, I remember fighting the urge to push him away but losing. I wanted to feel protected, I wanted to be held. Emotions flooded through me as I realised that I had no-one to answer to, no one to control me, no one to protect me. Only Steve seemed to be able to feel my emotions. So I cried has he held me.

Eventually Steve had to go home, he would no doubt be in bother with his mum and dad, but they were nice parents and Steve wouldn't be beaten or locked in a loft, he would be told off and made to do some work in the garden: he wouldn't be beaten until he bled and begged not to be hurt anymore.

Over the years, I had developed a deep fear of the dark and now that my emotions were calming, my nyctophobia began to kick in. I can't remember what time it was when Steve and I started the short walk back to Hampton Place, but I was glad of his company. With every noisy step we took I expected to hear my father's voice, screaming at me for being late. I imagined him hiding behind walls, or in the damp overhanging bushes, waiting to leap out and drag me home for a beating. Even though I knew my father was in prison, my deep fear of him would not leave me and I remember feeling terrified that, if he didn't get me before I reached Hampton Place, he would surely be waiting there, drunk, when I did.

Steve left me at the top of Hampton Place; it was only a few yards from the dark passage that lead to the back of the dark, damp house that I called home. When Steve finally thought I was calm enough and he had pushed his luck as far as he dared with his mum and dad, he gave me a hug then turned and ran towards his own home. The sound of his shoes hitting the pavement started to fade, dulled by the heavy mist that was now forming. It was as if the world was squashing me, the drizzle was stopping but now dense smog remained, hovering over the dark, damp, street. When I reached the end of the passage, panic suddenly surged through me: I stared into the sheer darkness of the passage; it was like looking into the abyss. No lights, no noise; only blackness. I turned around as panic began to rise, fully intending to walk away, but all I saw was deep, silent, smog rolling in great clouds along the street. The combination of smoke and fog seemed to be making deep orange coloured patterns around the gas-lamps. My imagination was now rampant and every where I looked I could see my father staggering towards me. He was at the top of the street, at the bottom of the street, stood in the passage opposite where I was standing. Though his legs and feet moved as if he was walking, but the image of my father did not come any closer, it was as if he was trapped in sort of smog filled bubble. I remember shivering with fear, anger, loneliness, helplessness. I wanted to scream and run, but I was too afraid to do either in case my father somehow escaped from the fragile bubble. Less than 24 hours earlier I had been trapped in a children's home, feeling just as desperate, just as scared, just as lonely and shaking with the intensity of my emotions. Sliding down the wall of the passage, I started to cry again. Closing my eyes tight shut and putting my hands over my ears, I curled into a ball and pressed myself against the cold rough Yorkshire Stone wall. I remember feeling the edges bite into my back as I tried to become invisible to the night and the images of my father. I remember repeating over and over to myself that he is in prison, he is in prison . . . my father is in prison. And I remember the opening my eyes and the sheer terror that surged through me when I saw my father emerging out of the smog walking towards me.

It only took a brief moment full of sheer terror for me to realise that the man that was slowly emerging from the dark smog into the dull orange glow of the gas lamp was not my father. But it was long enough for me to piss myself. I knew the man; he lived a few doors down the road and had been a friend of my father's. He had almost passed me before he realised that I was there and I remember he jumped slightly at the sight of me. He didn't recognise me at first, I must have looked very different from the last time he had seen me, then his voice broke the silence with a friendly '*hey-up lad . . . what you doing sitting on the floor . . . you'll freeze your nuts off*' I don't know if it was the relief that it was not my father or the friendly sound of the mans voice, but I started to sob again. The man stood for a minute then sat down beside me on the cold damp ground and ruffled my hair. The man meant no harm, he was simply showing concern for a young lad . . . but I pulled away from him as he moved closer and I caught the stench of beer on his breath. My head spun, and scrambling to my feet, I ran into the darkness of the passage, I remember the man pleading that he wasn't going to hurt me, and I remember feeling that it wasn't him that I was afraid of; it was the stink of beer I was running from.

The passage was only about 4 yards long, but even in my blind panic to escape the images of my father and the stench of

Just Once, When I was little

beer on the mans breath, it seemed much further. I remember the sound of my shoes echoing of the damp dark walls as I raced the short distance. Then suddenly I was through. I burst into the house, my home, and there, crowded in the small dimly lit room were my siblings. I hadn't seen them since the day of father's arrest; I remember the looks of terror in their eyes as I slammed the door shut behind me, shutting out the images of my father that I felt sure had followed me. I didn't stop, I didn't rush in and hug them, and there were no tears of joy at the reunion. I don't think I even smiled at any of them. I just remember breathing heavy and feeling tears running down my face and I remember seeing my mother sitting exactly as where she had been when I left hours before. I remember wanting to attack her, I wanted to hurt her; I wanted to make her feel *something*, anything. But she just looked at me with empty eyes. I almost knocked my younger brother over as I ran to the bottom of the stairs and then run as fast as I could up them. I wanted to hide, I wanted to escape; not just from my family; but from the world. I remember hiding behind a bed in the attic, squeezing my self into a corner. And I remember sobbing as I tried to handle the confusion of emotions than ran through my brain. I hated my mother deeply, and longed for her to hold me and make things better. I was terrified of my father, the mere thought of him made me shudder, and yet I wanted him to come back so everything would be ok again

So deep was my sadness that it was only when my sister came to bed much later that I realised I had been sat in almost total darkness. And yet I was terrified of the dark.

I have no fixed, reliable, memories after that first night back with my siblings, or even the following few days. I can only recall not being able to accept that my father was no longer there, no longer a threat. The house had not been touched since the day of my father's arrest and I remember seeing his brown suit hanging behind the bedroom door, I remember it stank of beer and cigarette smoke and I remember sleeping on the bedroom floor but I can't remember why. I remember reliving the night my father tried to knock me off the roof, when I had told a lie and said I had burgled the neighbour's house.

The beating I received had been inevitable from the onset and, even today, I still feel deep anger for betraying myself. It was all there in that house, the smells, and the sounds, the filth . . . the memories. Why had someone not realised the further damage that returning the children to *that* house would cause; and that their nights and days would be full of the terrible memories and images that were in every room.

Why did someone not realise that we were children and we needed help; security and a cuddle. Instead they returned us to the very house where we had suffered terrible abuse; and to a mother, a known criminal, that didn't give a shit about her children. Why?

Everything was different yet little had changed. We still lived in filth, we still went hungry. Father had gone, yet he was still there in every room of the house, his smell, his clothes, and his anger. Every unknown noise in the house would set off a chain reaction of fearful looks among the children. Even with the bedroom light left on all night I was terrified of sleeping. Sleep was when my father became real to me and I would wake up screaming, escaping from nightmares that I remember to this day. And I wasn't the only child. Every night muffled screams could be heard, and I knew what they were dreaming and why they screamed.

I seldom stayed in the house, I would stay out until the last of my mates went home then I would return to Hampton Place and find somewhere in the still overcrowded bedrooms. Often I would sleep on the floor fully dressed, I had no pyjamas and my small stash clothes were in a corner sticking of piss. The clothes they had given me on my release from the children's home were at the bottom of the pile. They had been there since I returned. And I would never wear them again.

My mother soon recovered from any trauma she may have suffered over previous months. Within days of the family reunion she was bringing home strangers. Some tried to befriend the children, yet the only response they received from us was to be told to fuck off or simply ignored. Some tried to boss, even bully the children, the response they received was far worse. One 'accidentally' fell halfway down the stairs when he tried to catch me after I had called him a cunt. It may have been the ever present, overflowing piss bucket being thrown at him that sent him tumbling back down the stairs and limping out of the house.

I hated Hampton Place and was glad when, only a few months after returning to the place, we were evicted. But this time the eviction would be different.

Mother's habit of ignoring all warning letters or visits from landlords and having not made any plans as to where the family could do a 'moonlight flit' to, meant that we were literally kicked out of the house one day. I remember the knock on the door one morning and three or four big blokes simply walking in and start to carry the pitiful furniture out of the house. The men sorted the few items of any value and put them in a van; there wasn't much, only the old television and a radio that belonged to a neighbour.

I remember standing at the end of the passage watching my mother crying her false tears. She was telling anyone that would listen about how badly we had been treated in life. She told them how we, 'her lovely children' had been abused and how no one would help her. She told how cruel the landlord had been. She told them how she had paid the rent and how the landlord had asked for sex and she had refused him and that's the real reason we were homeless. But the few neighbours that did listen to her had seen and heard it all before. And they knew mother for what she really was; they had seen the constant stream of men, she had lied to them all before. She had literally begged, stole and borrowed from them. And they were just glad to see the back of her and her thieving kids.

After the neighbours had heard enough and had walked away, I think it finally dawned on mother that we had nowhere to go. I walked back along the passage to see if there was anything worth salvaging from the pile of stinking furniture that had been thrown onto the pile of rubbish that was already there. I remember the stench that came from the piss soaked rotting mattresses; and I remember seeing my father's brown suit jacket sticking out from under the grimy settee that I had used to escape his beating; the night I betrayed myself. I remember feeling a deep sadness. The pile of rubbish was what was left of my life, it was my family's life and I knew it was the end of us. I was 12 or 13 years old and still too young to make any sense of it all. I remember touching my father's jacket before I turned and walked away, struggling to stop myself from crying and wishing he was here.

Steve was on holiday and staying with a relative in Sheffield or I would have simply left what was left of my family and gone to find him. But instead I stayed with my siblings and my mother. I wanted to walk away from it all. I wanted to leave all the misery that was etched into the faces of my younger siblings behind me. I wanted to leave all the memories and start my life again. But I could not. I knew I had to stay.

Walking around like refugees, we must have looked a sorry sight. We weren't going anywhere; we were simply wandering around the damp streets of Bradford getting wet and hungry going nowhere. Mother eventually realised that she had to do something. The damp day was turning into an even damper evening and the younger kids were starting to cry and cling to the older children. Mother suddenly went in to a telephone box we had walked past several times. I could see her talking and crying, she was pleading with someone about the terrible state we were all in, she kept breaking into deep sobs that even had me convinced for a while. Then as suddenly as she had gone into the phone she came back out again, all signs of her deep utter despair vanishing in a split second. I remember her saying we had somewhere to sleep for a couple of days.

We were to be the guest of the centre for the homeless.

The only good part about the place was that it was situated only a few hundred yards from where we were standing. The place looked bleak and run down, a place to be avoided. I had walked past the place hundreds of times and watched the 'guests' wandering around outside picking up cigarette butts and begging pennies off passersby. And that's where our mother was taking her children. But she even fucked that up.

As we entered the building the first thing that hit you was the strong smell of bleach. It made me gag. The walls were a deep blue colour and all the floors were covered in deep green tiles, even the low swinging lights had a deep grey shade over them. The inside of the place was even more depressing than the outside and, as the children were huddled in a group of misery, I wished with all my heart that I was somewhere else.

Thanks to my mother; I got my wish.

Mother, when asked my age by the bloke that was filling in the forms my age, had told him that I was 13. Even though there was a huge sign in front of us stating clearly that a male child, over the age of twelve, could not stay there. The bloke stopped writing and glared at mother and shook his head. The man had obviously being willing to allow me to stay but, once he mother had told him my age, he had no choice. Mother, at last, realised her mistake and tried to back—track but a woman had suddenly appeared and, with the same arrogant manner as the matron at the children's home, almost threw me out of the building. The woman didn't care that I had nowhere to go, and mother's crocodile tears had no effect what-so-ever on her. The man behind the desk suggested contact the council to get me put in a children's home for a few days. I remember almost swearing at the man, but instead I quickly told a lie that my mother just as quickly endorsed. I told the man I could stay at an aunts that lived just round the corner and that I would run round there and see if she would put me up, if she couldn't then I would come back and tell them. I remember thinking that once I was out of that building I would not be returning. Though I did return later; it would be after I had endured a night that, to this day, can fill me with a variety of emotions; sadness being the stronger of them.

Standing outside the dismal building, the stench of the place was even stronger than the stink of piss and filth that clung to my clothes and filled the air around me. Sitting on a low wall I remember looking up and down the street and realising that it was getting dark, the usual smog was already forming under darkening clouds. Then, to make matters worse, it started to rain; and any relief I felt about 'escaping' from the homeless shelter quickly left me, my fear of the dark increasing by the minute. I was scared, hungry, cold, wet and miserable. I was homeless and without a family. And I felt utterly alone.

I sat on the wall allowing the light rain to soak me, I was waiting for my mother to come out and tell me what to do, where to go. I was waiting for her to come out and make things better. But I knew she wouldn't do anything, she was in the building and I knew she would not be bothered about her son outside. And, has I realised the truth, I started to cry. Leaving the wall behind I started walking towards Manchester Road, the only place I knew that had the new electric street lighting, cars and people.

Has I walked with my head down against the damp air and growing darkness, I remembered a song that I had heard many times before, a song with words that really meant something to me and seemed to reflect much of my life.

"The Sound Of Silence" by Simon & Garfunkel has powerful lyrics that I knew off by heart; and I started to quietly sing them has I wandered towards Manchester Road. Already I was jumping at every strange noise, and there were plenty of them. Cats seemed to be everywhere and every few yards one would suddenly dash out from under a hedge or a terrifying meow and growl would split the night air and increase my terror. In an attempt to scare the cats before I got near them I started to stamp my feet as I walked, but my soaking, threadbare shoes made little noise no matter how hard I placed each step. So I started to sing louder, increasing my pace until I was almost running.

Reaching Manchester Road was like walking out of a dark room into sunlight. The smog had become dense and the rain had settled to a constant drizzle that gently found the few last dry spots on my body. I remember a being caught in the headlights of a car that was turning onto Manchester Road from a side street; the sudden dazzling light hitting my eyes meant that I couldn't see for several seconds when the car drove on. When my vision returned and I looked up and down the road all I could see was smog; even the streetlights struggled to make an impact. I remember standing still listening for any sound; but there was nothing. No cars, no people, even the cats had stopped their noise. I walked slowly, my senses heightened by my fear of the dark, until I reached a row of shops that were still open; the lights attracted me like a moth. One of the shops had closed and the recessed doorway was dry so I decided I would sleep there; there were people, noise, and light so it seemed the best option, the only option.

I watched a woman with two young children go into a shop a few doors away from where I was sitting huddled tightly against the cold, she was laughing with them. The children were dressed in warm clothing; they were happy, safe and loved. They were a family, they were happy, and they belonged to each other; while I belonged to no-one. My family no longer existed, if it ever had, in the true sense of a family. There was more love and commitment being shown by the woman and her children in that brief, fleeting moment than I had ever been shared by my own family. I started to cry, and then I started to get angry. When the small family came out of the shop, I had to fight a growing urge to run at them and destroy their happiness, I wanted to scream at the woman but didn't know what I wanted to scream. I just wanted to stop their happiness, their laughter their lovely life. I remember watching the woman holding her children close has they crossed the main road. The smog and drizzle hid what little traffic there was. I wanted a bus to hit them.

Slowly the shops closed and the traffic became even lighter; I found myself crying, feeling shame that I had wanted the woman and her children to die horribly. I didn't and I desperately regretted the horrible thoughts that had flooded my mind. I had buried my head into my folded arms and in my misery I hadn't noticed that I was totally alone; when, at last, I did raise my head, I realised I was totally and utterly alone.

All the traffic had stopped, all the shops had closed and all the lights had been turned off. The smog seemed to move, forming shapes has it drifted passed the streetlights. I started to sing again, almost at a whisper I started to sing "*The Sound of Silence*" I felt like I was praying.

The more I sang the words, the more I could hear the music in my mind, and the more I realised just how much they reflected how I felt. I tried to focus on the words, leaving out the ones that didn't seem to fit; I tried to think of anything that would allow me to mentally escape where I was. but it was useless, all the thoughts would, eventually turn to my father.

I dare not lift my head; I dare not look into the darkness of the night and see the smog and the shapes it formed. I knew that there were monsters hiding in darkness, perhaps even my father. I had pushed myself as far back has I could into the shop doorway, making myself as small as possible. I sat huddled in a tight ball; but the cold was still getting through and I couldn't stop myself shaking. I started to sing louder, the same words, the same song were muffled has I pushed my face into the small tatty jacket that I was wearing. I remember the stench that was ingrained in the rotting fabric; I remember it made me feel homesick. The stench of piss and filth gave me at least some comfort, but only for a short period, then the memories started.

Has memories came unbidden into my mind I started to cry again. None of the memories or images made me smile. I could see the tent in Sedbergh, I could see the loft my father had locked me in when I had toothache, I could feel my father's hands holding me face down, I could smell his breath and hear him grunt. I had to move, I had to run somewhere, anywhere, I had to stop the memories, the images. Has I slowly lifted my head and looked at the darkness, terror gripped me; the drizzle and the smog had combined into a terrifying soup of darkness. I could only just see the opposite side of Manchester Road. There was not a sound; my world was one of total silence. Then I was running, I remember my clothes sticking to me, my grubby trousers ripped has I ran down Manchester Road has fast has my legs could move. I was in full flight to nowhere.

A car passed slowly by and I looked at the driver has I ran past in the opposite direction. He was leaning forward staring into the dense smog and I remember the shocked look on his face has I flashed by; a few seconds later I heard a crashing sound has the car hit something. It was only then that I realised that I was running down the middle of the road. I must have gone there to avoid the shop doorways that hid the monsters that wanted to tear me limb from limb, or my drunken father.

I didn't stop running, I could not, I didn't stop sing, I dare not, when I stopped singing the silence returned.

I ran until I could run no more and I eventually came to a staggered stop, breathing deeply I stood with my hands on my knees afraid even to look up. I had idea how far I had run, only that I was still on Manchester Road. I stayed staring at the road for several minutes and it was only when I heard a vehicle approach that I forced my self to straighten up just enough to see the side of the road and get on to the pavement. I didn't want the driver to see me, in my mind I thought it could be my father; searching for me to beat me to death, but I also remember wanting it to him, come to save me.

It wasn't long before the cold, damp, night air reached my bones and I started to shiver. I was so cold that I began to ignore my fears and started to think about somewhere warm, I could think of nowhere so I started to walk down the middle of the road again, all I could see was the smog, illuminated by the street lights, and the only sound was me singing *The Sound Of Silence*. I was petrified.

I remember obtaining two bottles of very cold milk from somewhere. Hunger and thirst helped me ignore the pain in my teeth has I drank one too quickly. I tried to save one for later, but the bottle was too cold to carry and my gloveless hands couldn't grip the damp glass. I can't remember if it was anger or frustration that made me throw that bottle of milk, but I remember the vividly the shattering noise it made has it smashed into the road seconds after it had left my hand and disappeared into the smog. It was as if the night had exploded and I immediately went into panic mode. I started to run again, the sound of my pounding feet bouncing back of the houses was feeding my desperate urge to run. I remember the smog bound, damp night air tasted like dirt when it ran into my mouth has I gasped for air. I didn't know where I was running to, I just ran down the centre of the road, my senses were stretched and reacting to every sound or movement, imagined or real. I was crying has I ran, yet I was still singing that same tune . . . over and over '*The Sound Of Silence*'

I was staring at the road when I fell, I can't remember how I went down, whether I slipped or simply fell from exhaustion, I simply can't remember. I remember lying on the cold hard tarmac sobbing, I had cut my knee and scraped my hands but it wasn't the physical pain that caused me to cry, it was my utter despair. Only a few weeks, or was it months!, before, I had been a virtual prisoner in a children's home and I was almost broken emotionally by the psychological bullying of the staff and the physical bullying of my peers. But a young woman had saved me and shown me love when I thought there was none left in the world. I lay there sobbing, wanting '*my angel*' to save me again, I wanted Uncle John from the Cinderella home, to ruffle my hair and protect me. But there was no one, no one just to make things better, no one to hug and hold me. I stayed on the cold ground listening to a vehicle approach. I would stay there and let it squash me, let it run over my head and kill me. I had seen a cat try to escape from under a bus has it pulled away from the bus stop on Leeds Road, the cat didn't make it and it was crushed under the huge back wheel. The images of the cats brains and guts overrode any desire I had to be squashed so I got to my feet and stumbled to the side of the road. I watched has the vehicle drove slowly passed, its headlights causing the smog to glow and swirl making shapes again, but I was getting used to the monsters that the smog created, the only image that I didn't want to see was that of my father. every time his image started to form, I closed my eyes tight shut for several minutes until I was sure it had gone.

I had no idea of the time, the sound of the town hall clock had been muffled by the smog and my constant singing, but it was the middle of the night and the cold had really started to bite into me. I was hardened to the cold, my parents had seen to that, often we had woken in the winter to find the piss soaked bed covers covered in a thin layer of ice, but I was not prepared for the bitter cold that hurt me bones. Then I heard a low humming noise that sounded like another vehicle being driven slowly, but the noise was constant; then I realised what was making the noise, it was one of the many wool mills that seemed to be everywhere at the time. And I knew where I could get warm.

As my pounding feet carried me nearer to the mill the noise increased from a gentle hum to a loud roaring sound. I staggered to a halt, the warm air from the vent mixed with the cold night creating a dense swirling fog that I clung to my already soaking clothes. The noise from the vent drowned out even my singing and it was like walking into a darkened room the smog parted in front of me and closed around me like a blanket. I remember feeling warm, the vibration from the vent was strangely comforting and I remember feeling dizzy, light headed and struggling to stay awake. The warmth and the constant humming sound slowly sending me to sleep. Then a the whole world seemed to explode into light and noise when a large wagon suddenly turned the smog into swirling chaos as it turned into the factory gate that was only a few yards along the dark street.

I started to shake again as panic gripped me and terror ran through my body. I struggled to my feet, I felt sick with hunger and my head spun has I tried to make sense of it all. I started to run again, this time I knew where I was going, I was going to where what remained of my family were: I started to run towards the homeless shelter. *I remember screaming out loud that I would waken the fat cow up, I would drag her out of bed, I would tell them that she had lied, that she was an only child and didn't even have a fucking sister.* One way or another I was going to make sure my mother walked those streets with me.

The smog was still heavy and the drizzle still soaked everything it touched but I no longer cared, eventhe darkness no longer scared me shitless. I was filled with nothing but anger, and even though my soaking clothes chaffed at my skin and the smog and rain mixed with my tears and stung my eyes, I ran to the shelter as fast has I had ever run, my only thoughts were to get my mother out of there so she could share my misery. And I didn't care how I did it or the trouble I would cause her.

By the time I reached the hostel I was totally exhausted, both physically and mentally, I was drained. My head felt light and I remember leaning against the door and retching; the milk I had drank earlier came gushing out of my mouth and splashed down the big door, after a few seconds I started to kick the same door, my foot slipping on my own vomit. I kicked and kicked, the whole world seemed to echo with the sound of it; lights started to come on through out the building and I could hear footsteps thumping towards to door. I didn't care that people were shouting, I remember thinking it was comforting to hear voices, even angry ones, I didn't want to be alone any longer, I didn't care if they threw my mother and my siblings out of the hostel, I didn't care about the trouble I was causing. I just didn't want to be alone anymore.

The heavy door swung open, the light almost blinding me. I remember shouting, crying, that I wanted my mum. Then the whole world swam and I felt like I was floating and the last thing I remember was hitting the wet pavement.

The next thing I remember is a woman undressing me and washing me with a damp cloth. I could not resist and I don't think I even tried to, even though I was naked. The smell of the place was still overwhelming but I didn't care as kept falling in and out of sleep. I remember sitting on a low chair in a office eating jam and bread and drinking tea out a heavily scratched plastic mug, I remember there were teeth marks on the edge where someone had chewed the thing. It didn't bother me; I'd drink tea out of much worse. I had been given, and dressed in, a pair of heavy oversized pyjamas. They were blue stripped and stiff with starch, but they were warm and clean, and I remember that the people in the office were very kind, a young woman had put her arm around me and was stroking my head, but I couldn't stay awake and she held the plastic cup to my mouth for me, it made me feel like a baby, but I didn't care. I was warm, dry and safe and I fell into a deep sleep.

I remember waking the following morning wondering where I was, I wasn't scared, I felt safe, warm and dry . . . I hadn't pissed the bed! and I remember checking the sheets in disbelief. I looked around; I was in a small room that reminded me of the police station they took me to when my father had been arrested. It was painted in the same deep colours as the rest of the building but the smell was different, the smell was one of clean blankets and toast. Within minutes of waking up the door was opened and the woman that had cuddled me to sleep entered with a huge pot of tea in a plastic mug and a stack of heavily buttered toast. My mouth flooded with saliva has she placed them on the small table at the side of the bed, the tea was blistering hot, too hot to gulp down as I had intended to do, but the toast was wonderful, dripping in butter that ran down my chin has I gulped the warm toast down. There was no jam to put on the toast, just salt, and the woman told me to try a bit of salt on a slice, and I have put salt on my toast ever since. It was the best breakfast I had ever had, I was relaxed and the horrors of the night before had faded to the back of my mind, to remain there in my memories until later, when they would come back and haunt me. In that room, I was happy, warm and safe. Then my mother walked in.

She was oozing false with concern about her 'little boy' and kept trying to hug me, I just wanted to smack her in the mouth and didn't respond to her false tears of concern. I knew, the woman in the room with us knew, everyone knew it was all false. My mother was covering her arse and trying to be, in the eyes of the hostel workers, the loving mother concerned about her young son, but we all knew she was nothing of the sort.

The atmosphere changed dramatically when the bossy woman from the day before turned up. She was not amused with the situation and she wanted answers there and then. I remember her going on about me and what was I doing there, it was not allowed . . . blah blah. The other staff just looked away from her and got on with what they were doing. Then the woman turned her attention to my mother. I smiled when I saw my mother take a backward step when the woman took a step towards her; the woman did not break step has she took my mother firmly by the arm and walked her towards her office. I nearly laughed out loud when I saw the pleading look on her face

I can't remember how we came to be, with a great dollop of irony, living in an old shop on Manchester Road, but we did. Mother had be given a severe lecture by the boss of the hostel, but it had had little impact, as soon has we were out of the building she was up to her old tricks and showing with great pride the packet of cigarettes she had stolen from the office desk. I knew they probably belonged to the woman that had cuddled me and held me close, I had seen her smoking, I wanted to snatch them of my mother and return them, but I just shook my head in disgust. Someone from the council had given my mother the keys to the old shop, it was supposed to be an emergency arrangement to keep 7 kids off the street, the place was an absolute shithole, even though I was used to rundown, derelict homes, this one really was the worst by some margin. It was riddled with mice, the walls were wet with damp, the roof had more tiles missing or loose than in place; then, to complete the effect, we dragged all the old, soaking stinking furniture that had been thrown out of Hampton Place by the bailiffs the day before. It was to be our home for about six months.

The building had no bathroom only a battered outside toilet that was plastered in other people shit, electricity on the ground floor only, it had been turned off to the upper two floors due to the danger of the rain hitting the electric lights, the only good thing about the place was that nearly all the other buildings in the row were empty and provided wood for the fire and scrap metal to weigh in at the local scrap yard. For the first few depressing days we kept the fire going, burning old tables, chairs, floorboards, in fact anything that would burn. We also found a couple of gas meters that hadn't been emptied. We were so busy I don't think I noticed how filthy I had become. Having no bath was just the reason mother needed to totally ignore our hygiene, I don't think I washed from one week to the next, and it was only when Steve's mother virtually threw me into the bath one day and I felt disgust has I watched the filth cling to the edge of the bath and the sludge that Steve's mum had to swill away when she dragged me out again. I vowed then to get some kind of wash every day.

I can't remember going to school while we lived at Manchester Road, I was still a pupil at Fairfax Grammar yet I cannot remember attending whilst I lived there, I seemed to spend most of my time pulling out lead piping from the empty houses or taking lead off the roofs. In time I got used to the old

Just Once, When I was little

shop and in many ways I began to enjoy my new-found freedom. Perhaps too much, I was beginning to run wild and had started to vent my aggression by fighting; I would fight anyone that wanted a scrap. I was never a bully though; I detested bullying and would often intervene on the side of a lad being bullied. And, anyway, it gave me another reason to have a fight.

Robbing the lead off the roofs was stupid for a more than one reason, the missing lead allowed the rain to pour through the holes that were appearing all along the roof tops, and there was the constant danger of over confidence that could lead to falling off the roof. And one day I almost did just that.

Steve didn't need to steal, he was an honest lad nurtured by excellent parents that both worked hard to keep their son feed, clothed and out of trouble. I don't suppose I was the kind of lad Steve's mum or dad would have chosen has their son's best mate. But the never once said anything, they showed me only kindness and warmth; however I doubt they would have forgiven me if I had killed us both, and I very nearly did.

The old shop on Manchester Road had three floors to the front and, due to the cellar, four floors at the rear. From the attic we used to climb out, nick the lead and then climb back in again, it was so high from the back garden that I only ever looked down once, and that was more than enough for me, it was a terrifying drop to the rubble covered ground below. To fall would mean certain death; but that didn't deter any of us, until the day I climbed out of the attic skylight and went out on to the roof even though it had been raining. I had reached a chimney about four houses down, I had slipped a couple of times and that had made me carefully nervous. Steve had climbed out after me and was almost with me when I pulled a good sized lump of lead away from the chimney. Holding it boastfully up above my head to show Steve the thing slipped out of my hands. Instinctively I reached to grab it; the sudden weight of it has I caught it almost pulled me to my feet. I felt my feet start to loose grip. I felt Steve's hand grab my clothes. I felt us both start to slip forward.

I threw the lead to one side and spun my body reaching for the chimney has I did so. I grabbed the crumbling bricks just hard enough and for long enough for us to grab the apex of the roof. It took Steve and I forever to get back to the skylight. And we never once even stuck our heads out of the thing again.

When we were back safely inside the attic we both laughed and acted as if it meant little. But we both knew we had been lucky; it had happened so fast, just a few seconds, but even today I don't like looking up at buildings, the memory of the near fall is one that can make me shiver almost has much has memories of my father.

Manchester Road, in many ways, was a major contributor during my formative years. I adjusted to a life without my father's sexual brutality and relied not at all on my mother, who seemed to be quite happy collecting new boyfriends and spending their money. Steve and I became inseparable, we would often meet in the morning and hang out all day until well in to the night. Steve and his parents helped me to realise that some people were good, that there were nice homes and nice parents. Just by being themselves they had shown me what a family could and should be like.

Something strange happened to Steve while we lived at the old shop; he allowed a lad to beat him up and didn't even fight him back; Steve took punch after punch and didn't even cry out. The lad was nothing special, a couple of years older than me, but not a '*hard man*' by any stretch of the imagination and I'd seen Steve fight bigger and harder lads even when he knew he would come off worse. Steve didn't back down; but that day he did.

The lad was called Mick, I had seen him about and I think he had been a boyfriend to one of my sisters. But he wasn't a mate, I didn't like him for some reason and I would have battered him if Steve had just said the word, but he didn't. Mick had followed Steve and I in to the old shop. Steve watched Mick walk in behind us while I asked him what he wanted. Steve just said that it was between Mick and himself and that I had to keep out of it. I remember being baffled because Steve looked worried and Mick was smiling and it took several dark looks at me from Steve to stop me jumping on Mick when Mick pushed Steve into a chair and started to punch him in the face. It didn't take long for blood to appear on Steve's face and his eyes started to swell. I just kept yelling "what the fuck is going on?" but Steve kept telling me to keep out of it, he looked as if he would thump me if I went for Mick.

After several long agonising minutes Steve, at long last, raised his hand and looked at Mick. I thought for a moment that Steve was going to fight back, but he just shook his head and Mick backed off and, without saying a word, walked out of the shop. I asked Steve what the fuck had just happened, but he would refuse to talk about it and, even though it caused many arguments, he never did tell me why he allowed that piece of crap to lay into him like that. It was the only time Steve had not fought back; we had countless scraps after that day and not once did he show the slightest reluctance to return blows.

Somehow I acquired a brown medium sized dog; I don't remember how or when the mongrel came into my life, but we became firm friends. Prince was every young lads dream for a pet, he seemed to read my moods better even than Steve and never left my side; he even slept on my bed keeping the rats and mice away. And he liked a good scrap. Prince was an influence of a different kind to me, he would wake when I did, he would eat when I did and he would sleep when I did. He became a constant companion that didn't ask questions when I sulked, when I cried, even when I woke from my constant nightmares, screaming or kicking out, Prince was there at my side. Just by being there Prince had a calming effect on me, we would often wander off and sit in the park watching the world drift by. The mongrel made me feel safe; all he wanted was food, water, a safe place to sleep and love. Bit like me really. In many ways, life was ok. I had food, a bit of money from the lead that we now only took from inside the derelict houses, and I had my mates. Then my mother fucked it all up again; and I ended up locked up for three weeks when she persuaded me to take the blame, again, for a crime she had committed.

Mother hadn't stopped her thieving, if it wasn't nailed down and guarded by police with guns, she would nick it. She would sneak into offices or shops and steal what ever she could; often my sister and younger brother were reluctant partners in her crimes. One day the police came to our humble home and turned it over looking for stolen goods. I remember watching them grimace has they looked under piss soaked blankets or looked through the piles of rubbish strewn about the house. I couldn't help but laugh when one of the burly officers nearly fell over when several mice ran out from under an old mattress, but I laughed once too often and one of the coppers slapped me on the back of my head. It didn't stop me laughing, I couldn't; the sight of Bradford's finest jumping at the slightest movement was just too much. I stopped only when they looked under some clothes near mother's bed and found a radio. If they had not been so scared of the vermin and looked a bit harder they would have found a lot more of mother's stash. But they were happy they had found something and promptly frog marched me down the stairs. It wasn't my radio, it wasn't my mother's either, well not legally anyway. She had stolen it a few days earlier but it wouldn't work and should have been dumped, but mother's intelligence was never her strong point, so I, along with two of my siblings and our mother, were taken to the local nick to be interviewed. We had all been loaded into a big black van and it was during the short trip to the nick that she begged me to take the blame for her crime, telling me that the family, including me, would be taken into care. I knew that she was right of course, there would be no option for the authorities other than placing us all 'in a place of safety' she assured me I would get probation or a fine, or even just a slapped wrist. It wasn't her false tears that persuaded me, it was the thought of being sent to a children's home that forced me to agree. So I was arrested when I told the police I had nicked the radio and was given bail and told I would be going to court in a few weeks time. When I got home later and told Steve, he nearly slapped me, calling me every name he could muster. I remember him screaming at me that '*she*' had done it again, and I remember thinking that my best mate was right.

    Setting off for court the morning of my appearance, I felt sure that it was not going to be a good day. Even though my mother had assured that I would only get a fine and that she would pay it; I still had a gut feeling that I wouldn't be coming home that day, I remember giving Prince a hug before I got on the bus, leaving him sulking has the bus pulled away, he hated being parted from me but I knew he wouldn't chase the bus, he had been told to go home and I knew he would do has he was told. I think the only reason I didn't start to cry was that my mother was sat at my side; and I would never cry in front of her, I had cried out to her when my father was beating me, abusing me, and she had done nothing then and I knew she would do nothing now. So I held back my tears, turning the feeling of sadness into anger; and I remember the feeling of disgust I felt towards my mother has she lit a cigarette and started to bite her grubby nails. Sitting so close to her on the leather seat, I could smell my mother. She was filthy and reeked of old sweat and filth; I was going to court, she was supposed to speak up for me, and I knew I would not be coming home that night.

Because I had pleaded guilty my appearance in court should have been a short affair, I should have received a fine or probation or even a suspended sentence. Instead I was sent to a remand centre for three weeks for pre-sentencing reports to be made. Suddenly a burly bloke in a uniform came and took me firmly by my arm. I wanted to kick out, I wanted to run, I wanted my mum to stop what was happening. But I knew she wouldn't, I even started to tell the magistrate the truth, but the bloke holding me just pulled me away. I looked back at my mother with desperation in my eyes, but she just looked at the floor and started to bite her nails again.

Later that day, after several hours in a holding cell below the court, I was driven to Tong Park Remand home situated about 20 miles from Bradford on the far side of Keighley. As I was being bounced around in the back of the prison van, all I could think of was the children's home that had proven to be a living nightmare. The children's home was supposed to be a place of protection, Tong Park was for bad lads so I'd worked out that it was going to be far worse, and it was initially, yet it turned out to be far different and in many ways was, probably, the best place I could have been sent to. But I wasn't to know that as I sat in the back of the van on my way to the place; the urge to cry was immense, but I didn't, there was no one to cry to. I was alone again. My family, friends and my dog would be getting on with their lives while, to pay for my mother's crime and keep the family together, would spend, at least, the next three weeks in prison.

When the van pulled up outside Tong Park strangely my first impression wasn't one of fear it was one of admiration. The old building looked wonderful in the autumn evening and even when I was walking, escorted, the short distance fro the van to the large front door; I couldn't stop looking at the elegant leaded windows and tall imposing walls. I remember feeling nervous but not scared and as I entered the building I was struck by the wonderful dark wood that seemed to be everywhere. There was a heavy smell of polish that competed with the smell of food. I could hear plates and cutlery being used and suddenly I felt very hungry and wondered if they would feed me; all I'd had to eat and drink that day was a dry sandwich and a cup of lukewarm tea while I waited for the prison van to bring me to Tong Park and I my mouth salivated at the thought of eating.

No one spoke to me as I stood at the bottom of a long, winding staircase. I had been told to stand on a mat and wait, they didn't tell who, what, why or for how long I had to wait there. But I knew I didn't have an option so I stood exactly where I had been placed and waited in silence fascinated by my new surroundings with my hands behind my back. I had waited no more than 10 minutes when a big bloke came out of a downstairs office and motioned for me to go with him. He set off walking towards another office further down a corridor so I set off walking towards him. My heart jumped when the man suddenly bellowed at me to run. His voice seemed to bounce off all the walls and for several seconds all other noise in the building stopped. The noise of the cutlery and plates ceased and time seemed to freeze and I hesitated for a second but quickly responded when the man bellowed even louder "*NOW BOY*" with a burst of speed that bordered on running I made my way towards him, catching up with him in a matter of seconds. He then gave me my first indicator of what life would be like during my time there when he shouted at the top of his voice that I was to run the every time I was told to be or go anywhere.

I also received a hefty wallop for not answering quickly enough and not calling him sir; which I was supposed to do every time I was spoken to or spoke to any of the staff. I suddenly felt very homesick.

I was taken to the 'head mans' office and I was told to stand to attention in front of his desk and to keep my gob shut. I did exactly as I was told. I knew instinctively that I would never win a battle with any of the staff at Tong Park. So I stood in silence has the man behind the desk told me the simple rules of Tong Park. *Do has I was told. Do it quickly. And never ever answer back.*

Standing in front of '*the boss*' with my hands behind my back, reminded me of the children's home; yet even though the two blokes in front of me seemed huge, and should have felt more threatening, I found that I could handle what they were saying. It somehow didn't seem personal to me, I was realised that I was simply being given the same talking to as all the other waifs and strays that I had yet to meet

After my short, sharp talking to I was marched to the dining hall to get something to eat. I remember feeling relieved that the noise of the cutlery had stopped and the dining hall was, or so I thought, empty. It was far from empty; when my escort opened the door, it seemed that hundreds of eyes were suddenly focussed on me. I couldn't stop myself from stopping in my tracks; it was as if I had walked into a wall. There were no plates on the tables, and nothing to distract eyes to anywhere else but me. I felt like running, but the firm hand on my shoulder gripped even tighter and I knew I could do nothing. The lads in the room were to be my peers for 21 days and nights, and they looked anything but welcoming.

I was made to sit, squeezed, in the middle of two lads about my age and a plate of sandwiches was brought to me by another of my peers. I had suddenly lost my appetite, but the man that had escorted me stood over me and told me to eat, so reluctantly, I did. After a few minutes the man left the dining room and this was the signal for all eyes to turn back to me. I felt like crawling under the table, I hated being the centre of attention and the lads sitting either side of me must have taken my nervousness to be fear so they started nudging me, testing me to see if I could stand up for myself. They quickly found out that I could, I had been bullied far worse and I simply opened both my arms and knocked them both off their seats. The sudden crash brought my escort rushing back into the dining room. He looked at the two lads, and then looked at me. I tried to look the picture of innocence but it didn't work, all three of us were told to go to the bottom of the stairs. The two lads involved with me told me with their faces that being sent to '*the bottom of the stairs*' was a punishment and not a good thing. Maybe to those two, and the other lads, it was, but I thought it was great. Before we reached the stairs we were handed a cloth and a tin of polish and told we had two hours of punishment and to get on with it. I had no idea what 'it' was so I just followed what the lads were doing and took the cloth and wax from the man.

Our 'punishment' was a well established 'attitude adjuster' and involved waxing and polishing the huge staircase from top to bottom, spending, at least, two hours making the old, dark wood shine. I had to stop a smile spreading across my face; only that morning I had been miserable, I had felt homesick and alone, I had been 'sent down' for three weeks, and now I was stood in front of a huge staircase trying not to smile. It was not a punishment for me; I would have polished that beautiful, elegant staircase for nothing and for no other reason than I wanted to. I almost ran to the first step.

The two lads with me must have thought I had fallen and banged my head; they had no idea that not only did I want to polish the seemingly endless wooden staircase, but it was helping me adjust to my new surroundings. We spoke in whispers as we polished and I found I liked the two lads. They told me who to avoid, what the rules really were and the type of things they did at Tong Park. The nudging at the dinner table was just to test me and see if I was 'hard or soft' and their way an introduction to the place; they were telling me about the pecking order that established who was 'top dog' and who the 'bitches' were. They assured me that I would be meeting the *top dog* soon; telling me he was a bully and I should watch my back. I didn't have long to wait.

Just Once, When I was little

When the two hour punishment came to an end, I didn't want to stop. I didn't polish the winding staircase, I caressed it. I loved the smell of the wax and the feel of the wood and by the time I handed back the polishing rag and wax, I felt relaxed. The place was spotlessly clean and, other than the initial dressing down by the head man and the bit of bother at the dinner table, I felt the maybe my stay there wouldn't be too bad. And it wasn't; by the time I left Tong Park I had learned a lot about myself. But I had to meet the head by first and pass some kind of test, but looking back at the long, winding staircase, I didn't give a shit.

The first night in Tong Park was not unpleasant. For supper I had a large mug of hot milky cocoa and a lump of fresh baked bread smothered in butter and jam. Even though I received a couple of wallops to the back of my head from the burly staff for not responding fast enough to an order or not saying 'sir' when spoken to, I still found being in that wonderful old building fascinating. The dormitory slept about 8 lads and was spotless. I had been given a bed near a window that overlooked the wonderful countryside and, after I had received another wallop for looking out of the window for too long, I was handed my bedding and told to make my bed up, I didn't have a clue. The beds were in two neat rows and so neatly made the dorm looked more like a hospital ward, there wasn't a crease to be seen on any of the beds. I was told that my bed MUST be as neat as the others and I was shown, only once, how to make my bed and fold the clothes I had been issued just before I had had a bath. It took me some time to make my bed the first night and it was only after one of the other lads had shown me how to tuck the sheets in that I achieved it to a standard that the staff member grudgingly approved. I didn't sleep much that night; I was still a bit homesick and missed Steve and Prince. I remember sitting on the edge of my bed and looking over the darkness of the fields towards some houses that were on the other side of those fields. There were lights shining in many of the windows and I remember wondering about the families that lived in the houses. Were they watching television? Were they sitting in front of a warm fire? Was there a mother hugging her children? Was there a dad reading to his children before they fell asleep? I felt sad; but not too sad, and I was about to go to the toilet when a voice whispered that I should get into bed and pretend to be asleep as the night staff would be checking soon and if I wasn't in bed then I would be in deep shit. Within a few minutes I heard the muffled footsteps of someone walking along the landing. Doors being opened and closed quietly; I quickly climbed under the blankets, just seconds before the dormitory door was opened. After a few seconds, the door closed and all was quiet again. I could hear the footsteps descend the freshly polished staircase. Then I must have fallen asleep because the next thing I remember is being shaken awake by the lad from the bed next to mine; and the first thing I noticed when I had finally opened my eyes proper was that I hadn't pissed the bed. I was so surprised that I felt the full length of the bed, looking for the wet patch, but there wasn't one. I had fallen asleep without going to the toilet and I hadn't pissed the bed; and I felt proud of myself, for the first time for a long time, I felt pride.

The mornings in Tong Park were little short of organised chaos, all the dorms emptied at once and all the lads tried to get to the bathroom at the same time. The result was a long queue of lads standing with their legs crossed waiting to use one of the many toilets. It was in that queue that I met first met the 'Top Dog'. He was a big lad with the first signs of a beard growth and about 2 years older than me, he was hard faced and a bully. All the lads moved out of his way and even the staff seemed to allow him to push his way to the font of the queue and didn't interrupt or stop him when he 'accidentally' bumped into me. I wasn't sure what to do. It wasn't fear that stopped me responding by punching him in his mouth; I just didn't know what punishment I would receive if I did. The staff seemed to take little notice and so I just fell back against the landing wall and did nothing, holding my temper and overcoming the urge to fight back. I later found out that this was a mistake, the lad had taken my reluctance has a sign of cowardice and the other lads thought the same and, in their eyes, I was the bottom of the pecking order.

Tong Park's purpose was not just punishing the lads there; it was also to instil discipline of a different kind. Over the following weeks I was forced to think for my self when facing a problem. The staff would set us tasks that needed more than childish enthusiasm. We built small sheds without instruction; the shed, when built, had to withstand being drenched by a hosepipe while being shaken by two burly members of staff. We would have to work as a team to dig holes, climb over fences, and serve meals. We were also encouraged to stand up for ourselves and avoid being bullied; this part of the lessons came has a bit of a shock and a big relief when the '*Top Dog*' decided, after only two days, to turn his attention to me.

I had not been ignored as such but every time *Top Dog* was present then the other lads made it clear that I wasn't part of the gang yet, I was, after all, on the bottom of the pecking order. That all changed when we were playing football.

I had only been in Tong Park a couple of days and, though I was still a bit homesick, I had settled down and was learning all about Tong Park and its few rules and I was glad when I found out we would be playing football. I desperately wanted to be out in the open fields and run until my lungs stretched.

The bullying started when I was in the changing room. I was putting on the shorts I had been given when I suddenly felt an arm around my throat pulling me backwards. It was *Top Dog*. He pulled me towards the door and then let go of my throat; he started to push me; almost bouncing me off the door, but I didn't react even though I could feel anger building inside me. I didn't want to miss playing football and I knew that, no matter who started the fight, I would be punished.

The door suddenly burst open sending me crashing into the bully. It was a member of the staff. He was a big bloke and easily pushed the door wide open; pushing the bully and me over the damp tiled floor and into a tangled heap with ease. I just lay there waiting for the man to explode and start to dole out the punishment I expected. But he did nothing more than look at me, shaking his head slightly has he did so. I was baffled by this and it took a few seconds for me to respond when he told me and the bully to get off the floor; so the man simply grabbed my arm and hoisted me clear off the floor, I felt like I was flying.

The next memory is of being on the football field. The countryside was wonderful, the smell of autumn filled the air and I was playing football; or at least trying to. The bully was doing his best to flatten me, and he was having some success. He was older and bigger than me and he knew what he was doing. Almost every time I got the ball, and a few times when it was no where near me, he lunged into me. I had a small cut to my head, my legs were scraped and bruised and I was covered in mud. I remember wondering why the staff didn't intervene and put a stop to it; but they didn't do anything, they just stood there, and the man that had hauled me off the changing room floor just kept looking at me, almost staring, and shaking his head slowly. Then 'top dog' really came in hard. My whole body seemed to change direction; I flew through the air and skidded to a halt, sliding through the mud. My left leg had several long deep scratch marks running from my knee to my ankle, the pain seared through me and I felt the anger that I had managed to control thus far, flare up. For the first time I retaliated. Jumping to me feet I ignored the pain in my leg and wiped the blood from my head wound, spreading it across my face. I remember screaming at the bully and charging towards him; then I stopped when I saw the staff all staring at me. I thought I was in trouble; I felt it was unfair; I'd taken all the crap from the bully, I'd allowed him to humiliate me, and now I was to be punished. The man that had pulled me of the floor in the changing room and had stood staring at me was now walking straight at me, he looked furious and I stood waiting for the inevitable slap, he had worked out that I enjoyed waxing the stairs so I knew my punishment would be something I would not like. The bully backed away smiling; I stared at him, all I wanted to do was punch his face in, then I felt the powerful hand of the staff member pulling me away.

The man walked, half dragged me, over to the edge of the field; I was fully expecting to be punished, however, as we reached the edge of the field, his suddenly let me go and turned me to face him. "*How much crap are you going to take . . . don't think we will step in . . . you need to sort this . . . now*" He spoke quietly but firmly, my head spun. Was he saying I should fight back? Was he telling me it was ok? Then he uttered the few words that would guarantee a response "If *you don't fight back, they'll think your soft . . . a coward . . .*" I didn't give him chance to finish what he was saying; I pushed him away, not caring about any punishment. My mind had suddenly filled with the voice of my father. "*I'm not a fucking coward . . . I'm not . . .*" *I* walked away before the tears that filled my eyes had a chance to start running down my face. I remember the rage that flooded my whole body; it was anger that was making the tears, not fear, and, as I ran back onto the pitch, I had only one thought. No more bullying; whatever the cost.

I was only back on the field a matter of seconds when I saw '*Top Dog*' start running towards me; he was running with a triumphant smile on his face. My head seemed to explode and, has the bully got about 15 feet away, I ran at him. The confusion on his face has I ran at him replaced his sick grin; he seemed to slow down, I didn't. I slammed into him taking him off his feet. He was bigger and older; but I didn't give a crap. He was a lot smaller than my father, he certainly couldn't hurt me like my father did, and I wasn't scared of him. I was in a place where I knew no fear. We hit the muddy ground together all the time I was punching his face, he couldn't do anything to stop me; he tried to curl into a ball to protect himself. But I just kept screaming at him, screaming that I was not a coward. I think every punch I landed on 'Top Dog' was aimed at my father's face.

In a matter of seconds, that seemed like minutes, 'Top Dog' was shouting for me to stop; it was only then that the staff stepped in and dragged me off the lad. My head was still spinning and anger still filled my whole body; but the all the staff at Tong Park were all big blokes so even though I kicked and screamed at them to let me go and carried on kicking, they had little problem in controlling me. I didn't care what the staff did to me; everyone now knew that I wasn't a coward, and I had flattened, with some ease, the lad that was supposed to be my nemesis. But I was shocked when the only words spoken by any of the staff were "*about time . . .*"

Brian Mynott

Has I limped away from the crowd that had gathered around the prone figure of the bully, the man that had been staring at me, walked over to me telling me to stand still. I was still expecting to be punished and held my breath, wondering what was going to happen next. My temper was still flaring but under control and I stopped as ordered as if I had hit a brick wall. But the man started to talk to me about bullying. I told him, sharply, that I was *not* a bully and, after smacking me on the back of my head for not including 'sir' in my response, he told me he knew that I wasn't, and neither is he now, he said has he pointed to the lad being helped to his feet. We stood and talked for what seemed an age. He knew about my father, he knew much about my life outside Tong Park. I began to feel comfortable talking to the man; he reminded me of Uncle John, the wonderful giant of a man that looked after me at *The Cinderella Home* in Morecambe. I asked him why none of the lads knew any of the staff's names and why we had to call them 'sir' every time we spoke. Its just the rules, he said, it helps discipline and avoids familiarity with the inmates. It was the first time I had been called an in mate and the man's words suddenly made me realise the reality of where I was. I spoke to the man about my life, even telling him how I ended up at tong Park, how I had taken the blame for my mother, because I was stupid and because I didn't want to return to the children's home. I remember crying, not heavy sobs just tears that felt warm when they ran down my cheeks. Amazingly the man ruffled my hair, and I could tell that he believed me and, as we turned back towards the others he stopped me and looked straight at me and spoke to me; the words he uttered, in a quiet voice, helped me to accept where I was and understand what the staff there were trying to achieve *"you're here youngster, it don't matter why or how, so lets just see if we can make life a bit better for you for when you leave eh!"* strangely, I didn't want to think about leaving.

Much changed that day. But it wasn't until I started to queue for my tea after the match when all the lads moved out of my way, allowing me to go straight to the front, that it dawned on me that I was now '*Top Dog*' I remember thinking that I was too small to hold such a lofty position in the pecking order and feeling confused at what I was supposed to do. But I needn't have worried, all the lads, even the now ex '*top dog*', simply accepted things had changed; I found out later that evening that I had certain responsibilities that came with the status I had acquired. This included controlling bullying between the inmates; it wasn't hard for me to enforce this part of my new responsibilities. I detested bullying then as I do now, but I also had to ensure that new inmates understood the ways of the remand home, I found this part difficult because it made me appear to be a bully myself, but I understood the reasons for this and found this understanding allowed me to act the part of being a bully of sorts. But I don't think I made the best bully come mentor Tong Park had ever had, though I doubt I was the worst either.

Life pretty much ran smooth for most of my time at Tong Park, there were a few incidents that I recall, some fondly and some not so nice. One of the 'nice' memories is of Bonfire Night. It was November 5th and the staff had clubbed together and bought a decent sized box of fireworks and all the lads had been on their best behaviour, watched closely by me, to ensure that we could watch the display after tea. Standing outside that wonderful building, the smell of autumn filling the air, was magical. The fireworks, though pathetic by today's standards, lit up the faces of the people standing around. Nearly all the lads there were from similar backgrounds to myself and, like me, found a kind of security in the discipline of the place, and watching their faces light up with each firework, made me realise that we were all little more than children. All the staff and inmates stood watching the fireworks, and I remember looking out over the fields and seeing bonfires blazing away, I imagined the people that were standing around watching their own bonfire night displays, and for once, I wasn't riddled with jealousy. Tong Park was a disciplined place, you could get a quick smack for even a minor offence or you could end up polishing wood until your arms ached because you didn't say 'sir' when the staff spoke to you. But the place also offered a kind of security that many of the lads there, including me, and never known. I never once felt bullied during my time there and admit to receiving punishment simply because I wanted to polish the stairs! I was feeling settled for the first time in years, the clean bedding, the constant washing, the food, the fresh, smog free air and the friends I made, and the fact that I didn't piss the bed once during my stay there, helped me to smile again, I felt freedom in my imprisonment.

I was into my second week and enjoying the windy, crisp, and cold but sunny morning. I was clearing the long driveway of fallen leaves, I was looking into the deep blue sky watching birds struggle against the wind, the same wind that kept blowing the leaves back to where I had just swept them from, it didn't bother me, I could have stood there all day sweeping the leaves and didn't care how many of them escaped from the pile. I didn't have a care in the world, but it was Saturday, visiting day, and, for the first time since I arrived at Tong Park, I felt like running away. My mother had turned up to visit me, and as I watched her walk towards the main door, I remember saying aloud *"what the fuck does she want"*

Within a few minutes I was summoned to go to the visitors' room, I didn't want to go, I didn't want to see her, I didn't want to smell her, I wanted to stay away from my mother and the life she represented.

The reunion was a sickly affair, and I knew that the hugs and kisses she smothered me with were false. She wanted something; I just didn't know what that something was.

The only time any of the lads were allowed to smoke was during visits and the room soon filled with the smell of cigarette smoke as the lads, some little more than children, including myself, smoked one cigarette after another. My mother had brought two packs of twenty Park Drive and I smoked until I felt sick, all the time she watched me, each time our eyes met she gave me a sickly smile. I remember wanting to scream at her to get it over with and tell me what she wanted. She had to catch at least three buses to get from Bradford to Tong Park, she had bought two packets of cigarettes and some chocolate, what ever my mother wanted must have been very important: to her at least.

As the time for the visits to end, mother started to twitch and I could tell that she was trying to say something, something that she didn't want to say but knew she must. Then, with only a few minutes of visiting time remaining, she dropped her bombshell. She, my wonderful mother, wanted me to take the blame for yet another of her crimes.

I nearly picked up the chair I was sat on and belted her with it as she tried to persuade me that it would not count; if I added it on to my other crime, she pleaded, it would be '*taken into consideration*' and I would only get a bigger fine . . . a fine that she would pay. I really wanted to hit her with the chair. I didn't agree and just stood up sharply, knocking the chair over as I did so.

It took me a few days to recover from my mother's visit; all the old feelings and memories had come flooding back to me. Was she so stupid, was she really so uncaring about her son, her children? I knew the answer. My mother thought only of herself.

My mother's unexpected and unwelcome visit, and the reason she had come, had left me in a foul mood and many of the lads stayed out of my way. I was looking for a fight and they all knew it and it was only after I had grabbed a lad by his throat for no real reason, and the staff member that had spoke to me after the fight on the football pitch, the man that understood me, grabbed me and pulled me to one side, that I stopped. The man stared into my face, reminding me that he didn't like bullies; he reminded me, also, that I had told him that I *wasn't* a bully. Suddenly the anger turned to sadness and I started to cry; so the man stood between me and the rest of the lads that were stood nearby so they couldn't see my tears. He knew about my mother, he knew the problems I had in dealing with my mixed up emotions. I told him she hadn't *come to see me* I told him what she had come for. He ruffled my hair and took me inside, away from the prying eyes of my peers.

I was as mixed up and angry has the day I had arrived. I was angry, sad, I both hated and loved my mother with equal passion and it was confusing me to the point of madness. I know realise I just wanted a mum, a mum that loved me like

Steve's mum loved him. But I didn't understand then; I was little more than a child. The man sat opposite me and listened, never once did he stop me swearing, never once did he even try to stop me talking. And I told him everything, what my father had done, my time in the children's, the hunger, the night I walked up and down Manchester Road and the terror I felt as I did so. I cant remember how long we sat in his office, but it must have been a long time because the bell sounded to tell everyone that dinner was being served. As we stood to leave, I still felt sad, but different and I smiled as I said "thank you sir" he smiled back at me and, ruffling my hair again, said *"Bill . . . my names Bill . . . if you tell anyone you'll spend the rest of your time here polishing every bit of wood in the place"* he saw me smile *"now come on . . . lets get some food eh!".* He ruffled my hair again. And I felt the sadness and anger lift.

As it drew nearer to my court date, it became obvious that I would not be coming back to Tong Park after the hearing. Bill, as I know knew him, had dropped enough hints, though I don't know if he thought that it would make me happy, or if he was preparing me for my return to my previous life. I think now that it was the latter. I remember not wanting to leave Tong Park and its disciplined regime, and even then I found it ironic that I would miss a prison; and that, in essence, is what Tong Park was, a prison, and yet I hated even the memory of my time at the children's home; a supposed place of safety.

Though I didn't once use Bill's name during my stay at Tong Park, the fact that he had told me made me feel special, which was really an alien feeling to me, and it made my last few days there both sad and happy. I'm sure that Bill told a few of the lads his name, and I'm sure the lads he told felt the same feeling that I had done, but it doesn't in any way dilute the value of that simple but hugely influential act. Tong Park did not have the same impact on many of the inmates. Some even bragged about what they had done ion the past and what they intended to do when they were released. Many of the inmates found the discipline too much and spent hours crying every night, though they were generally ignored, sometimes other, hardened lads, would scream at them to shut the fuck up, calling them girls names or a 'puff'. Unless I felt it was going to go too far, I stayed out of it, Bill had shown me what I already knew, that bullying was a terrible thing to endure. But he also *taught* me that dealing with it on your own, was not always a bad thing.

On the day of appearance in Bradford Juvenile Court, I woke early. It was autumn and the dawn seemed to take forever to bring light to the world and I sat on my bed, my dry bed, and looked across the fields towards the road that ran between Skipton and Bradford. The street lights glowed brightly and didn't have the smog hanging around them that the lights of Bradford did. The air was clean and fresh and I remember having a desperate urge to walk through the fields: even in the dark. I remember having a desperate desire to be free and walk through the park with my best mate Steve; and an equally strong desire to stay where I was. In Tong Park, I felt safe. I had friends and felt that, in many ways, I belonged there; but being free included going home, back to a life of chaos and filth.

Eventually the dawn arrived and Tong Park started to come alive. I could hear the kitchen staff preparing breakfast and the smell of toast started to filter through the building. I remember thinking that my next morning I would waken in the mice riddled damp, filthy surroundings of my home in Bradford. And things would smell very different.

When it got to 7am the whole of Tong Park burst into life as the dormitory lights were turned on by the staff. The lights were bright and, with help of the bellowing staff, the inmates struggled out of nice warm beds shielding their eyes, it was the same every morning. Except Sundays, then it happened at 8am.

I didn't dress in the usual uniform that all the inmates wore, I couldn't, the clothes had been taken off me the previous night and I had been told I would get my own clothes in the morning. When my own clothes were handed back to me, I shuddered. Even though they had been washed, my clothes still held a faint smell of home; and it wasn't a pleasant smell, and I knew that when I sat at the breakfast table, those sat near me would also smell it, they would smell me.

Bill wasn't working the day I left Tong Park. He should have been, but he wasn't, and though I knew is name I wouldn't use it and ask where he was, so I never found out why he was not at work and I regret that I didn't get chance to thank him. But, today, looking back, Bill must have known the good he did for me and I think that was all he needed, though I don't think he would have realised the influence he would have on me many years later. As the car taking me to court pulled away from I couldn't take my gaze away from the wonderful old building. I had arrived there only three weeks before; I was scared, homesick and utterly sick of my life; when I left I had changed. Meeting Bill had had a profound affect on me, our long talks: well, Bill listening and me doing all the talking would be a better description, had been the first time I had really spoken to anyone so deep. I felt calm and in control and I didn't fear the future so much. My nightmares were less frequent and less terrifying. And I hadn't pissed the bed even once. Though I remember thinking it would all mean nothing when I got returned home; nothing would have changed there, and the slight smell reminded me of my real life.

I watched Tong Park for as long has I could; and I felt genuine sadness when I could see the old building no more.

As predicted I received two years probation. My appearance in court only lasted about 10 minutes; my mother was there, and the smell of my home on Manchester Road was much stronger. I should have been happy, I should have run out of court laughing, feeling free. But I didn't, I remember waiting for the bus feeling subdued. Nothing had changed; I could smell the smog that lingered with the autumn mist. It was a cold day and standing at the bus with my mother I felt a cold blast of air cut through my paper thin trousers, I looked up and down the road, it all seemed so bleak and muggy. I was cold, miserable and hungry; it was the first time I had felt like that for three weeks. I remember staring at my mother; she was biting her grubby nails, and I knew she was still upset that I hadn't taken the blame for another of her crimes, because she didn't even offer me a cigarette. I couldn't stop looking at her, she was my mother by blood only and I think it was standing at that bus stop that I began to realise that I desperately wanted a '*mum*' a mum that would protect and cuddle me. and it must have hurt then, as it does today, to realise that the woman that was my mother, would never be the mum that I so desperately needed.

The bus arrived and my mum took me upstairs so she could carry on smoking; the evening was turning to night and the bleakness of Bradford started to suffocate me. I looked through the dirty bus window. There were no fields, no clean air, just soot blackened houses and damp streets. I remember thinking about Tong Park trying to remember what they would all be doing. I remembered the fireworks. And I wanted nothing more than to go back to prison.

Prince went crazy when he saw me getting off the bus, my sister told me that he'd hardly moved for three weeks and kept watching people get off the bus, but even that wonderful reunion couldn't stop me almost retching when I walked though the door, back to my previous life; the place stank of filth. My three weeks in Tong Park, and the wonderful smell of polish and toast, had made my nose sensitive to the smell of the house again. I felt ashamed of my own home; of my life.

I was great meeting up with Steve later that evening; the big lump squeezed me so hard when we met that I nearly fainted. We walked the streets doing nothing but talk. Prince was, of course, with us and life felt a bit better. We walked and talked for hours and it was very late when I returned home. I was knackered. The early mornings at Tong Park had knocked my biological clock out of sync; but going to bed that night was awful. The smell, the noise of the countless rodents scurrying about the bedroom, the filthy blankets, the damp walls; before I had gone to Tong Park, that house, that bedroom, were my normality and I was used to my life, didn't like it, but I was used to it; now I just felt disgust. It took me some time to drift off to sleep; Prince was in his usual place at the bottom of my bed keeping the mice off the bed with an occasional growl, his presence also helping me to feel safe and keeping the nightmares at bay. When I awoke the next morning there was no smell of toast, no fields to look at, and I had pissed the bed.

My life soon returned to 'normal' and within a few days I had got used to the smells and the rodents. Mother went to court for the crime for which she wanted me to take the blame, the courts must have realised, probably with the help of the local council, that if she was 'sent down' then there was the problem of what to do with her seven children; so she was given probation. I cannot recall what the crime was, at the time I wasn't bothered, but the relief that mother had not been sent to prison was immense. Not because I was glad for her, I really didn't care, the relief was there only because of my fear of a return to a children's home. I was, in many ways, settled living in a derelict shop on Manchester Road; its amazing what a child can become used to; however, as was normal in my life, the family was on the move again.

The old shop had eventually become unliveable. This was as much due to the actions of my family speeding things up, we had 'recovered' just about every ounce of lead and copper from the buildings and the rain now poured through the roofs, even the mice had started to find it hard to keep dry. So, with more than a bit of regret on my part, the family moved homes again. Fortunately our new home was only a mile or so away so I didn't have to start making new friends or fight the local lads.

Havelock Street was, by the standard I was used to, ok. It was a typical back-to-back house with, like Hampton Place, a passage leading to the houses to the rear. The house was neat, tidy and clean and the previous occupants must have, to my young mind, been quite well off. There was no bathroom and the only toilet was to the rear but the house itself was decorated and rodent free. Just a few hundred yards away from the house there were open fields that you could access via what was locally known as '*The Cat Steps*' and I would spend many hours in those fields; sometimes messing about with my siblings and mates, but mostly just sitting doing nothing but think. At the top of the *Cat Steps* was a small pig farm, the strong smell of the place making the area reek, especially on warm days; but I didn't mind, it made me feel as if I was really living in the countryside. At the side of the pig farm there was a small garage that repaired cars and vans. The garage was to become another important part of my life; allowing me to begin to mature, to *grow up*. Within a few weeks of moving to Havelock Street I had pestered Geoff, the garage owner, to let me sweep the garage floors and wash the cars. I was, by now, the ripe old age of 14 and going through a delayed puberty and working with Geoff helped me to cope with the strange changes that were happening to both my mind and my body. All my mates had pubic hair; some even had started to grow their first feeble attempts at a beard whilst I was as smooth as the day I was born. I now know that this was because I had spent most of my life in a state of hunger and stress and this had delayed things for me; however I didn't know that back then, I thought that there was something wrong with me and it knocked my confidence for a while. Every day I would search for any sign of a pubic hair. After several weeks, when I felt confident in Geoff, I ask him how old he had been when he first grew a beard. Geoff knew immediately what I really wanted to know "*you mean when did my balls drop and grow hairs down there . . . and when will yours*" I started to stutter that I didn't meant that; but he just laughed and said he was about 15 when he grew '*pubes*' but I knew he was telling a white lie, he had a full beard and hairy arms, but I knew he meant no harm and was trying to reassure me.

I have always had a great attachment to music throughout my life and one day I was cleaning a customer's car after Geoff had serviced it when I first heard a record that would remain a favourite of mine to this day. "*All In The Game*" by *The Four Tops* was being played regularly on the radio. I found the tune wonderful and happy and, after hearing it only a few times, I knew every word and used to sing along. Even when I hear the song today, some 40 years on, I smile and think about the *Cat* Steps and Geoff's garage.

Working for Geoff gave me my own money, it wasn't much, but it was mine, I'd earned it honestly and it drove my mother nuts that I wouldn't give her any of it. I wouldn't give anyone any of it; it meant more than just money to me, and I would hold on to it and was quite miserly, only spending it when I was desperate.

Life was going ok, I had my own little job, the countryside, my mates and, eventually, my first pubic hair. I remember looking down one morning and seeing a few little dark hairs just starting to grow, I almost screamed out loud, but realised my siblings would soon realise why I had screamed. For a few months I was quite happy, then mother screwed everything up again, however this time I don't think I recovered for many years.

It all started when mother decided to write begging letters to celebrities, telling them how destitute her poor family were, how her children had suffered at the hands of their abusive father, providing graphic details of his crimes. She would tell the celebrities that we were destitute and desperate and needed money. When I found out I nearly thumped my mother; I couldn't understand how she could tell strangers about my being raped. How she could tell them about her daughters being abused? I went crazy for a few days, fighting any lad that fancied a scrap, and some that didn't. I was starting to calm down, putting it down to my mother's ignorance and stupidity. But then I found a letter that turned my world on its head and my head explode with anger and confusion. The letter was from my father and, as I read the letter, it was obvious that she had been writing to him. Though my mother had watched when my father beat her children; and though my mother had lied to the police telling them that I was *always falling down stairs* or that I was *always fighting with my brother* giving a reason for every bruise or cut my father inflicted on me or my siblings, the letter hurt me far more. I remember crying, screaming out loud as I read the words of my father *"forgive me . . . I've had help . . . it was great to hear from you . . . don't deserve you . . ."* I ripped the letter into a hundred pieces and started to smash things. I remember smashing a small table and picking up one of the legs that I had broken off. I am sure that had my mother walked through the door at that moment, I would have beaten her with it. I threw the leg at a mirror; it didn't smash so I tried again and failed again. So I screamed obscenities at the useless piece of wood and threw it against the wall, the wood bounced off the wall with some force and just missed my head before it hit the front door with a loud bang.

I slammed the door shut behind me. I wanted, needed, to fight. So I went looking for one.

It didn't take long to find what I was looking for. At the end of the street a group of lads were messing about. They had seen me and I knew that if I carried on walking towards them then at least one of them would say or do something to challenge me. I was still the 'new boy' of the area but, due to my working in the garage and the pig farm, I had hardly set foot beyond the end of Havelock Street, so I had yet been 'tested' by the locals. Well, they would now have their chance. I was alone, smaller than most of the gang; I was, in their eyes, easy pickings. But they had no idea just how wrong they were.

As soon as I was near enough to hear their insults and warnings, they started. The usual '*what you looking at . . . what you doing here . . . fuck off back to your pig farm . . .*" I didn't even slow my stride and punched the first one full in the face. Then it all went blank. I remember nothing until it was all over and lads were running away from the maniac. I had blood on my clothes and I was shaking, my fists were grazed and bleeding; and they were running away, and I remember screaming at them to come back I wasn't finished, I needed to fight until *my pain* had gone. So, with tears of anger streaming down my face, I started to chase the small gang along Great Horton Road towards Queensbury. I was almost begging them to come back and fight; but they carried on running, and I stopped. I couldn't go on; but it wasn't because I was exhausted. I just couldn't go on. My head was full of the words contained in my father's letter and I felt empty. I remember sitting down though I don't remember where and I remember sobbing. It was as if my father had returned home and I felt bitterly let down, not just by my mother, I felt let down by the whole world. Then I felt the hair on my head being moved and instinctively swung a fist thinking someone was touching me. I heard a yelp and realised quickly that it was Prince. That set me off sobbing even deeper. I hugged him, crying as I said I was sorry over and over again, but Prince didn't care and within seconds was licking my face thinking he had done something wrong; the next thing I remember is walking towards the Cat Steps with Prince. We almost ran down the steps to the fields, I wanted to be alone with my dog and make sense of my confused world but Steve was there, and I think it was the only time that wasn't pleased to see my best mate.

Though I didn't want to see Steve I started talking to him. He knew I was hurting and gently kept asking me what was wrong until I finally let go of my anger and started to cry again. I remember talking quietly between sobs, telling my best mate what my mother had done. Steve didn't really respond, he just sat and listened. And it wasn't until I had finished talking and stopped crying that Steve spoke. Then he only spoke one word. Bitch.

Later that day I returned home to face my mother and confront her. Even though I had calmed down a lot there was still enough anger in me, helping me scream at my mother. I screamed abuse at her, telling her, at last, just what I thought of her. It came out in a great wave of emotion. How she covered and lied for my father and how she sat there and did nothing while he beat and abused her children. I remember repeating the words of the letter, over and over again. Asking why?

I screamed abuse, I smashed things, I cried in anger. And, when I had run out of swear words and my anger lessened, my mother did nothing; it was as if I had not spoken a word.

We lived in Havelock Street for several months, longer than most other houses we had lived in and, other than my mother's constant boyfriends and the school truant officer; we were left very much alone. I spent much of my time working in Geoff's garage, on the pig farm or in the fields at the bottom of the Cat Steps. It was taking me less time to recover from my mother's antics and I took little notice of what she was getting up to. We seldom sat down to meals together as a family, in fact we seldom had a meal at all and we still fended for ourselves most of the time. Most of the money I earned at the garage was spent on food and clothes. My sisters would also contribute and it was they that really ran our house; with little or no support from my mother. My older brother had been looked after by nana since father's arrest and so had escaped the horrors of the children's home and the terror of walking alone, at night, up and down smog bound Manchester Road in the middle of autumn; he had remained in the background since the day of father's arrest and, as such, did little to help his younger siblings. Our aunts and uncles had also moved out of our lives on the same day as our father, leaving seven children to fend for themselves. With no discipline or guidance, slowly, we were becoming feral. School became a very low priority and there was no structure to our days. Often I would stay out all night without anyone even noticing I wasn't there. I was constantly fighting and had built up a reputation. Steve and I had gathered a small but tough group of mates and we were slowly evolving into a gang. We were a motley group of leather jacketed lads. Studded belts and steal-toe capped boots was our uniform and we stood by each other what ever trouble we got our selves into. And we seemed to attract trouble daily.

Havelock Street was where I, biologically, matured. Puberty crept up on me and I remember the morning I noticed my first pubic hairs. It was as if I had discovered a diamond. It meant so much to me; I was at last going to be like all my mates. No longer called 'baldy balls' behind my back; however, with the onset of puberty I developed strange urges that I didn't understand and muscles that grew where I didn't know I had them. I was now a young man.

No longer being a 'boy' impacted on me in many ways. I not only started to behave differently but I was also felt somehow different and was slowly becoming aware of sex and what it was. In the late 1960's children made up their own theories of what sex was. If you held a girls hand too long then you made a baby was just one of many such theories. To me however, the realisation of what sex *really was;* was disastrous. I started to realise just what my father had *really been doing to me*. And my nightmares became deeper, darker suffocating.

I think it was about that time that I started to block out my childhood. Not just the horrors of it; but the good times, but fighting memories is a terrible personal battle and one doomed to failure from the start. The only thing my battle achieved was to increase the anger and confusion that was, now, ever present. In trying to forget the cruelty and privation of my childhood, I also buried all memories of Uncle John at the Cinderella, my 'Angel' at the children's home, in fact any memory from my childhood, good or bad, was met with the same resistance. Because each memory, even if initially a nice one, would result in memories of my father and make me shake with feelings of disgust, guilt, despair and fear. My only escape was fighting. And I had to fight almost every day; not just to inflict pain and release the terrible pressure I felt in my head, but also to receive the physical pain that took away the anger and self hatred I felt. But whether I received pain or gave it, the release was only temporary; even though sometimes the relief lasted only moments. Because of the powerful emotions that were dominating my life I struggle to recall much of my time at Havelock Street after I discovered the letters between my parents. Reading *that* letter from my father to my mother had opened up a wound, or started a fresh one, that wasn't healing. In fact it was acting as a channel for the rest of the shit that made up my life and I spent most of my days, and nights, in a kind of haze, as if I was somehow detached from the rest of the world. In many ways my time at Havelock Street and the events, and realisations, that occurred while I lived there, shaped the next decade or so of my life. I cannot remember why we moved from Havelock Street, though it was probably the same reason as all the other times, not paying the rent, but one day I was informed that we were moving to a council house on Canterbury Estate. I cannot remember leaving Havelock Street. I don't remember saying goodbye to Geoff and his garage or the *Cat Steps*; in fact I don't remember the day we moved from Havelock Street to Tamar Street on Canterbury. But I remember the shit my mates and I kicked up when we started establish ourselves there.

Canterbury Estate was, and remains, one of the toughest council estates in Yorkshire; and it was, probably, the last place I needed to be. I was angry with the world, searching for the violence I needed to keep the emotional agony and nightmares at bay and, though Canterbury Estate may have been the last place I *needed* to be; I certainly wanted to be there.

I cannot begin to recall all the fights my gang and I were involved in during those first few weeks. Every day and night saw us fighting with the local gang; but never once did we even try and avoid a confrontation, in fact we went out of our way to make sure we 'accidentally' bumped into them. The fights weren't vicious, they were more 'hit and run' affairs and eventually the locals gang realised that I now lived on their estate and I wasn't going anywhere. They also realised that we would stand our ground and fight; and that it would far better all round if we stopped kicking the crap out of each other and joined forces so instead of fighting one night we started to talk instead. There was the usual pecking order to establish but that didn't take long and was resolved with only a few scraps between the new friends. There was never any doubt who would lead the gang, there was only Steve that could have challenged me but he had always accepted that I could think on my feet and had got us out of a hundred scrapes. And there was also never any doubt who would be my second, though Steve and I were only fourteen years old, we were quite formidable and no one questioned or challenged Steve's position. In many ways, I had built a new family. A family made up of teenage thugs barely out of childhood, almost all from broken homes, almost all had lived lives of violence and privation, and almost all had their own nightmares to live with.

We were 'Bikers' or 'Greasers' and out uniform was leather jackets, studded belts and steel-toe-cap boots. Many of us had motorbikes, thundering old BSA Bantam's or Triumph Tiger Cubs that, by today's standard, were slow ponderous machines, but back then the machines were the business and when we rode together the noise the machines created filled me with pride. Our collective enemy was the 'Mods' and we would spend many hours chasing after them. They rode scooters that made a noise that did not carry the same threat as our bikes, they attached mirrors to almost every bit of their machines and, with their fur trimmed parka, we thought them a joke, but some of them could scrap and, on the few occasions we caught them, we would find ourselves in a real set-to and have to battle our way out. But we didn't care, we would fight, get battered and bruised, heal and then get at it again. Surrounded by violence and being part of a gang it was inevitable that girls would soon become an issue. Of course I had boasted of doing all sorts of things with dozens of girls, but every time a girl tried to get close to me or started to flirt, I would make some excuse or other. I tried to work out what was wrong, I couldn't understand why girls scared me; and then one night I was introduced to the wonders of marijuana.

I had tried sniffing glue for a while, but I didn't like it, it gave me nothing but an headache so I had soon packed it in. I had heard of marijuana, it was all the rage in the 60s, and I had often caught the smell of it when the gang were together. The first time I tried I thought my brain had opened up. I remember I laughed at anything, I remember Prince running round my legs wondering what was happening, I remember a girl of about 18 flirting with me, I remember her kissing me, I remember getting into bed with her, I remember having wonderful, fantastic sex, I remember having sex over and over again that night. And I remember crying like a baby afterwards.

The following day was filled with images of the previous night and the feeling of the girl's nakedness. I realised that day that in wasn't scared of girls, I was scared of sex. That day I had sex again with another girl, a clumsy affair but I felt almost addicted to sex and really didn't care whether the girl had enjoyed it or that it was clumsy and took place in the toilets in the park. I simply wanted sex and I didn't care whose girlfriend I had sex with. The only dark part of the following day was when on of my mates had slapped me on the back and told me he had started to think I was a 'puff'; he had no idea the button he had pressed, and he was totally off guard when I slammed my forehead into his face. I had suddenly exploded as the memory of Sedbergh flashed unbidden into my mind. As I looked down at the lad, I wanted to kill him, but Steve grabbed my arms and spun me around and dragged me away. He knew I was about to start crying.

Later that day I went for a walk in the local park to rid myself of the anger that still raged through my body. I was alone except for Prince. Prince always judged my mood right and walked at

Just Once, When I was little

my side as if he'd been told off; when I sat on a bench he placed his head on my knee, his sad eyes seemed to see my pain. I sat and cried for a while, struggling to force the memories that a few words had brought flooding back. I remember standing and starting to run. I remember singing as I ran but I can't recall what the song was. I remember running around and around the park until my lungs hurt. Then calmness returned, but it was an uneasy calmness that didn't rid me of the feeling of anger. I remember saying to my self that I would prove that I wasn't a 'puff' that I would have sex with as many girls as I could. With that I set off walking back to Tamar Street.

That night I had sex again and the next night and the next night; every night, and sometimes during the day, I had sex. So it came as no surprise when I eventually pissed someone off that wasn't part of my gang. The lads in the gang had a very liberal attitude to sex and didn't seem to care that I was screwing their girlfriends. But when I had sex with two sisters; their brother was not happy at all, and it set me up for my very first 'pub fight' and send my emerging reputation through the roof.

Although I was still only 15, I looked at least 3 years older and had no real problem getting into pubs and even though I had found out that the girls brother was going to 'rip me to bits' 'kill me' and piss in my skull, and that he went into the pub that Steve and I were about to go in to, I didn't give a crap. In fact I was more than ready to go up a league, fighting lads my own age had become boring and very few that knew me or my reputation would stand and fight. So the thought of fighting a 19 year old both scared me and attracted me in equal measures. I was more than ready. I had no idea how big the 'man' was, some of my mates had said he was huge, at least 6 foot tall and 'hard as nails' but as I entered the pub I didn't care. Perhaps I was looking for the pain so longed for; perhaps I was hoping for it.

Steve was nervous when we walked in and I could see the relief on his face when he saw that the pub was nearly empty with no sign of my new found enemy. I had left Prince at home, I knew that if I went down he would have stood his ground to protect me, but I didn't want protecting. I wanted the fight. I desperately wanted the fight.

I knew that lad had walked in, Steve's expression gave it away, and in an instance every muscle in my body tensed, I had to fight the urge to turn and look at the man I knew I would soon be fighting. I had to fight the urge to run at him. I looked at the table, messing with the half empty pint glass trying to give the impression that I was calm. Suddenly the ashtray seemed to jump as the man slammed his fists on the table Steve and I were sitting at. The sudden noise startled me and I couldn't help but jump. He saw me jump and saw it as a weakness. He was screaming abuse and kept leaning towards me has he announced to the world what he was going to do to me. He would teach me to shag his sisters and brag about it. I wouldn't be walking out of the pub. I remember feeling a strange calmness, I wasn't scared but I knew that it was only a matter of seconds before he thumped me, but I wasn't angry and simply sat there waiting for the fight to start. Then the man said the words, though he meant them only as an insult, would ignite my fury that, even though he was much older and bigger than me, would be the downfall of both him and his reputation. He kept screaming at me to look at him, I knew he wanted me to lift my head up so he could smash his fist into my face; he called me a bastard, a piece of shit. *Then he called me a coward*. My feet urgently searched for something to press against that would give me the leverage I needed to do what I was about to do. I sensed that he had stood back so I looked up just long enough to see his face. He looked into my eyes and saw the hatred in them and I knew that he would lean back towards me, as he did so I looked back at the table. I felt his face about a 12 inch from the top of my head. He called me a coward again. The face of my father appeared in my mind. I launched myself with all my might, the top of my head slammed into his face. I felt his teeth scrape my scalp. I heard him collapse on the floor. I remember standing over him. I remember seeing the blood ooze from his nose and mouth. I remember spitting on him. I was 15, little more than a kid, and I had just beaten a man with a reputation; a reputation that I had taken from him; and now had to live with.

The size of the gang was increasing and, with the motorbikes available, we decided to form a proper biker gang. It took a few days to decide on the name of the gang, we didn't want to piss of the 'real' bikers such as the *Satan Slaves* or *Hells Angels*, both of which had gangs in Bradford, nor did we want to join them, though the reality was that we were still too young and not in their league. After a few discussions we decided on '*The Demon Kings*' and within days we had our own 'colours' which were cropped Levi jackets that had had their sleeves removed making a waistcoat with our name on the back surrounding a image of a skull. It seemed to change the dynamics of our gang; it seemed to change almost overnight. We no longer bothered with the kids and our fights were now far more vicious as we fought 'Pakis' 'Skins' 'Mods' for their 'turf'. We had been barred from all the local pubs and had to suddenly descend on pubs outside our area. This would often cause a fight when we suddenly walked into another gang's 'house' and told them to get the fuck out.

My time with the gang and the denial of my past and estranged me from my family, I only went home to give my wounds time to heal or to change my clothes or to have sex with a girl I had picked up. I was running wild but free, I was enjoying my status and reputation: and the violence. And then I met my first love.

If ever there was a wrong time in my life to meet my 'first love' it was during that period of my life. My emotions were bi-polar to say the least and I was riddled with abandonment and attachment issues and, other than a very few people and my dog, I trusted no one. But I couldn't help falling for the girl I will call Rose. Stunningly cute with long flowing deep black hair and a smile that would make vinegar taste sweet, I was smitten from the moment I set eyes on her. I couldn't make sense of my feelings at first. I had several girlfriends on the go at the time and none effected me like Rose did. So much so that I found I couldn't talk to her and I would blush when she was anywhere near me and, if she hadn't one day suddenly kissed me, I don't think I would have ever had the bottle to ask her out. But we became an item and it really was a magical period of my life. But the initial magic lasted only a few weeks; riddled with self-doubt and terrified of forming relationships of any kind, I started to test Rose almost from day one. I remember being unable to sleep and listening to Motown love songs. But I was convinced that Rose would dump me; that she would, like everyone else, simply abandon me. Even though I had affair after affair and she was still there, I couldn't shake off the deep fear that one day Rose simply would not be there. So I kept testing her, even sleeping with her best friend.

Rose brought a few weeks of calmness to my chaos and, in return, I gave her many months of heartache. I tested Rose until she had had enough. I remember thinking to myself when she told me it was over that I was right. That I knew she wouldn't stay. I remember shouting at her calling her names, insulting her. I was too young and too hurt to realise that what I had done. Rose had given everything she had to help me; but my fears and anxieties blinded me to everyone except myself. And, in a surge of new, misplaced anger, I went from fight to fight, girl to girl. My moods would go from sullen to violent in seconds, I became unpredictable, uncontrollable. Even Steve had problems calming my temper or lifting my mood. Prince was the only living thing I truly trusted and the little calmness I occasionally felt was when he was with me, he would simply sit with his head on my knee and listen. Never interrupting, never telling me how '*he saw things*' he didn't tell me to calm down, cheer up. Prince just accepted my moods.

Loosing Rose had an immense impact on me and, for a while, I blamed her for everything. Somehow I managed to blame Rose for all the crimes and shit I had lived through, and then I converted the anger into violence and began to lose all control. I seemed to be fighting every day and night, if I wasn't fighting other lads, I was fighting my nightmares. I was fifteen years old and still pissing the bed. Nightmares that were so powerful kept me from sleep. If I got drunk, which was often, I tended to become over emotional and would often, in my battle to keep images of my father from my head, stub cigarettes into the palm of my hands and start to scream with the emotional release the pain gave me. I was so lost in my world that I lost all sense of time or purpose. So much so that I only knew it was Christmas Day when someone told me; it hurt in a very different way, a kind of sadness overwhelmed me. I took Prince and walked towards the park noticing, now, that families were out walking, children were playing on the bikes while their parents looked on. Christmas had never meant the same to my family as it did to other families. To me it Christmas was full of fear as my father was almost permanently drunk; and I remember watching the 'happy families' with a deep sense of jealousy. The happiness I say in their faces simply reminded me of my own Christmas days and the misery that somehow seemed more intense by the happiness of others.

I have omitted many times more of my life than I have written; if I wrote about every fight and sexual encounter this book would be almost endless. I have written only about people and places that I feel influenced my life, both good and bad, and there was a police officer that put the brakes on me. I needed the brakes applying. I was running wild with no concern about anyone or anything. It started when I returned home with Steve and found the front door had been forced. There was no one at home and it was obvious that some one had burgled us; and I remember laughing at the stupidity of it, we had nothing at all for anyone to steal. Then I heard Prince whimpering. We couldn't make out where he was at first but I found him trapped in what was supposed to be the larder. My head exploded with rage when I saw my best friend struggle to stand; he had been hit hard on the top of his head and blood seeped out of the nasty gash that ran from his left ear to above his eye. I screamed that I would kill some one and started to smash the door only stopping when I realised Prince was cowering; he must have thought he had done something wrong, for the first time in a long time the tears I cried were for a reason other than myself.

I sent screamed at Steve to get on his BSA and get as many of the gang together as he could. I remember washing Prince's wound and tearing a sheet up to use as a bandage. I was crying all the time. Someone was going to pay and I had a good idea who that person was and I knew where he and his mates would be.

Steve returned after about half an hour with four or five of the gang and, within an hour there were about 15 of us. They all loved Prince, he was the gang's mascot and a friend to them all and they all wanted vengeance. We knew that no one on the estate would dare even think about robbing the house, but we knew a gang of villains that lived on Little Horton Lane about a mile from Tamar Street, we knew that they had been caught robbing off the estate. And we knew where they would be.

We knew that the small gang of thieves would be in or around a café in Foster Square near the train station. It was where they sold the stuff they had nicked and was a base for their shoplifting expeditions; we didn't bother where we parked our bikes, the fact that we blocked off half of Kirkgate, we just wanted to get at the person that had nearly killed Prince. The door of the café nearly came off its hinges when Steve put his full weight behind his boot and kicked it open and we saw straight away the lads that we were looking for. Tables and people were sent flying has we charged across the café floor. The gang tried to make a run for it but it there was no way out for them and, within seconds, they were being battered to the floor. The café owner, or manager, tried to stop the attack, but he soon stopped trying when one of the lads threatened to batter him with a chair. The lad we knew to be their leader was dragged across the floor and kicked every inch of the way. I wanted him outside where I could really vent my anger on him. Steve was trying to calm me; he knew I was ready to go too far, all the collective anger that had built up since Rose dumped me, was ready to be let loose. I often wonder if I would have beaten that lad to death. I know that I wasn't thinking; I know I wanted to beat the lad to death. But would I have done it? I will never know and I have a police sergeant to thank for that.

As I dragged the screaming piece of shit outside the café I was already punching him full in the face. I could not stop. Each punch was full of hatred and anger. Each punch slammed into his face that was rapidly turning to pulp. I let him fall to the ground and was about to start in earnest and beat him until my anger faded when a young copper came running up to me screaming at me to stop. I felt his hands start to pull me away. I turned my anger on that copper and stood and faced him; telling him to fuck off and keep his nose out of my business. Then I pushed him and he fell. And the next thing I remember is floating through the air and feeling powerful hands spin me around. It was a much older, bigger copper with 3 stripes on his arms; and he threw me about as if I was a rag doll. Then I was in the back of a van having my ribs bent by him.

"*You little bastard . . . . threaten one of my lads . . . I'll wring your fucking neck . . .*" I was bounced around the back of the van and it is one of the very few times in my life that I felt genuine fear. Other than a fear of my father, fear was alien to me, or so I thought. Blow after blow battered my ribs cage until I struggled for breath, I could feel fear growing and I admit that there was a point that I almost begged for the copper to stop *almost.* Suddenly the van stopped and the sergeant stopped thumping me. With one last final, and painful, wallop he let me go. When the van doors swung open I dare not move. Looming in front of me were the huge heavy gates of Bradford town hall; and the thought of being taken inside those gates terrified me; but the sergeant had a different idea. Picking me up by my collar he stared into my eyes "*if I hear, see or even think that you have threatened one of my lads again . . . you'll not see life outside again for fucking years and I will make you life hell . . . now get out of my fucking van*" I believed every word he said and, as I crashed on the pavement outside the van, I vowed never to threaten a copper ever again. Whether that sergeant was simply being an arse or whether he knew what he was doing, but either way he stopped me from doing something stupid. The mood I was in I may have caused the lad that had hit Prince serious harm, or even killed him. I may have hit that young copper and ended up in jail. But instead of being arrested and locked up, I was given a good kicking, a kicking that not only did I deserve but one that probably altered the path I was on.

It took several days before I could breathe without pain, but I suffered the pain without complaint. Some of the lads wanted to get some revenge on the cops, but I wouldn't allow it, as far as I was concerned the big sergeant had done me a favour. The lads that had broken into Tamar Street went into hiding and we saw very little of them and, the few times that we did, they ran like rabbits as soon as they saw us.

Though I was still hurting following Rose dumping me I soon settled back into the routine of fighting and chasing girls. My nightmares had lessened, but only because I slept little and when I did, it was often during the day when people were around. The gang were no longer satisfied to stay on the estate and we would often just cruise around Howarth Moor or Shipley Glen. Whenever we went to Howarth I would always go to the small church at the top of the village and sit and think about the Bronte family; especially Charlotte. Only Steve knew I had read Jane Eyre, but he didn't know I had read it twice. I somehow related to both the book and its author. Sitting in the church I could almost see Charlotte walking through the doors with her family, and in my mind, she always looked sad.

It was a strange, confusing period of my life. I was in a constant battle with my emotions; trying desperately to deny any part of my childhood. It was a battle that I often lost and my moods would change dramatically from one day to the next. One day, or night, I could be full of rage, hatred and anger looking for trouble wherever I could find it. Then the next day I could be sat on my BSA alone, over looking fields and meadows admiring the beauty of it. I would sit and stare at the sky at night wondering what it all meant; and I would think about all the people throughout history that had at looked at those same stars and thought the same. I would also often visit Bolling Hall Museum; a wonderful old building just a few hundred yards from Fairfax Grammar, the school I can't remember leaving. When I walked through the rooms of the people that had lived there hundreds of years before; in my mind I could see them, I could see them going about their daily lives, and I would, for a short time, join them in their world. But other times I would hide from the world, thinking about my live both as it was and how it had been. I saw no escape from either. I tried to look to the future but I only saw misery, and I felt trapped by who I was.

Just Once, When I was little

But with more than a touch of irony to it, I was to find peace of mind working on a farm in North Yorkshire.

Taking the blame for my mother's crime had landed me in Tong Park. My time there had helped me to understand parts of my self that I was struggling to come to terms with. I had been given probation as part of my sentence and had, more or less, kept my appointments but had had a few encounters with the police and my probation officer realised that it was only a matter of time before I would end up back in court and I would almost certainly end up in Borstal and he offered to set up a work placement me on a dairy farm in Pick Hill. At first I refused to leave my mates and my lifestyle. But eventually I began to like the idea of living and working in the countryside so, to the utter astonishment of Steve and the rest of my mates, I decided to leave Canterbury Estate and milk cows.

The farm was everything I dreamt a farm should be. The farmer's wife was a stocky young woman that seemed to live only to feed the men of the farm and her husband was a typical farmer. The farmer was so calm about life that I often wondered how he could manage the large dairy farm and all the other animals. During my time on the farm I learned to drive a tractor, milk a cow, dig post-holes and erect fences and I learned to shovel tons of shit! The river Swale runs through the land and I would spend hours sitting on the bank just enjoying the peace and quiet while enjoying the beauty of my surroundings. But best of all was the horse I got to ride. l can't remember the name of the medium sized horse but I remember it didn't take me long to learn to ride it and rounding the cows up for milking was paradise. Even though the cows would return to the milking shed simply by calling out 'Cush Cush' I still rode the horse round the fields as if I was John Wayne. I had my own bedroom and clean, sweet smelling sheets. I had regular meals. I had the freedom, after work, to do what I wanted. I was happy and could, at last, see a future. Then mother fucked it up.

My mother had been absent from my life, even more so after the letters I found that had been sent between my father and her, but it should have come as no surprise when she screwed my life up once more.

A few months before I went to work on the farm mother had started a relationship with a man called Bob; she had met him in Wakefield when she was on a night out in the town. He was an idiot, a bully and a lazy scrounging lump of a man that I avoided. My younger brothers were not so lucky. During a visit home for the weekend, it was obvious that my three younger brothers were being bullied by him, of course mother; true to form did nothing to stop it. Bob wasn't the sexual predator that my father was, nor was he as violent, but he was a bully and a loud mouth and I knew I had to return and put a stop to Bob's antics, my siblings had been through enough and though it hurt a lot to leave the farm, I made the decision to return to Canterbury.

From day one I was in Bob's face and the bullying soon stopped and a kind of normality returned to the house. I was soon back with my mates and soon back with the girls. But I carried in the back of my mind that I had found freedom on the farm and, thanks to my mother, had had to leave it and return to a life I so desperately wanted to leave behind.

Within weeks of my return I was back to my usual bi-polar mood swings. Bob always stayed out of my way when I was in a bad mood. I'd told him only once that if he hit one of my siblings again then I would put a shovel through his skull. He knew that, while I may have exaggerated a bit, I would cause him serious damage and so he kept his fists to himself. Then it was my turn to screw my life up by doing something that, to this day, I feel disgust with my self for doing. I slept with Steve's girlfriend.

I don't know why I didn't stop myself doing something that I knew as I did it, I would regret for the rest of my life, and I didn't even fancy Steve's bird; to me, it was nothing special, the girl meant nothing to me. But I broke Steve's heart; and Steve the worst thing possible when he did nothing to me. I told Steve what had happened the following day; I was sure he would batter me and I had made a promise to my self that I would not fight back. I was riddled with guilt and shame. My best mate just walked away from me and I'm sure that he was crying. Although Steve came back that evening, things had changed; I tried to say sorry, I tried to explain. But he just said it was done

Just Once, When I was little

with and wouldn't talk about it; later that night Steve and I got into a fight, not with each other but we took on a small gang of Asians that had started to hang out too close to Canterbury. No other members of the gang were with us; they had kept out of the way of Steve and I, they knew that we were both ready to batter someone. And we did, we laid into the Asians as if they had caused the silent rift that now existed between me and my best mate. I don't think neither of us was, in our minds, fighting anyone else but each other. I had never seen Steve so angry, he was taking blow after blow and ignored them, he just punched and kicked, he scratched and head butted anyone near him; and I matched his anger.

At the end of the fight, the gang of Asians ran off, some of them had to be helped by their mates. Steve and I stood gasping for breath; we both had cuts and bruises; our fists showed the usual signs of heavy fighting, my boxing skills had come in useful and Steve had found a new weapon when he used his forehead to break noses. We would fight many more times together, we would laugh and joke together, and he would still be at my side when I needed him. But things were never the same again. I had betrayed my best mates trust and I had ripped his heart apart, for nothing more than a quick, meaningless half hour of sex with a girl I didn't even fancy.

A few nights after the fight with the Asians I decided to go for a long ride on my bike. I didn't have much petrol so I took a length of hose and *borrowed* fuel from cars as I went. It was summertime and I rode around Skipton and into the Dales and I was enjoying the freedom of the open road, the smell of the countryside. I felt as if I could ride to the end of the world. Then I saw a sign for Sedbergh.

I pulled over into a lay-by and turned the engine off, the silence was sudden and my body still felt the vibration created by the old BSA. I kept looking at the sign; I tried not to, but I failed. I remember looking along the road wondering if it was the same road the old battered van had driven along as my father took his young family to a holiday from hell. It felt so long ago yet so recent; my mind began to flood with images and smells. I started to cry, I was a 'Greaser' a hard bastard, yet

I cried like a smacked baby. I remember standing there shaking screaming '*why, dad, why couldn't you be normal*' '*why couldn't you just be fucking normal*'

I remember falling down on to the hard concrete, I felt my skin being scraped off my knees, but I didn't feel the pain and ignored the blood that soaked through my torn jeans. I just kept screaming '*why dad, why*' cars went passed and some even slowed down, but they soon pulled away when I screamed abuse at the driver. I remember smoking a small tab of marijuana then wishing I hadn't, it seemed to access deeper emotions that filled me with fear when I felt them. I watched the dawn start to lighten the sky and birds began to give sound the approaching new day. I felt utterly fucked up. My emotions were all over the place, in some ways I was a streetwise hard-man afraid of no one that could be punched and kicked without the slightest hint of cowardice. But in other ways I was weak, my emotions controlled my every waking moment and terrified me whenever I slept.

After the effects of the marijuana had calmed down I rode into a nearby village and borrowed a tank full of petrol from a car and a bottle of milk from a nearby doorstep.

My life was slowly changing, I was trying to grow up but I was trapped by my childhood and I was having trouble dealing with my emotions and just being alive. Though I had never considered ending my life, there were many times that I wished I had never been born. Bob was starting to become a problem and I had to reinforce to him what would happen if he carried on. He had moved into Tamar Street and tried to assume the role as head of the household; there was no way I would allow that to happen and my mother did the only thing she was good at. She abandoned me.

One morning I had gone into Bradford with a few of my mates and when I returned the house was empty. Everything and everyone had gone. I remember opening the door with my boot and walking around the empty house, the stench of the place seemed even stronger. My mother and my family had abandoned me; but what really pissed me off, and broke my heart, was that they had taken Prince with them. They had taken away the only thing that could calm me; I felt utterly alone. Then anger kicked in and I went crazy and wrecked what was left of the shithole I lived in. I smashed windows, doors, cupboards. I sat on the bare floor thinking that my mother had, at last, done her worst. But she had not finished with me and I would, once again, end up in prison because of a crime she committed.

Mother had followed her usual routine when she left a house and had robbed the gas and electric meters and when the police turned up to see who was wrecking the house they arrested me for the theft. The cops couldn't understand why I stood there laughing with tears flooding down my face. They couldn't have known that my mother had screwed me again.

It was a bank holiday and the courts were closed so I ended up being locked in a cell in Bradford Town Hall for three nights. It was terrible for many reasons, I was only just 16, I was claustrophobic, I was scared, I was alone and no-one knew where I was. Those three nights locked up seemed to sum up my life and how I felt. I began to think that happiness didn't even exist in any form and those that seemed happy were all liars. I felt separate from the world and not just inside the dark cell I was in. I had broken the heart and lost the trust of my best mate and I had lost my dog. I had been born into a life I didn't ask for; I didn't choose my parents, I didn't choose any part of my life. Sitting in the cell I realised that my family, as crap as it was, had gone. There was only me, and I didn't know who '*me*' was. I remember thinking about Uncle John and The Cinderella Home and the happiness and security I felt there. But my heart almost broke at the memories, so I stopped. I cried my self to sleep every night and one night I must have woke up screaming because the cell was suddenly full of coppers and I was being held down. I remember one of the coppers bringing me a plastic mug of tea and sitting with me until I calmed down. It was a small gesture by the officer, but it was what I needed at the time; a reminder that some people did care. When he eventually left he left the light on, telling me that it would not be a problem if I needed to press the bell. It was a small gesture by the officer, but it was what I needed at the time; a reminder that some people did care and, though it register with me back then, the officer's thoughtfulness came back later in my life; but that was still decades away.

Tuesday slowly came around and the courts were at last open and I was let out of my cell. I spoke to a solicitor that seemed more interested in why I, at 16 years old, had been locked in a cell for three days and nights. I told him to shut up, the cops had been ok really and I just wanted it over with. I didn't want to sit and listen to him waffle. I had avoided being arrested so many times that I felt that my time had come even if it was my mother's actions that had landed me back in jail, I knew I would go down again and I hoped that I would be sent back to Tong Park. I wanted to be somewhere, anywhere, that I would feel safe. I hadn't 'given in' in the same way has I had during my time at the children's home, but I had stopped caring about my future; I just needed peace and quiet, I needed time to access who I was.

It was a short appearance in court; I pleaded guilty and didn't even mention that my mother had robbed the meters. I simply didn't care anymore. The judge seemed to spend more time reading than talking and I remember standing with my hands behind my back waiting for the inevitable, I was resigned to my fate. Not just in the court room but in my life; I had had enough of living in a confused state and feeling almost permanently angry. But I wasn't sent to prison or even a remand home. I was put under the care of the local authorities and would be placed in a *'place of care'* again. Even that didn't stir my emotions. It seemed to fit the way my life was; but I made a silent vow that, no matter who tried, or what the cost, I would not be bullied again. But the children's home was not like the one at Bradford Moor, in fact the home I was sent to would be the total opposite and probably helped me to break through the wall of misery that I had run into.

The home that was to be my home for the foreseeable future was an old building and was situated opposite Bradford Royal Infirmary; a building I was very familiar with, the A&E department in particular. The staff simply ignored my deep moods and uncooperative behaviour, or at least I thought so at the time, but in reality they probably had the knowledge and skills needed to help a screwed up kid and knew that I would not trust easily and that I was damaged. I was given my own room and allowed to walk about where ever I wanted to. I could have simply walked away, but had no where to go; there was nowhere I wanted to go.

During my time there one of the male staff members became a friend of sorts and would encourage me to join in the activities of the home and, also, help me keep a check on my temper; a temper that would see me react to even the slightest provocation or threat of bullying. The man was in his 40's and seemed to be able to judge, far better than I, my bi-polar moods and we would sit and talk, but only when I wanted to, about my life. I found I couldn't talk about my life as a child. My mind would not take me there; I could only talk about things that were more recent. I spoke about the letters but couldn't finish talking about them without feeling the same anger as I felt when I read them. The man seemed to understand the nightmares I was having time I fell asleep, he knew not to shake me awake, he knew to just call my name and let me come out of my nightmare slowly. He didn't even mention the piss soaked sheets; he would just help me change them for clean dry ones.

My bedroom window overlooked Bradford and I would sit by the window making out the areas that I had lived. There weren't many areas that I couldn't make out. I'd lived in most of them, and suffered in them all. I could make out Havelock Street and even the Cat Steps and, when night came, I could make out the street lights of Manchester Road and my mind would take me back to the night I walked and ran its full length in the smog, terrified of the slightest noise. In the safety of my room I found I could think about things without feeling the sickening fear that came with such memories, perhaps it was this freedom to think that fuelled the nightmares that made my childhood real again and would suffocate me. Even sitting the window I found I just could not access my childhood, it was as my life before my father's arrest was hidden behind a wall of dense fog and would run away when I tried to catch it. But when I slept memories of my childhood came out of the fog; making me feel and smell the things I couldn't when I was awake.

    I had been at the home several weeks when I was told that I had visitors and I remember shaking at the thought of it being my mother and Bob. The man that had become my friend must have seen the anxiety in my face and quickly told me that it was two of my mates. I thought it would be Steve and one of the other lads and almost ran to the reception area and almost fell through the door smiling at the thought of meeting me best mate again. But the smile left my face when I saw it was Rose, and I felt a surge of pain when I saw her holding hands with one of my old mates. It was obvious that they were a couple and I had to fight a great urge to batter; I wanted to rip him apart, but Rose smiled at me, that wonderful smile of hers that had the power to calm me. It didn't take long for me to calm down; even though I felt betrayed I knew that Rose and her new boyfriend had done the right thing by coming to tell me themselves. Seeing them holding hands hurt me in a way I had never hurt before and, when they left shortly afterwards, I went to my room and cried. Rose had been my first-love and the pain I was feeling was the same pain all teenagers must feel when their hearts are broken for the first time. Strangely, when I had finished crying in my room, I found I didn't feel the pain of losing Rose didn't hurt so much, the pain that had I accrued just by being alive, was stronger and simply absorbed the pain. It was just another shovel of emotional crap to add to the rest of pile.

    A few days after Rose had been to see me I was called into the main office to meet with a social worker.

    I was told that I was to appear in court the following week and that my mother would be there. I sat in the room and my head began to spin. I remember shouting at the social worker and my mentor asking them what the fuck she wanted. I was slowly beginning to change, I found I was staying calmer for longer periods than I was angry and I hadn't pissed the bed for several nights and now, once again, my mother was trying to come back into my life. Why?

    I spent the rest of my time at the home in a miserable state and I ended up fighting with one of the lads in there because he made some remark about me getting my hair cut. I felt ashamed after that fight, the lad had been a friend of sorts and I had attacked him, I think it was the first time I had ever apologised for thumping someone. The lad seemed to understand and accepted my hand when I offered it to him, and that was also something that I had never done before, other than when I was boxing, I had always been too angry to shake hands, I always wanted to carry on fighting.

My life was about to change again and I knew when I left the children's home on the morning of my court appearance that I would not be returning and a deep fear filled my body at the thought of seeing my mother again. Only a few months before she had abandoned me and left me to face life alone; leaving me to face, once again the punishment for crimes she had committed. I remember wondering what I would do when I saw her would I would scream my anger at her, would I slap her and thump Bob? But there was feeling that confused me utterly. I hated my mother; she had contributed equally with my father to destroy the childhoods of their children. My mother had sat and watched has her husband abused and beaten, she had made excuses for him when the police were called, she had abandoned me both emotionally and physically so often that I had lost count. Then why did a small part of me want to see her again.

When I got to the juvenile court I looked a totally different lad than the one that had attended the same building a few months earlier. My hair was cut neat and tidy and I was wearing my first ever suit. Physically I was totally different; I looked like a smart young man. No longer a long-haired '*greaser*' from one of Bradford's hardest council estates, I felt clean the stench of my clothes were a thing of the past; however my emotions were as complex ever; always hiding just below the surface and, when I saw my mother the emotions were as mixed has they had ever been.

When she saw me, my mother stood up quickly and walked towards me holding her arms out ready to embrace me, but I was having none of it. Even though a part of me wanted to run into her arms and for my mum to make everything ok, another part of me knew that it was all false, and my mind swam back to the day I returned from the first children's home with my *Angel* and the emptiness if her eyes; and I knew that whatever my mother appeared to be, she certainly wasn't the loving mother that the people around us must have thought her to be, so I simply ignored my mother and sat down next to the social worker and waited to go into court.

The magistrate was a woman and, like the previous magistrate, she sat and read through a mound of papers then asked a few questions. My guilty plea had speeded things up a bit and it wasn't too long before we were told to stand up as she left the room to consider my punishment. And it wasn't long before she returned and shook my world to its very core.

I don't know what my mother had told the social services, but whatever she had said had influenced the judge. I was given a £30 fine and told I had to reside in Wakefield with my mother. I started to shout in protest but the magistrate told me to quieten down and explained that if I didn't accept her sentence and the conditions she attached to it, then her only option was Borstal. I was tempted to take the latter, but I knew that I didn't want to spend the next six months of my life in prison so I reluctantly accepted my fate.

My mother told the social worker that it would take a few days for her to arrange a bedroom etc and I couldn't go 'home' until it was sorted so I was taken, unexpectedly taken back to the children's home for a few days. That night I cried and cried. I cried until I fell asleep. I remember waking up covered by my blankets, I had been fighting my father's cropping hands again and I was sweating heavily. The room seemed to be crushing me and I had to fight a great urge to run away. I wanted to run to Malham or Morecambe, I wanted to run to Haworth and sit and stare at the moors. I didn't want to go 'home' I didn't want to live with my mother. I didn't want to live in Wakefield; I wanted to ride my BSA with my mates. I remember getting dressed quietly; I had made up my mind to flee, to escape. I would live on the streets, anywhere, I would steal milk to survive, I would do whatever it took. But when I tried the door it was locked. For the first time during my stay there, they had locked my bedroom door. I tried the window and found it locked too. So I sat on the windowsill and looked out over Bradford, my eyes taking in the street lights I had walked past. Then I started to cry again. In many ways I was still a boy, I was scared, anger and very confused and couldn't make sense of what was happening.

The following morning I was not allowed to go outside, I was now a prisoner in every sense and I felt trapped and responded by slamming doors and threatening the other lads. Then my mentor did something that stopped me.

I was sitting sulking in the kitchen, cursing the world and all that lived in it. I had stopped talking to anyone and trusted no one; then my mentor and friend came in and made me a cup of tea. I ignored him at first, but he just sat opposite me until I calmed down. Then he stood up and gestured for me to follow him and, after a token resistance, I did as he asked and we walked toward the door leading to the outside. He opened the door and walked outside, again gesturing for me to follow him and, again after another token resistance, I followed him outside into the fresh air. We sat on the bench we usually sat and talked and he handed me the cup of tea that he had made; he waited a few moments before he started to talk to me, waiting until I had calmed down. He told me that I could run if I wanted; but he told me he would be sacked if I did and, anyway, where I would run to? He told me I could live a life on the streets of Bradford but how long would it be before the police caught me? I knew he was struggling to find the words he wanted to say to me and it made me feel better because he had tried. I didn't run away, I would not be the cause of the man losing his job, he had been good to me and had helped me by understanding that I was in a mess.

I remember the day I left the home, it was like leaving the Cinderella Home again, I felt deeply emotional because I knew that I was not just leaving the home; I was not just leaving Bradford. I was leaving behind my childhood and starting a new life. I should have felt emotions other than sadness; but I couldn't reach any. Bob had come across from Wakefield to pick me up and I was angry when Prince didn't bound out of the car, I missed the brown mongrel and asked Bob why he didn't bring him; he didn't reply, he just asked if I was ok. I didn't answer him and it was a long, silent trip to Wakefield.

Driving to Wakefield I went along streets and roads that had been such a big part of my life. I passed near to Ripley Villa and saw my self as a child there, and felt the shame of having to move when my mother burgled a neighbour's house. I passed Fairfax Grammar and had mixed feelings about the place. It seemed that every corner of Bradford held memories for me and most of them were terrible and I remember thinking that perhaps it wasn't such a bad thing. I could leave my past behind, start a new life where no one knew me. I thought that maybe the nightmares would stop and that I would be less angry. But I was so very wrong; and within minutes of arriving at my new home I would be thumping Bob and threatening to belt my mother and within 6 months, and thanks to my again to my mother, I would be back in prison. Things would not get better; they would get far worse. I was an angry, confused young man riddled with self doubt and confusion. Wakefield would pay the cost of my childhood and the violence it had bred into me and in the following years my life would be, in some ways, far worse than my life up to that point. I wasn't leaving my childhood behind, I was trapped in it. I wasn't leaving memories behind me, they remained as feelings that confused me until I had no idea who I was. And all that I considered normal would change.

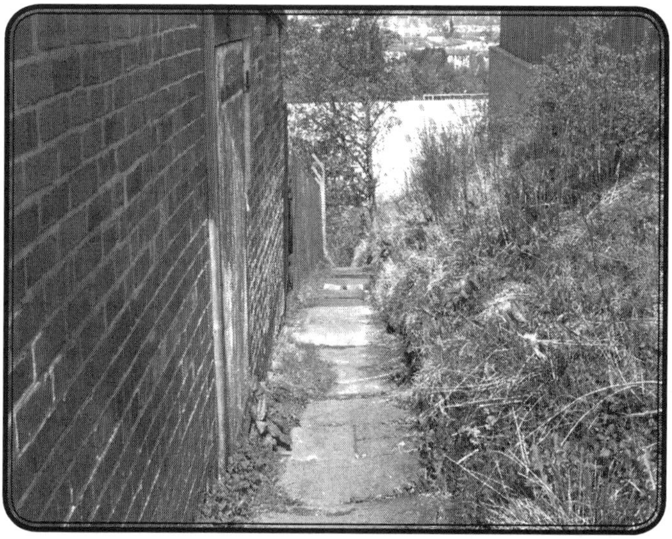

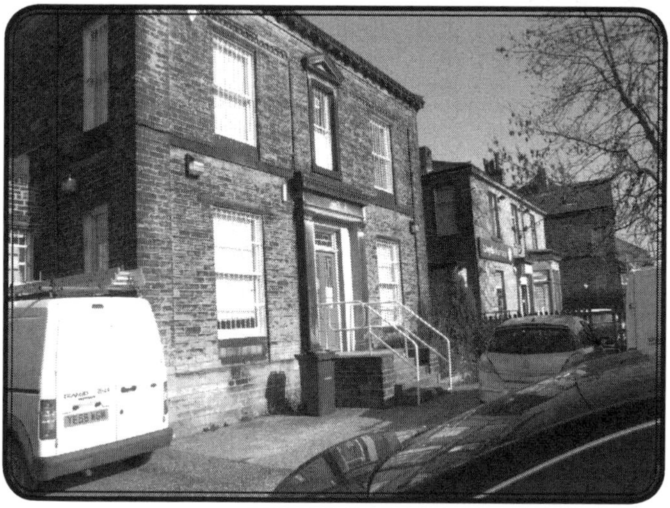

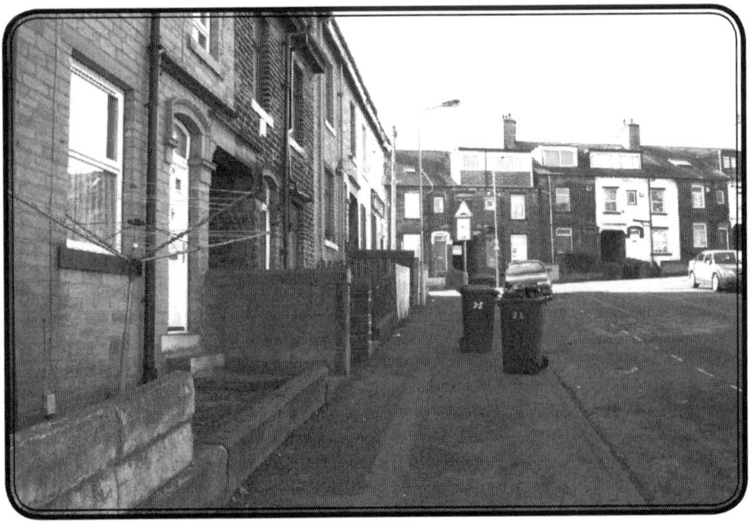

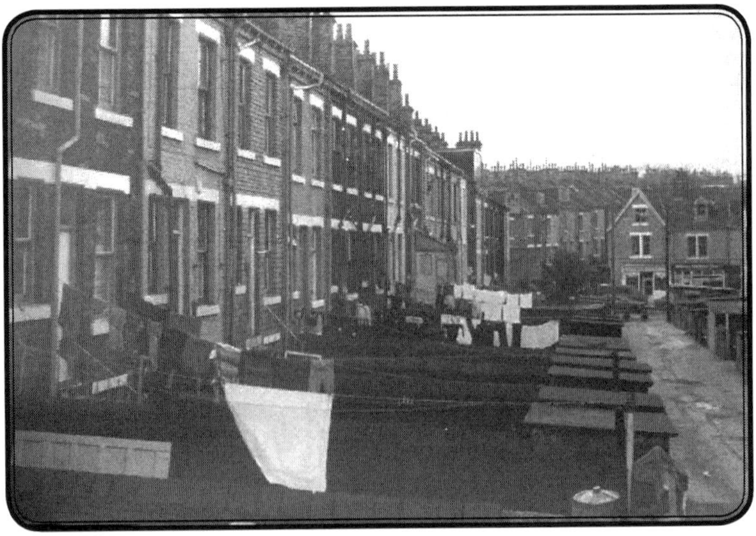

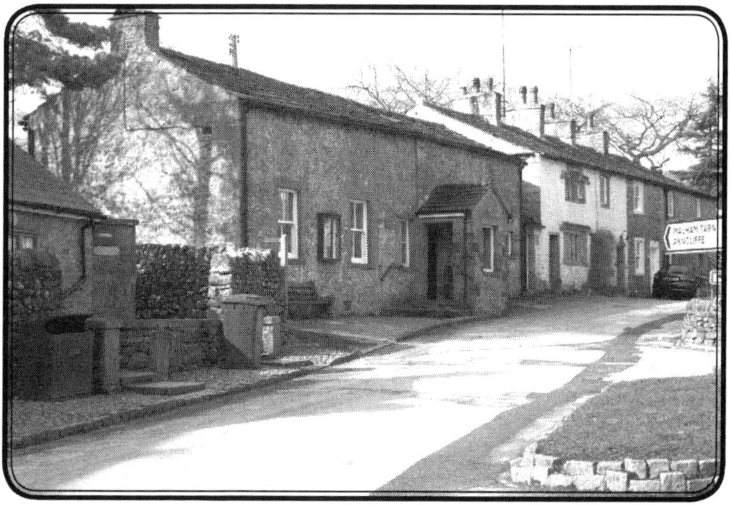
MALHAM TARN

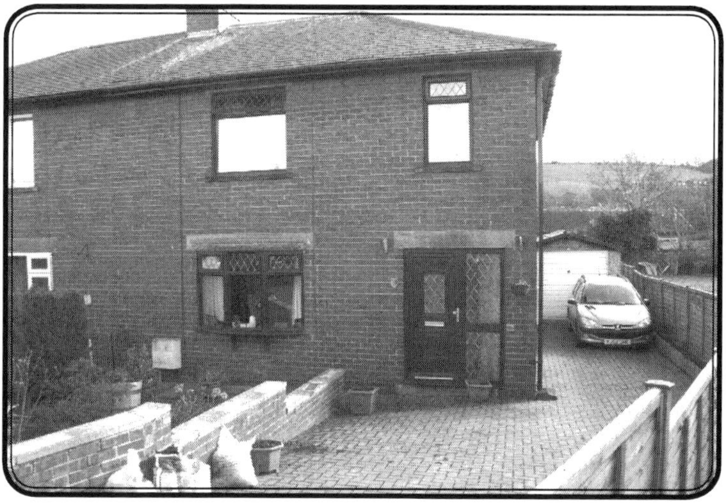

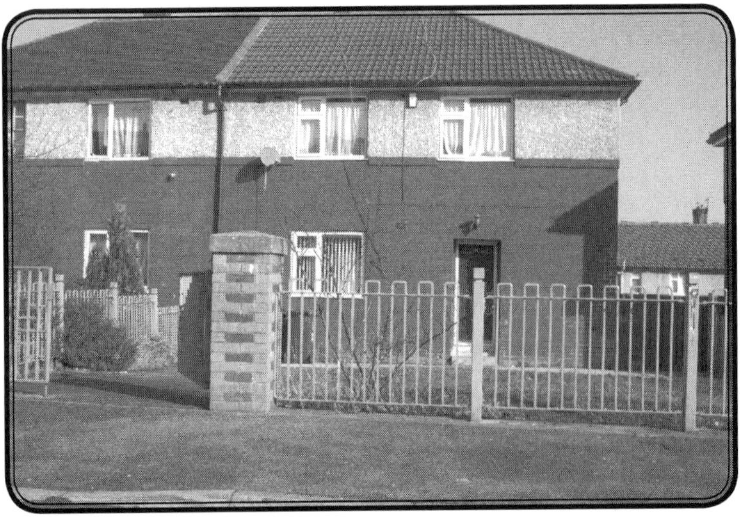

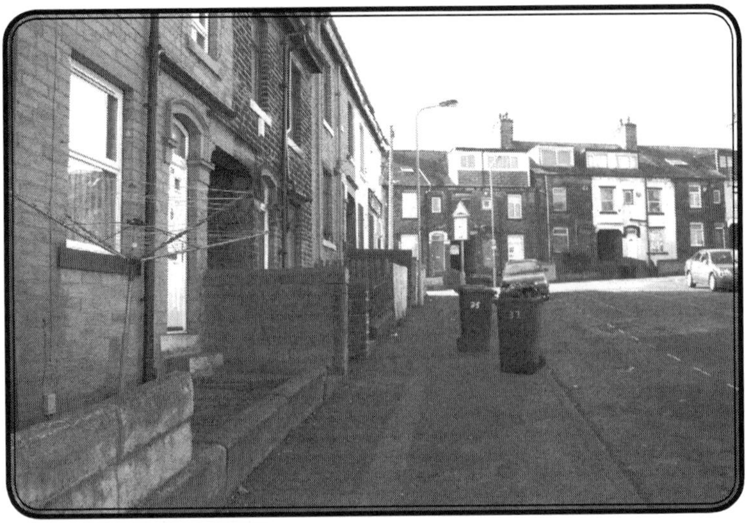

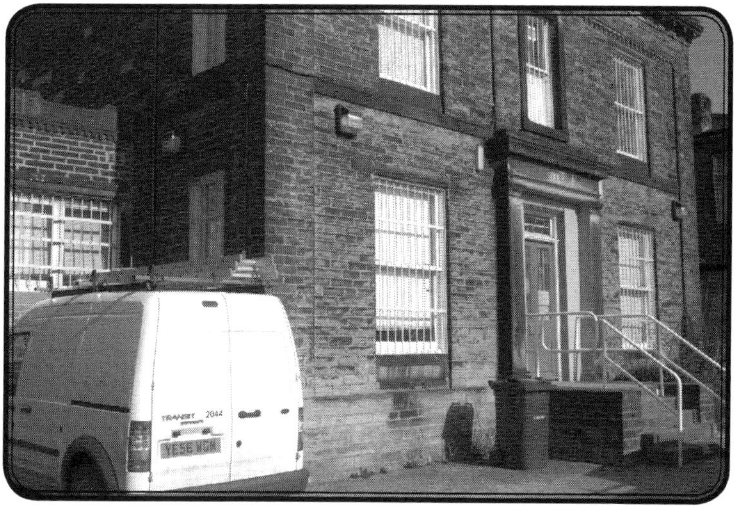
TRANSIT 2044

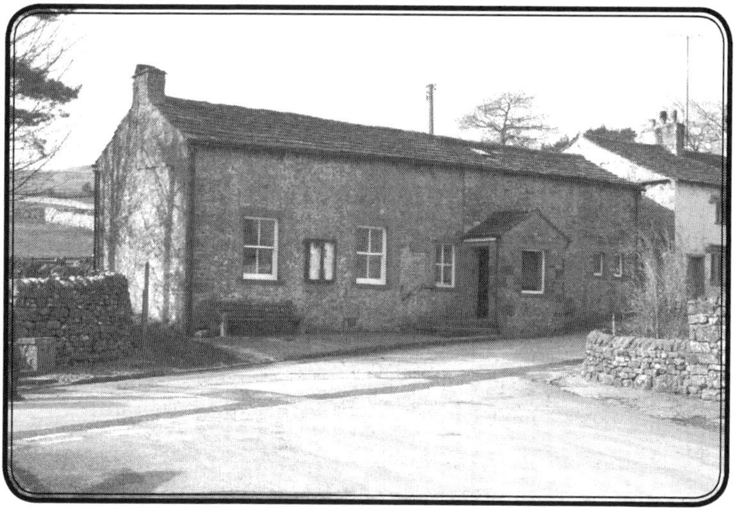

Just Once, When I Was Little

Written By

Brian Mynott

www.brianmynott.co.uk

Printed in Great Britain
by Amazon